THE BOOK OF THE
ROYAL SCOTS
A British Railways Illustrated Special

IRWELL
PRESS ≡≡≡

For Alec Swain. There is unlikely to be another man on earth to travel at 100mph in the cab of a Royal Scot; I hope to be prodding him into repeating the tale for many years to come.

Acknowledgements

There are any number of books and articles concerning the Royal Scots, many of them detailed to an absorbing degree. I've consulted several in compiling these notes and though keeping largely to the well-worn path set by others, this account does, I feel, manage to wander up a few hitherto little known byways. One or two wholly new elements have been introduced to the story, and I think this is probably the first account to draw on all the Board and Committee records held at the Public Record Office, Kew. As with *The Book of the Coronation Pacifics* (Irwell Press, 1998) the Engine Record is also something rather new. My worst excesses have been restrained with kindness and good humour by Allan Baker, Stephen Summerson, Alec Swain and Eric Youldon; Geoff Goslin and Ashley Butlin proved a help as usual and I would especially like to thank John Jennison and Brassmasters (purveyors to the gentry of fine etched brass LMS locomotive kits) for his efforts on the Record Cards.

Bibliography

BR London Midland Magazine, LMS Magazine, The Railway Gazette, The Railway Observer, The Locomotive, various record series at Kew – principally RAIL 418, 422, *Royal Scots of the LMS* (Ed. Doherty, Ian Allan 1970), *The Royal Scots and Patriots of the LMS* (Nock, D&C 1978), *The Stanier 4-6-0s of the LMS,* (Rowledge and Reed, D&C, 1977), *An Illustrated History of LMS Locomotives* (Essery and Jenkinson, SLP 1989), *London Midland Fireman* (Higson, Ian Allan 1972), *Loco Profile Royal Scots* (Reed, Profile Publications, 1971), *LMS Locomotive Names* (RCTS 1994)

CONTENTS

Cover. 46165 THE RANGER (12*TH LONDON REGT.)* at Carlisle Citadel, under that magnificent ecclesiastical screen, 15 April 1957. J. Robertson, B.P. Hoper Collection.

Below. 46105 CAMERON HIGHLANDER, one of the Scottish Scots, in transitional condition at Polmadie, though still basically in post-war LMS garb; the date is not recorded, though the BR number was applied from April 1948 and the new smoke deflectors did not appear until the end of 1952. (Note, on the smokebox door, the fairly awkward addition of the '4'). From the 'fire devils', both slung from the water column arm (woe betide anyone passing beneath!) and positioned on the ground, it might be winter. Photograph J. Robertson, B.P. Hoper Collection.

Works Official – ROYAL ENGINEER, a Queen's Park engine (with diamond works plate). It is not generally realised, but there was a further pair of tiny windows, up on the cab front above the firebox, just like on the 3F tanks, the 4F 0-6-0s and others. The much larger boiler on the Scots made them invisible from most angles. They were proper windows and were not just for ventilation, but they were hard to clean and not really much use – hence their early removal. With the eye of faith, they can just be seen on 6109, in its works grey at Queen's Park works.

iv

'Fifty Improved 4-6-0 Passenger Tender Engines'

It is with this first opaque reference in the LMS Minutes that the 'Royal Scots', celebrated across nearly four decades of active main line service, first made their own highly individual entry into the LMS story. And an unusual entry it certainly was.

It was not long after the company's formation that locomotive policy on the new LMS, if not floundering, was definitely acquiring an uncertain gait. The whiff of Pacifics was in the air, but Hughes' ideas vanished with his retirement in 1925, leaving only the 2-6-0 'land crabs' as an indication of what might have been. With Fowler's accession came ideas for a *compound* Pacific, which really put the wind up the West Coast operating people. By 1926, as has been recorded so often before, locomotive affairs on the LMS were mired in a confusion of unsuitable Claughtons, L&Y 4-6-0s and Midland 4-4-0s. Where the other new companies seemed to be forging ahead – Pacifics on the LNER, LORD NELSON ('the most powerful locomotive in Britain') on the Southern and all sorts of dazzling publicity on the Great Western, the LMS was going nowhere.

'Nowhere' can be perfectly illustrated by the Locomotive Renewal Programme for 1926, promulgated in June 1925. Under this, the company was committed to 150 Class 4 0-6-0s, a similar number of Class 3 0-6-0Ts, and fifty each of the Class 4 4-4-0 Compounds and the smaller Class 2 4-4-0s, at a total cost of £1,821,250. The average age of the LMS locomotive stock was then 27.43 years (up from a pre-Group average of 22.29) and when this current programme was complete, Hughes calculated that the average age would be down to 23.5 years. Some form of bigger engine was on the cards, though no one had a clear idea of what it would be. The Locomotive and Electrical Engineering Committee was informed that: '...*the question of the provision of an improved and more powerful type of passenger engine for the purpose of avoiding double heading and duplication of certain heavy express passenger main line services*' was under consideration.

Yet the hunt for a new, modern, main line passenger locomotive still seemed to lack urgency. At the meeting of the Mechanical and Electrical Committee in March 1926, Fowler reported that the fifty Compounds had been ordered from the Vulcan Foundry. There was no progress on the 'new passenger engines', as this rather startling extract confirms: '*Mr Booth asked whether anything further had been done regarding the designing of a more powerful type of passenger engine, and was informed by Sir Henry Fowler that the matter was still under consideration by Mr Trench and himself, the principal difficulty at the present time being that the engine he had designed, whilst suitable for the run between London and Glasgow Central, was too high for the loading gauge on certain of the lines approaching Glasgow St Enoch.*

'*It was desired that the same type of engine should run between Liverpool, Manchester and Holyhead, and it was on this point that he was in communication with the Engineer, but he hoped to be in a position to report further more definitely at the next meeting of the Committee*'.

The fact that Fowler had designed his first effort too big for large tracts of the LMS was not a good omen and it seems somehow significant that he never did report on the subject at the next meeting. There was clearly conflict in the higher echelons of LMS management; Fowler was no classical CME and design influence passed largely to Anderson at Derby. He, it has been demonstrated in many writings,

Wheeling 6155, one of the Derby batch, in July 1930. The works plates are still on the smokebox, though this was hardly the right place, if some illusion of keeping a loco's 'unique identity' was to be maintained – and the deflectors would soon render this site redundant anyway.

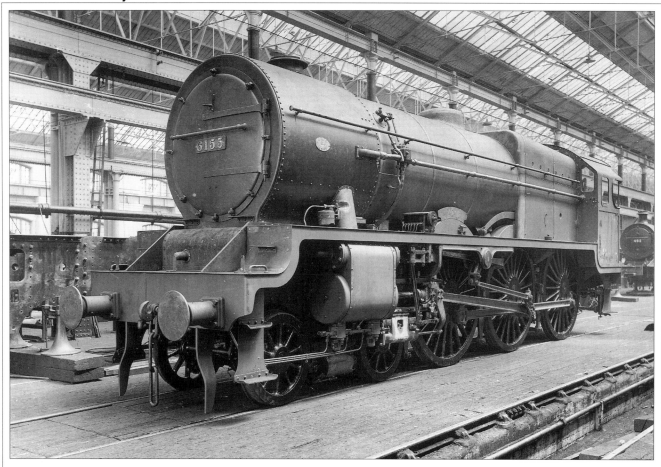

6155 fully wheeled at Derby, July 1930. The little cylinder on the footplating, immediately in front of the steam pipe, is the vacuum relief valve, which was only visible in the few years between construction and the fitting of smoke deflectors. It is bolted, by a flange, to the steam pipe and allowed atmospheric air down into the steam chest when the engine was coasting, that is, running with steam shut off. Otherwise the vacuum created within the cylinders would tend to suck smokebox char and other undesirable matter down the blastpipe into the cylinders, causing undue wear. It was the relief valves which made that *'chink-chink'* when coasting. The Derby Scots differed from the NBL ones in having a recess (very clear here) in the steam pipe; on the top of the equipment is a steam connection and the recess provides clearance for a spanner to be got on it. There is a thread for a pipe to be connected up, running along the footplating (usually tucked out of sight on the NBL ones though just visible in some pictures) but in this view it has not yet been fitted.

simply carried on with a straightforward Midland policy so far as locomotives were concerned. Trials in 1925 comparing the GWR Castle 4-6-0 with the new Gresley Pacific must have made an impression on the LMS, for in October 1926 exasperated elements in the company determined upon action. Braving the likelihood of the GW 'leaking' the advantages of its own locomotive (as it had done with the LNER Pacific the year before, in breach of an agreement and to Gresley's intense annoyance) arranged to borrow a Castle, and in that fashion settle its internal conflicts. During a month on the LMS, the work of 5000 LAUNCESTON CASTLE, then almost new, was so conclusive as to end any argument. The days of double headed Midland Compounds from Glasgow to

Newish Royal Scot, 6122 ROYAL ULSTER RIFLEMAN in original condition, in full crimson lake, at its home shed of Crewe North; behind is one of the first British coaling plants and over on the left a Claughton, BUCKINGHAM.

D E R B Y.

10th December, 1926.

TO THE CHAIRMAN AND DIRECTORS OF THE TRAFFIC
AND LOCOMOTIVE & ELECTRICAL COMMITTEES.

LOCOMOTIVE RENEWAL PROGRAMME.

After careful consideration we recommend that 235 engines
of the following types be built as renewals, viz :-

			Estimated Cost £
(A)	50	Improved 4-6-0 passenger tender locomotives	387,500
(B)	100	No. 4 class 0-6-0 freight tender locomotives	465,000
(C)	25	2-6-4 passenger tank locomotives	137,000
(D)	50	No. 2 class 4-4-0 passenger tender locomotives	250,000
(E)	10	No. 3 class 4-4-2 Tilbury passenger tank locomotives	45,000
	235		£1,284,500

(A) The following sets out the case for the proposed 50 improved
4-6-0 passenger tender engines. As mentioned in Traffic
Committee Minute No. 726, of the 17th June, 1925, a limited
number of an improved and more powerful engine than the
4-6-0 "Claughton" Locomotive is required for certain main
line passenger services. In view of this we have been
experimenting with a "Castle" class engine loaned to us by
the Great Western Railway, which worked in the Euston -
Carlisle service very satisfactorily.

Careful tests were made, which now allow us to know exactly
what is required, and it is proposed, as shown above, that
50 locomotives to satisfy these requirements be provided.
In order to obtain these at the earliest possible moment and
not to interfere with our present commitments, we propose
that these be purchased from The North British Locomotive
Company, who are in a good position to deal with the order,
and who would open one of their Works, at present closed,
to expedite delivery. They promise to commence delivery in
25 weeks, and to complete the order in 35 weeks.

Carnforth, followed by a leaking combination of Claughton and George V 4-4-0 for the less than glorious onward passage to the capital would have to end, and end soon. This was the pass that LMS policy had come to by the end of 1926.

LAUNCESTON CASTLE settled what arguments remained and provided a clear indication of the 'way ahead'. The future, very definitely, had a 4-6-0 looming large in it. At left the Derby memo setting out the 1927 Locomotive Renewal Programme, including the 'fifty improved 4-6-0 Passenger Tender Engines'. It is also interesting to see what engines were to accompany them into this new world.

So did the Royal Scots make their official entry onto the LMS stage, with a less than sparkling chorus line of 4Fs, 2Ps and – Tilbury 4-4-2 tanks. The story runs that the Great Western was not inclined to come up with a set of Castle drawings; certainly the LMS expected at one time that its own 4-6-0 would be *very* closely based on the GW design; only five days after the memorandum (left) the Minutes record that the CME had under consideration the design of *'an improved and more powerful type of passenger engine for certain main line passenger services'* and it had been possible to ascertain the company's requirements, which *'would be some slight modification of the 'Castle' engine'*. [My underlining]. However the locomotive was to look, it was recommended that the order be placed with North British 'at the earliest possible moment'.

What followed was quite remarkable in British practice; in that same month, December 1926, the order went off for fifty of the new locos, to be ready, straight off the drawing board, for service the following

6137 VESTA at Camden, after 1928-style alterations to numbering and lettering. From this time the Royal Scots (VESTA has small numerals for instance) underwent a sort of Darwinian evolution in terms of livery, expanding to fill every niche and then reverting to a much more closely similar style in the changed conditions of the 1950s.

London Midland and Scottish Railway Company.

Secretary's Minute Office,
L. M. S. R., Euston Station.

File No. 31314

Secretary's Office.
Euston Station.

EXTRACT FROM THE MINUTES OF THE Locomotive and Electrical
COMMITTEE OF THE 26th APPROVED BY THE BOARD OF THE
27th January 1927.

Locomotive Renewal Programme.

With reference to minute No. 355 of the
Locomotive and Electrical Committee of the 15th
December 1926; in reply to Mr. Booth, Sir Henry Fowler
stated that an order for 50 4-6-0 passenger locomotives
had now definitely been placed with the North British
Company.

The engine, which was an improvement on
the "Castle" class, would be of the three cylinder type
with a boiler pressure of 250 lbs., per square inch, and
a tractive effort of 32,000 lbs., compared with a boiler
pressure of 225 lbs per square inch of the "Castle"
engine and a tractive effort of 31,000 lbs. It was also
considerably more powerful than the "Claughton" Type.

The weight per axle was 21 tons, but
inasmuch as the engine would be better balanced this
weight had been accepted by the Engineer.

---

summer. Without the Castle drawings, the LMS made do with Lord Nelson drawings from the Southern, though very little use was made of them in the end.

By the time of the above memo, the 'slight modification' of the Castle had become – quite rightly – 'an improvement' over the Castle!

The LMS could not hope to do a task of this extent in its own shops, while North British had two well equipped works (a third had been closed) to carry out the task. Half of the Royal Scots, as the 'improved 4-6-0 tender engines' would be called, were built at the Queen's Park works and the other twenty-five at Hyde Park. Brian Reed in his *Loco Profile* account of the class (Profile Publications Ltd, 1971) describes the inevitable outcome: it was the first Hyde Park engine, 6125, that was made up in works grey for the official photograph. (The LMS was fond of this – see for instance *The Book of the Coronations*, Irwell Press,

1998). Betrayed by its oval Hyde Park plate, it was lettered 6100 for the official photograph. The real 6100 got the proper diamond shaped Queen's Park plate. Its record card shows 6100 with a 'date built' of 14 August 1927, though it was ready before that, for on 27 July Sir Henry Fowler informed the Board that No.6100 was available for inspection by the Directors that very day, on No.15 platform at Euston. The class name also dates from this time, Sir Henry suggesting on 27 July 1927 that as the engine would be working the Royal Scot train, the loco should bear the same name.

The Railway Gazette hailed the new engine as 'adding one more' to the recent examples of engines for 'heavy main line express duty', the others being, aptly, the Castle and the Lord Nelson. *'It will doubtless be found to fill admirably'*, it continued, *'all that the ambitious programme planned for the summer service demands'*. Things were hotting up; on Friday 17 June

1927 for instance the Up Royal Scot expresses from Glasgow and Edinburgh (at this time normally with two Compounds from the former and an ex-CR 4-4-0 or a Compound from the latter) passed Carlisle ahead of time, *The Railway Gazette* was moved to comment. At the height of the season the train was not combined but ran on to London in two parts, each with a Claughton, headed by an ex-LNW 4-4-0. Running separately throughout, on 17 June 1927 the Edinburgh train reached Euston ahead of time and the other portion got in dead on time. The stage was being set.

6100 was soon on trials, carried out between Euston and Carlisle, Euston and Crewe, Crewe and Carlisle and Carlisle and Glasgow, and by late November 1927 Fowler expressed himself 'thoroughly satisfied with the results obtained'. 'As a consequence', Fowler declared, 'it was quite clear that a considerable economy in coal and water consumption might be expected'. The new engine also went on show for the public, for a lot of interest had been aroused by its making. Edgar J. Larkin of the CME's Office, Derby, was one of the young Engineer Demonstrators which accompanied it to many towns and cities in England and Scotland over 1927-28, when 6100 or one of its sisters was admired by 172,484 visitors, raising £5,000 for local charities. One of the new engines attracted 14,000 visitors (can you imagine anything like this today?) at Glasgow Central while at Edinburgh Princes Street 10,000 more paid to see another Royal Scot. 6149 at Birmingham in December 1927 attracted no less than 16,000 people. A host of celebrities came to see the engines, from the Prince of Wales to Dixie Dean. The Lord Mayor of Leeds seems not to have quite been with it, asking if ROYAL SCOT was made in Britain. Edgar Larkin soon put him straight: *'I informed him with no little pride, that every cubic inch was British, and, further, that the LMS was on the National Roll.'*

The Royal Scots came into traffic in numbers from the end of August 1927 and the train with which they were to make the 'big splash' was being made ready too. The double heading was an interregnum before the new engines could be delivered. On Monday 26 September 1927 the Royal Scot train was to run non-stop from London to Carlisle with fifteen coaches, representing the longest non-stop trip in the world. The former double-headed job to Carnforth was 236 miles, but now the Carlisle run was 299¼ miles. The down train departed Euston at 10am behind, appropriately enough, 6100 ROYAL SCOT, while the up train was in the charge of 6104, later named SCOTTISH BORDERER. 6104 was in the hands of Driver William J. Scott of Carlisle, with Pilotman H. Warden

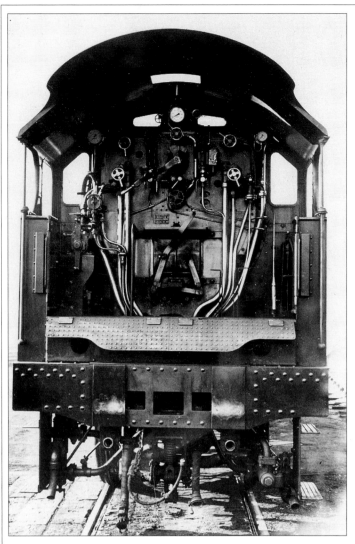

Cab view of ROYAL SCOT. The little 'top light' windows above the firebox, usually unremarked upon in accounts of the class, could not be more obvious from this angle.

and Fireman Chambers (it was his first visit to the capital). All three were afterwards guests at an informal dinner held at the Euston Hotel where Driver Scott was interviewed for the *LMS Magazine*. It is hard to imagine this today, but his only previous experience of the new Royal Scots before this vital prestige trip had a couple of return trips from Carlisle to Crewe! That day, more or less unconcerned, he had backed onto the train at Carlisle where the down Royal Scot had been brought in by 6128, with Polmadie's Driver Stevens in charge. Driver Scott had been 'a bit worried the coal wouldn't last' but 6104 had arrived 'in good order, and ready for another 300 miles home tomorrow'.

Many Changes - Parallel Boiler Days 1927-1943
From their inception in 1927, there was always something going on in respect of the Royal Scots. Derby had seen that many mechanical details were thoroughly 'Midland' and these were hardly hostages to fortune, while other amendments were made as the long life of the Royal Scots wore on. Yet the engines were a revelation when first they came onto the West Coast workings, and were a success 'from the off', working the heaviest and fastest trains.

A steady programme of improvements to West Coast services was foreseen for the 1930s, the apotheosis coming with the streamlined Pacifics and the Coronation Scot train. These were to replace the Royal Scots on the most important trains, though in the event of a Pacific being unavailable the job fell to a Royal Scot, and very ably they coped too. In 1930, however, Stanier and his Pacifics were still far in the future and the immediate need was for more of the big 4-6-0s. Twenty more were built, 6150-6169, this time by the LMS, at Derby, in 1930. They were largely identical to the earlier North British examples and all seventy engines came truly into their own from 1932 when West Coast services were generally speeded up, with even heavier loads. The reason for the second batch appearing from Derby was price. North British had not made a good deal of money on the first Royal Scots, probably because of the special efforts it had made, and felt compelled to raise its quotes on any

6123 with the more familiar large numerals. This puts the date at post-1928, when the changes began to be made, but before about 1932, by which time the class had got coal rails on the tenders. The smokebox works plate has disappeared.

A poor view, technically (it probably suffers through being a copy) but a striking one. The scene is Euston in the 1930s and is obviously posed – there would be ructions at the blowing off of one engine, let alone three. The noise must be truly deafening as 6100 (back from the USA), 6203 PRINCESS MARGARET ROSE and 6109 ROYAL ENGINEER announce their presence to the world.

A pair of beautiful new 'uns, at Crewe (with the North shed in the background). These two, 6141 and 6142 with blank nameplates, are surely on delivery from Glasgow, such is their scintillating state, with glistening 'Turplat Noweld' forged steel buffers by George Turton Platts & Co. of Sheffield. The engines seem to have gone off NBL to Polmadie in pairs, for reception by the LMS, so presumably some at least some carried on to Crewe in similar fashion.

6112 SHERWOOD FORESTER at Derby (even the backdrop is a row of highly polished locos, and you'll not see buffer stops cleaner than that anywhere) about 1935. This would be for the unveiling of its regimental crest.

new engines, despite the Great Slump having hit the world. Fowler decided in January 1930 that he could build them cheaper 'in-house':

'TO THE LOCOMOTIVE & ELECTRICAL COMMITTEE

Gentlemen,
ADDITIONAL "ROYAL SCOT" LOCOMOTIVES
In anticipation of the approval of the Directors the Executive Committee have agreed to commencement at once being made with the building of 20 additional "Royal Scot" engines, which will form part of the Locomotive Programme for 1930, to be submitted to the Directors at a subsequent meeting.

The urgency in this case was owing to the desirability of some of the additional "Royal Scot" engines being available for the heavy summer passenger traffic this year.

Owing to the high price quoted by the North British Locomotive Company, who built the existing "Royal Scots, the new locomotives should be built in this Company's Workshops'

A few days later, on 30 January 1930, Fowler ordered the commencement of the twenty new Royal Scots 'in anticipation of the approval of the Directors'. The reason, as the earlier memo quoted above makes clear, was the price; the Locomotive & Electrical Committee acknowledged this, but made the curious observation that '*The precise cost of building these locomotives in the Company's Workshops at Derby had not yet been*

ascertained', so Fowler must have been confident 'his' Royal Scots would come in under price. The Committee would receive a full report on the cost of the twenty engines 'on completion' in which case, it might be a bit too late…

The engines were delivered between May and November 1930 so in terms of speed Derby was not put to shame by North British, though the deliveries were spread out somewhat. Yet it was a pretty polished performance, with a programme that called for the frames of the first to be laid down on 5 May 1930 and the first engine to leave the Erecting Shop for the Paint Shop less than three weeks later on 23 May (see J.B. Radford's *Derby Works and Midland Locomotives*, Ian Allan, 1971). Derby would be acutely aware of any odious comparisons with North British and the programme was adhered to, to within a few *minutes*! It helped that the boilers were built at Crewe, but they were numbered in the Derby series.

Once the twenty Royal Scots had been delivered from Derby, Wood and Hartley had to report upon the costings. It looks exactly the sort of document which is intended to be less than crystal clear, with 'variable out of pocket' and 'non-variable constants' as well as other bits of witchcraft, though it contains the interesting sentence: '*The building in the Company's Shops resulted in an economy of £32,338, but the overall cost of building exceeded the Contractor's price by £4,422'*. A big factor was the 'extra war wage of 6/6d' paid by the LMS; various incomprehensible factors

were listed but the simple picture seems to be thus: 1927 NBL cost was £7,725 (NBL figures from Reed's *Loco Profile*) or, less reliably, £7,744 (from the Engine Record Cards). Wood and Hartley's 1930 report show the 1930 contract price as £8,085 which Derby, with a figure of £8,306, exceeded by £221 per engine. The Record Cards for the Derby locos show *£6,467* and at this point I abandon the accountancy to those who know better!

Coal Consumption
At first, the Royal Scots returned very economical figures, though the savings varied as Drivers got to grips with new techniques of working, using full regulator and short cut-offs. The unprecedented hard work to which they were put, however, allied to 'Midland' engineering features belonging to a more sedate age, made for trouble. Within a year or two, coal consumption was soaring, nearly doubling in some instances on the London-Carlisle run. The problem was already known as the Derby Royal Scots were being built. The last fourteen of the Derby ones got four piston valve rings in place of the single one fitted to the earlier engines and improvement was apparent straight away. The earlier single ring suffered a build-up of carbon and did not remain steam tight, allowing an increasing part of the steam which did the work to pass through un-utilised. The Fireman was hurling more and more coal into the box to less and less effect. 6158 got *six* rings at Derby, together with some minor changes in the valve events, and these arrangements were

6145 CONDOR at speed on Bushey troughs. The notion that the Scots were based upon the Lord Nelsons can rightly be dismissed (in Reed's phrase) as 'persistent rumour'. In any case it should be LORD NELSON itself rather than 'the Nelsons', for the Southern engine was a lone prototype from August 1926 to June 1928, by which time the Royal Scots outnumbered it fifty to one!

made standard, applied to all the rest as they came through works. E.S. Cox in his contribution to *Royal Scots of the LMS* (Ian Allan, 1970) gives a truly startling figure, describing a reduction in steam wastage due to steam leakage from 80% to 8% over the period of a piston and valve exam. While the two types were running, Royal Scots fitted with six rings were returning half the coal consumption per mile of their sisters equipped with the original single ring.

The following Minute of 20 May 1931 summarises the experience; so impressive were the results that it was proposed to fit the piston valves to a further 1,657 locomotives: *'The Chief Mechanical Engineer reported that when the "Royal Scots" were built, they were fitted with the type of wide piston ring which had been standard up to that time. Owing to the greater width of these valves and the higher steam pressure employed, it was found difficult to keep them steamtight, and as this was closely bound up with the question of coal consumption, an investigation was made into the whole subject, and a new design of piston valve was prepared having a number of narrow rings instead of the single wide ring.*

Authority was obtained for the "Royal Scot" and "Claughton" engines to be fitted with the improved type of valves. The results obtained had been very satisfactory. A saving of 11½% in coal had been obtained, comparing a "Royal Scot" with the narrow rings with a similar engine having the old wide ring. Moreover, after running 34,000 miles without attention to valves, the

coal consumption of the narrow ring engine had only deteriorated very slightly compared with what our experience had shewn with the wider rings.

In view of the above results, authority was now asked to extend this alteration to cover a further 1,657 engines, comprising the more important main line types at present fitted with wide ring piston valves. The cost of fitting the 1,657 engines concerned was estimated at £43,000, and it was intended that the engines should be equipped as they pass through the shops, the work being spread over from three to four years.

In estimating the savings, an allowance had been made from the total coal used annually by the engines for the amount used for lighting up and standing by, on which no saving could be expected. The saving would be realised whenever the regulator was open, whether the engine was running on the main line or shunting. Taking this saving at only 6% as against 11½% on the "Royal Scot" tests, bearing in mind the lower pressure of engines which it was intended to fit, the total annual saving was estimated at £47,600.

Approved, and recommended to the Board.'

Bogies

The bogies fitted to the Royal Scots had the same side spring control as the Compound 4-4-0s. This was an unsuspected error, and in due course the rather more boisterous behaviour of such a big 4-6-0 would demonstrate the drawback, disastrously. The Royal Scots, when swaying through the

wrong sort of trackwork, would build up an unstoppable movement, insufficiently constrained from the front end. 6131 PLANET derailed in this fashion, hauling The Midday Scot at Weaver Junction on 14 January 1930. As Reed in the *Loco Profile* points out, there then followed the unusual circumstance of the Accident Inquiry being conjoined with another, thought to derive from the same cause. A few weeks before, a Lord Nelson bogie had jumped the rails with an up boat train behind the engine and the Inquiry in both cases suggested a strengthening of the bogie side-control springs. This was a precaution, however, and Cox describes as 'the purest chance, quite unconnected with the findings on the mishap' when Derby increased the value of the springing to two tons, in order to combat a rash of broken springs.

Axleboxes and More Bogies

In any talk of the disadvantages of 'Midlandisation' on the LMS it is the sad fate of axleboxes that immediately arises. Derby practice was of course followed as regards the axleboxes of the Royal Scots; they at least had fairly generous bearing surfaces but NBL had to use the Midland model of manganese bronze castings for the body of the box, with brass strips dovetailed in and bridged with white metal to serve as the bearing medium. Cox relates that this was thought to offer efficient heat dissipation but the small engine history of Derby had not afforded any experience of the heavy lateral thrust experienced on a big engine running fast. The resulting

CHIEF MECHANICAL ENGINEER'S OFFICE,

EUSTON STATION.

March, 1934.

"ROYAL SCOT" ENGINES - ALTERATIONS.

There are 70 of the "Royal Scot" engines in traffic the first of which was put in service at the end of July, 1927. Since these engines have been working they have given a good deal of trouble with hot boxes and bad riding. In 1931, there were 75 cases of hot coupled axleboxes, and in 1932, there were 95, and there have been numerous complaints of rough riding which has necessitated bringing the engines in for Service repairs before they were needed.

Because of these difficulties it was found necessary to introduce cross stays between the horn cheeks of the intermediate and trailing axles to prevent the frames spreading and in March, 1933, it was decided to replace the manganese bronze axleboxes, (which were originally fitted on the "Scots" and which constantly required renewing,) with cast steel axleboxes having gun-metal crown brasses.

This work was put in hand immediately to enable engines undergoing general repairs to be dealt with in order to overcome the troubles that had been experienced during the summer of 1932. As a consequence the number of cases of hot boxes fell to 43 in 1933.

It was intended to ask authority for these two items when making a further recommendation to your Committee for improving the riding - complaints of rough riding being still frequent - by the provision of new bogies of the bolster bearing type and new laminated bearing springs.

I am now in a position to make this report and shall be glad if the Directors will approve the action already taken in regard to providing :-

		Estimated cost.
1	New steel axleboxes;	£6,742
2.	Cross-stays to the intermediate and trailing wheels, which includes new horn blocks and horn clips, and consequent re-arrangement of ash-pan;	£ 4,539
		£11,281

and approve of the recommendation to provide the new bogies and new laminated bearing springs, the whole of the work to be carried out as the engines pass through the shops for repairs and which I anticipate will take two years to complete.

The total estimated outlay to carry out the whole of the aforementioned modifications is £46,853 for the 70 engines. The scheme involves additions to the Company's existing capital assets and the Chief Accountant's allocation is :-

	£.
Works & Equipment Maintenance Fund (Revenue Account - ultimate effect)	Dr. 27,059
Capital Account	Dr. 19,794
TOTAL	Dr. £46,853

(Signed) W.A. STANIER.

(Initialled) H.H.

wear, loosening the brass pieces, brought bad riding; the white metal broke up and hot bearings inevitably resulted, with increasing frequency. This would not have come to pass had LAUNCESTON CASTLE's axleboxes been copied instead and as soon as Stanier came on the scene, the Swindon style of box became standard. He summarised the gloomy state of affairs to the Mechanical & Electrical Committee in a memorandum of March 1934, which is reproduced left.

An interesting postscript to the Memo above comes no less than five years later – the CME reported that the work had indeed been done (presumably within the two years promised) but at a cost of £29,540, or £17,313 *less* than the authorised estimate of £46,853. This pleasant surprise came about through using the original bogie wheels and axles for the new bolster bogies and to a modification in the design of the spring gear. The original bogies had had steam brakes, worked by a cylinder fixed between the two wheels, rather like the Compounds. This equipment was done away with when the new bogie work was done in the 1930s, for the system was found to offer little benefit in exchange for the extra maintenance and the awkwardness of access.

Axlebox repairs remained frequent compared to other LMS classes but lest we be too hard on how the Royal Scots were shod, it is worth repeating Cox's point, that of all the three cylinder engines for which suitable records are available, the Royal Scots suffered fewer inside big end defects than any. Funnily enough, one particular three cylinder type which showed particularly badly against the Royal Scots was – the Jubilees.

Not many locomotive failures find their way into the official, minuted record but motion failures, especially inside ones, could be dramatic. Such was the case with 6154 near Auchterarder near Perth,

Smoke deflection antics, none of which, thankfully, proved effective. KING'S OWN played HUMORIST for these vaguely Italian-looking efforts while 6151 (below, opposite page) THE ROYAL HORSE GUARDSMAN got something almost too horrible to contemplate.

on 27 February 1936. A faulty inside big end caused heating so pronounced that the brasses disintegrated. The piston head was forced through the cylinder cover at the back end, fracturing the cylinder; the slide blocks of the cross head were broken allowing the cross head to come clear of the slide bar, and the rod was then forced up, to strike the cross stay between the frame, making a gap one foot two inches wide almost immediately above the driving axle where the frame stay was fixed. The striking of this stay broke the connecting rod, and that portion still coupled to the driving axle rose vertically and pierced the bottom of the boiler barrel (the hole in the barrel being roughly 8 inches in diameter) 'puncturing the boiler tubes to a depth of some six rows'.

6154 was on a Crewe North job, one which later went over to the Pacifics. The unfortunate Crewe North Driver later died in Perth hospital. It was always said that this incident prompted the removal of the crosshead vacuum pump and its replacement with a large ejector, though it is not clear why this should be so.

Smokebox, Smoke Deflecting
The vast Royal Scot smokebox was another Midland inheritance; it was 'built up', a technique that was somewhat out of date even in 1927. According to Cox, this was because Derby had had unpleasant experiences trying to fit 'drumhead' front

tubeplates, though these were being used increasingly elsewhere in the country. The Royal Scots thus got a tubeplate secured to the barrel by an angle ring. This needed a smokebox larger in comparison to the boiler than otherwise might be, and explains the painfully short chimney. The smokeboxes deteriorated through the 1930s, and this was an important factor in the decision to rebuild the Royal Scots, of which more anon.

That big smokebox and the small chimney bought that most intractable and alarming problem, that of smoke drifting into the 'dead' air behind the chimney. When conditions so conspired, smoke could obscure, possibly dangerously, the Driver's view of signals. Half hearted experiments were made from 1929 with various configurations, foreshadowing the tinkerings with the A3 HUMORIST on the LNER a few years later. Smoke obscuring the Driver's view was one suggestion in the Inquiry conclusions following 6114's infamous derailment at Leighton Buzzard in 1931 – see *British Railways Illustrated*, Vol.8 No.7, April 1999.

6141 got a sort of collar for a while, 6100 had a kind of trough fitted on top of the smokebox in front of the chimney (6133 got a variation of this, hooded over) and 6161 suffered indignities on a par with HUMORIST. 6125 had an insubstantial hood fitted while 6151 got a curious arrangement of deflector plates running down the

front of the smokebox in a most peculiar fashion. The Leighton Buzzard suggestions did not really carry much conviction – the Inspecting Officer was concerned to point out that the real cause was the lack of Automatic Train Control (ATC). This was out of the question because of the cost, but the LMS found it useful to seize upon the smoke deflection problem. It grasped the nettle by adopting big, generous plates. Only these, the Southern was demonstrating at last, could shift the big volumes of air needed to heave smoke clear of a locomotive. The new Royal Scot plates were first fitted in 1931 and the following year were pronounced a success:

'MECHANICAL AND ELECTRICAL ENGINEERING COMMITTEE
27 January 1932. The CME reported that to overcome the trouble which has been experienced with exhaust steam from the chimney of "Royal Scot" engines and the "Claughton" engines, fitted with large boilers, drifting downwards and obscuring the driver's view of signals, three engines were fitted, as an experiment, with the arrangement of side or deflector plates alongside the smokebox which had the effect of inducing an upward current of air alongside the boiler in front of the cab windows.

In view of the success of the arrangement and having regard to the importance of taking immediate steps

to rectify the trouble, instructions had been given, with the approval of the Vice President, for the sideplates to be fitted to the 70 "Royal Scot" and the 22 "Claughton" engines concerned as they pass through the sheds or the shops, the estimated outlay being £788. Approved.'

The Royal Scots all got their deflector plates within a few months; straight at first, they were later curved inwards at the top, in at least two different styles.

Drop Firegrates

On 27 March 1930, before the Derby-built engines came into service, the drop firegrates of the existing engines were proving troublesome. Fowler reported that 'owing to warping and cracking' they 'had been a continual source of trouble to the Motive Power Department'. An alteration to the design had been tried and proved satisfactory, and Fowler recommended that all fifty Royal Scots be so equipped, at a total cost of £558. This was obviously an optimistic assessment, for in March 1933 Fowler asked for authority to *remove* the drop fire grates from the Royal Scots and fit cast iron firebars instead. The new drop fire grates had not been entirely satisfactory and 'gave a certain amount of trouble'; they would be removed from the Royal Scots as they passed through the shops for repairs and cast iron firebars of the Midland type fitted, at an estimated outlay of £320.

The old FURY, as THE LONDON IRISH RIFLEMAN, approaching Crewe from the south about 1928 – the stock appears to be still in LNW livery. Note oval NBL Hyde Park plate, bogie brake cylinder, long drain cocks and vacuum pump operated off crosshead – and where are the headlamps? The Royal Scots at this time were the very apple of the LMS eye, though the bad riding and hot boxes were beginning to tell. They were also plagued by broken slide bar bolts, as well as frequent fracturing of the Monel metal firebox stays. At this time, a Scot would be in the Repair Shop at Polmadie every week or so for attention to one or more of these ills, and the situation must have been the same at Camden, Crewe and so on. The picture demonstrates well the aesthetic discordance set up between that high shouldered firebox and cavernous smokebox, and that rather puny tender. Photograph B.P. Hoper Collection.

Tenders

The tenders of the Royal Scots were standard, unprepossessing 3,500 gallon ones of the time, which detracted from the look and aesthetic balance of the locos – at least to the eyes of later generations, brought up on the Stanier design. They were of limited capacity for so important a class; this deficiency soon became apparent and the twenty Derby examples were provided with coal rails to get extra coal on board. This was extended over 1931 and 1932 to the rest of the class:

'LOCOMOTIVE AND ELECTRICAL COMMITTEE
29th October 1931

The 20 "Royal Scot" engines Nos.6150-6169, built at Derby in 1930, were fitted with additional coal rails on the tenders and these coal rails have been found to be a great improvement especially for those engines engaged on the long through runs.
The workings of the "Royal Scot" engines between Euston, Liverpool and Manchester have been tightened up, and as the margin between the outward and return trains on most cases is only four hours, it is considered necessary that all these engines should be well coaled up on the outward trip.
At the request of the Chief General Superintendent, the Chief Mechanical Engineer asked for authority to fit, as the engines pass through the shops for repairs, additional coal rails to the tenders of the first 50 "Royal Scot" engines Nos.6100-6149, the estimated cost of the work being £514.'

Come 1936 it was decided to replace the originals with new Stanier high sided nine ton, 4,000 gallon tenders, which seemed to suit them better, giving a wholly more balanced look. A Locomotive and Electrical Committee Minute of 25 March 1936 took the process a step further. In order 'to provide a safe margin of coal and water' for the Royal Scots working their through runs, the CME recommended that the tenders which, with their new coal rails, carried 5½ tons of coal and 3,500 gallons, be removed from the Royal Scots and used instead on Jubilees; the 9 ton, 5,000 gallon tenders of these engines were to be 'redirected' to the Royal Scots. The transfer would require 'certain alterations and additions to the tenders and locomotives concerned' at an estimated cost of £5,880.

That, mercifully, is about it; the substitution of new tenders took place through 1936-37 and there was not the sort of complicated interchange thereafter that was seen on the Jubilees and other classes.

Tenders lead fairly anonymous lives, and are rarely implicated in accidents, though the tender fitted to 6154 (curiously also the engine suffering the deranged motion at Auchterarder – see above) featured in one derailment of the time. On 17 April 1934 6154 was working the 5.40am express from Glasgow to Euston when it was

derailed at Penrith. On examination it was found that the right leading tender spring was broken and several plates missing. The Research Department considered that the failure was not due to composition or structure of the material but to the development of cracks due to the combined corrosion and erosion of the spring plates, a contributing factor being the lack of any lubrication between the plates. This condition was regarded as exceptional; the method of lubricating the tender plates, prior to the spring being assembled having hitherto, generally speaking, been satisfactory. It does not seem to have manifested itself again.

Names

'Sir Henry Fowler stated that fifty of this type of engine had been ordered and inasmuch as this particular engine would be used for working the train named 'The Royal Scot' he suggested the engine should bear the same name, which, after discussion, was agreed to'.

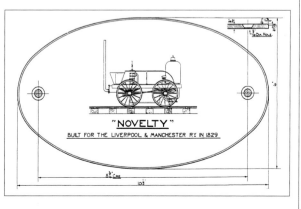

"NOVELTY"
BUILT FOR THE LIVERPOOL & MANCHESTER RY IN 1829

London Midland and Scottish Railway Company.

Secretary's Minute Office,
L. M. S. R., Euston Station.

File No. 3134

Secretary's Office,
Euston Station.

EXTRACT FROM THE MINUTES OF THE LOCOMOTIVE AND ELECTRICAL
COMMITTEE OF THE 24th APPROVED BY THE BOARD OF THE
25th October, 1928.

Naming of "Royal Scot" Class Engine.

Sir Henry Fowler informed the Committee that he had sent to each of the regiments represented in the "Royal Scot" class a photograph of the engine bearing the regiment's name, and he had received many expressions of thanks from the Commanding Officers.

ROYAL SCOT was the only one to carry a name when delivered, the others apparently coming out simply with the backing plate – the subject of the Royal Scot names has been covered endlessly elsewhere (the RCTS *Locomotives of the LMS* volume has no less than a dozen pages devoted to them, a fascinating exercise in itself). The first mention I have found in the archive comes on 26 October 1927, with Sir Henry announcing to the Locomotive and Electrical Engineering Committee that *'he was satisfied with the results which had so far attended this class of engine'*. After some consideration the following list (as spelt in the minute) was approved and recommended to the Board:

Always assiduous in preparing the ground, Fowler had arranged for a pamphlet to be printed explaining each name 'for the Directors' perusal'. Various amendments took place, altering most of these greatly. Fowler later had the highly attractive idea of fitting small plaques to those named after historical locomotives, with line drawings of the originals. Scrupulously polished, they often wore away like the face of a Queen Victoria penny!

The 'famous locomotive' names were removed in the 1930s, beginning with 6138 FURY which was destined, with unfortunate aptness, for the high pressure 6399. From 1932, OSTRICH, NOVELTY and the rest were given regimental names. A

ROYAL SCOT	METEOR
HIGHLAND CHIEF	COMET
ROYAL SCOTS GREY	LIVERPOOL
BLACK WATCH	PLANET
LOTHIAN	PHOENIX
ROYAL SCOTS FUSILIER	VULCAN
SCOTTISH BORDERER	ATLAS
CAMERON	LIVER
GORDON	SAMSON
ARGYLL	GOLIATH
SUTHERLAND	VESTA
SEAFORTH	FURY
LONDON SCOTTISH	AJAX
LOVAT'S SCOUTS	HECTOR
GUARDSMAN	CALEDONIAN
ROYAL ENGINEER	MAIL
GRENADIER	BEE
ROYAL FUSILIER	OSTRICH
SHERWOOD FORESTER	CONDOR
ROYAL WELSH	JENNY LIND
COLDSTREAM	COURIER
LANCASHIRE WITCH	VELOCIPEDE
PERSEVERANCE	LADY OF THE LAKE
SANSPAREIL	JEANNIE DEANS
NOVELTY	IONIC

number of regiments offered badges and these were characteristically unveiled by the Colonel, after which no doubt, there was a very agreeable lunch.

Split Bushes
On 23 January 1935 trouble was reported from the split bushes fitted to the leading coupled rods on the Royal Scots. Stanier recommended that they be replaced with side brass bushes, which had proved satisfactory on other classes of engines and which would 'enable a saving of £477 per annum to be effected'. As usual, the work would be carried out as the engines passed through the Works for repairs, to extend 'over a period of approximately three years' (it didn't – see *Slipping and Sanding* in the section *A New Engine*) and the cost was to be £1,015.

Side Draught Screens
These were the little folding protective screens, a few inches wide, set between the cab windows which gave some rudimentary protection for Drivers straining to see forward. Stanier recommended on 27 February 1935 that the Royal Scots and 52 three cylinder rebuilt 'Claughtons' be fitted with side draught screens on the outside of the cabs, similar to the screens provided on new locomotives recently built, such as the Jubilees. These modest screens, Stanier reported, 'had proved of considerable benefit to the drivers'. The estimated cost of the work (again, to be carried out as the engines passed through the shops for repairs) would extend over a period of about two years, and cost about £560.

Atomiser Lubrication
On 23 October 1935 Stanier reported that all new engines were being fitted with atomiser lubrication to the piston valves This was found to considerably reduce carbonisation and also minimised the normal wear on piston valve heads, rings and liners. He accordingly recommended that the Royal Scots and the Patriots be so fitted, at an estimated cost of £1,620. The principle was simply that of introducing a 'spray' of lubricating oil into the steam passages.

Speed Indicators
On 27 October 1937 The Mechanical and Electrical Engineering Committee approved the fitting of no less than 998 'express locomotives' with speed indicators. New and accelerated express passenger services meant that, paradoxically, there were additional maximum permissible speed restrictions imposed by the Chief Civil Engineer. Consideration was therefore given to *'the desirability of fitting an instrument which would both indicate and make a continuous record of a*

speed of a locomotive'. Twenty 'express engines' had been fitted with such a device. The Mechanical and Electrical Engineering Committee did not propose to recommend the fitting of speed recorders generally 'owing to possible margins of error and the difficulty and cost of checking such records' but it did think it advisable that 'an electrical type of speed indicator' should be fitted to 'the 998 locomotives working express passenger trains'. This widened definition of LMS express passenger engines involved a cost of £23,000.

There the matter seemed to rest, until 25 January 1940 when a memorandum was submitted reporting that *'as a result of the experience gained from the "Stone Deuta" type speed recording instrument fitted to eight "Royal Scot" engines and "Hasler" type instruments to 12 Princess engines it was decided not to fit speed recording instruments to engines as a whole and authority was therefore obtained to fit 998 engines with electrical type speed indicators'.* The War ensured that these developments faltered but speed indicators did – after a fashion – eventually appear on the 'new' Royal Scots (see later, taper boiler days).

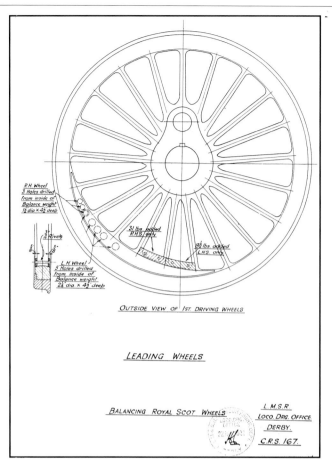

LEADING WHEELS

BALANCING ROYAL SCOT WHEELS

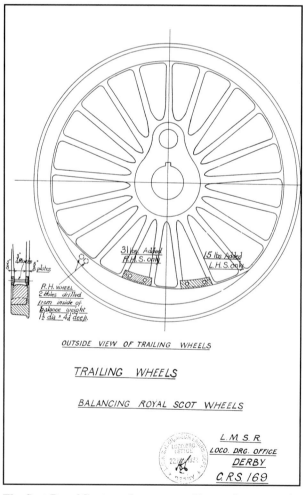

TRAILING WHEELS

BALANCING ROYAL SCOT WHEELS

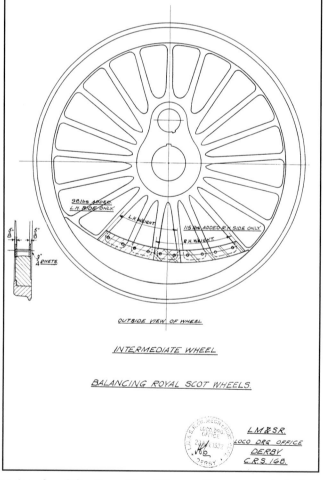

INTERMEDIATE WHEEL

BALANCING ROYAL SCOT WHEELS.

The first Royal Scots underwent, really, an almost continuous series of modifications. The riding problems prompted a fair proportion of these – take the wheel balancing for instance, an ordinary enough subject but vital to good running. A 'fine tuning' exercise in 1932 left the accompanying diagrams, which show how it was achieved. The basic balance weight was built into the casting, but additions and deletions (the latter by drilling out the required amount of metal) were necessary. Some of the photographs hint at this work – good hunting!

That front end, now long vanished; seldom could a 'rebuild' look so different...

Euston, March 1934. Back home, ROYAL SCOT kept the American paraphernalia for a while; the headlamp came off after a spell but the bell stayed on until the engine's rebuilding. Its fate is unknown, though the later CORONATION bell was in the Paint Shop at Crewe for years, and is now in the ADTRANZ hospitality lounge there. The bell and its mounting left no room for the middle lamp iron, which presumably meant ROYAL SCOT could not act as a royal engine at this time! Photograph G.E. Rossiter.

A Royal Scot Goes West

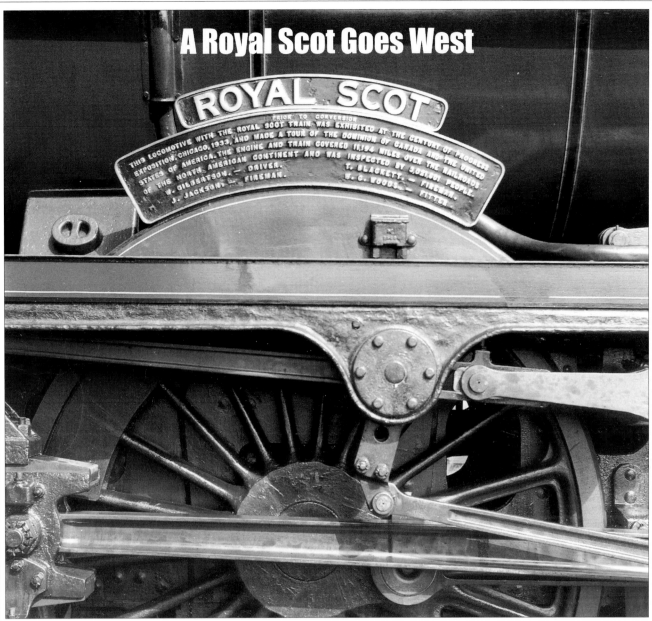

The plate recording the American tour - this was retained after 6100 was rebuilt, with the caveat 'PRIOR TO CONVERSION'. Photograph R.C.Riley.

America beckoned the more enlightened officers of our railways in the 1930s. Enormous technical interest was stirring over here in the affairs of the New World and many professional and personal contacts were being made. An invitation to send an LMS locomotive and train arrived from America, and the obvious choice was a Royal Scot.

Now Stanier, not long on the LMS, had misgivings about the Royal Scots, as a letter reproduced by Essery and Jenkinson in *An Illustrated History of LMS Locomotives, Vol. 5, Post Grouping Standard Designs* (Silver Link, 1989) reveals. In it, Stanier's brother is writing to his own son Tom, concerning 'Uncle Will's' appointment to the LMS. Apart from a wonderful image of Stanier, stricken by an excess of Scotch being carried down the Athenaeum steps, it reveals that Stanier thought the Royal Scot boiler 'no good'. He was to make sure that if one of these locos was to go

abroad, representing both the company and himself, it would carry his personal stamp, being reshod and getting a new bogie, as described in the memorandum of March 1934 reproduced earlier. 6100 was the first Scot to get this treatment. But was it? Much fun has been had down the years with its identity. For years the story has gone that 6152 was the engine sent, substituted for 6100. Reed has his doubts, hinting darkly that 6152's card is the only one missing, and Cox, teasingly, simply says 'a suitable unit was selected for shopping'. 6152's Record Card does in fact exist, and bears no comment that could link it to America, while 6100's has a scrawled comment 'AMERICAN TOUR YEAR 1933'. There are none of the precise notes that are found later in the case of the Pacifics, when DUCHESS OF HAMILTON stood in for CORONATION.

Some writers hold that 6100 temporarily switched identities with

6152, others say it was a permanent switch; Peter Rowledge has written that 'in the main' it was 6152 that went, *'though many components came from others of the class in shops at the same time as the engine was under preparation'.*

So you can take your pick. The Record Cards, incidentally, support none of these contentions, though I'm far from claiming these as 'clinchers'.

The point is, the engine that did go was very different in its mechanical condition from either 6100 or 6152 – or any other Scot of the time! It sailed from Tilbury with its train in April 1933, to land at Montreal for re-erection by the Canadian Pacific. The tour lasted from 1 May to 25 May, to arrive at Chicago in time for the World Fair. Over 11,000 miles were run in North America, though without the local ATC it was limited to 40mph. Its tender (it had been destined for the third Pacific) was fitted with Timken

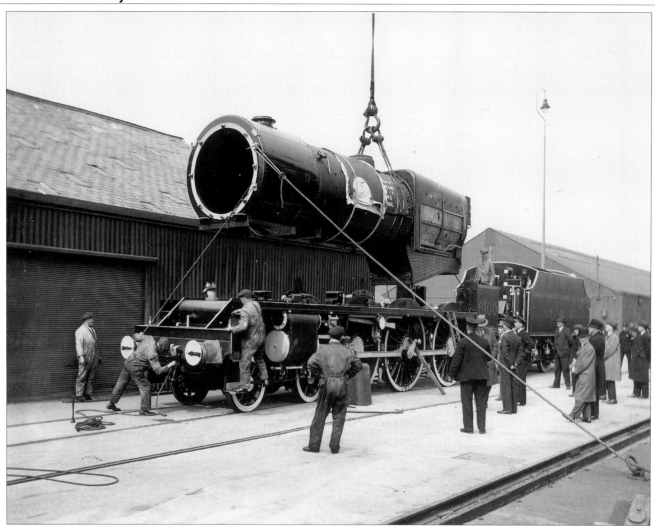

ROYAL SCOT was partly stripped for the journey to Tilbury, to ease the task of 'de-erecting' it once there. The small picture (caught by a tipped-off Mr. L. Hanson) shows it heading south behind 4F 4065 at Northampton Castle station on 3 April 1933, a slightly fuzzy picture but historically interesting. The train behind will contain its collection of spares, everything from brickarch bricks to smokebox door. The main picture show the boiler being separated from the frames at Tilbury dockside.

roller bearings and the loco suffered no failures, though after 3,000,000 visitors, as Reed records, its train was near-wrecked by souvenir hunters. The engine had an electric headlamp fitted at Derby and had the familiar horizontal plate on the smokebox THE ROYAL SCOT, but a Westinghouse pump was not needed, the engine hauling its own train of LMS vehicles. 'Over There', to coin a phrase, it got a hand operated warning bell and a cowcatcher, both of which came off when the CP workshops 'de-erected' it for shipping back home. It arrived back at Tilbury on 5 December.

The Engine Card for 6100 show a works visit 4 Jan 1933 to 2 March 1933 with a pencilled note 'Special For American Tour' perfectly timed for the American trip. 6152's Card shows it entering works in July 1933 when *a Royal Scot was in Chicago*, only coming out of works in August 1933, with its sister still 4,500 miles away intriguing light-fingered visitors in Chicago.

The mystery deepens, for the engine that went to America had the Derby style of motion bracket, which was different from the NBL one, while 6152 later sported a Derby one – a swap was the obvious conclusion, or

was it? All through the Royal Scot story parts and bits have been added or removed willy-nilly, as they became available from the mix of parts in works – and why shouldn't they? That was the idea of a 'standard' class after all. Was the motion bracket a chance red herring – or even a joke?

Whatever the engine's identity, the tour was adjudged a huge success; at the Mechanical and Electrical Engineering Committee meeting of 20 December 1933, Sir Harold Hartley (the Engineering Vice President) stated that the successful journey of the train through Canada and the United States had been *'very largely due to the absolute freedom from mechanical failures, which he considered was owing to the foresight in preparing the locomotive and carriages. Mr. Stanier said that*

realising the train would be away for a long time and doing a very big mileage, he and his staff had taken very special precautions in preparing both the locomotive and the coaches to meet the exceptional conditions. The Committee congratulated Mr. Stanier upon the foresight and care shown in preparing the train which had resulted in such a wonderful success.' Perhaps one day another letter from Stanier's brother will turn up...

The 'chassis' airborne for stowing on the SS BEAVERDALE, with the boiler still on the quayside.

On tour at Albany, New York State; most pictures show it without the cowcatcher, though it was certainly in use for part of the trip – the cowcatcher after all was the reason for stowing the coupling high up on a special hook on the bell mounting, rather than on the drawhook as was the more usual practice.

The hideous beast, which must have run up the lowest mileage of any main line locomotive in British history – and, moreover, not earning a single penny in the process.

High Pressure Dead End

E.R.O. 14005.

LONDON MIDLAND AND SCOTTISH RAILWAY COMPANY.

HENRY FOWLER,
CHIEF MECHANICAL ENGINEER.

TELEGRAPHIC ADDRESS:
"FOWLER, c/o BESLINE, DERBY."

TELEPHONE No. 1100.

CHIEF MECHANICAL ENGINEER'S OFFICE.

PLEASE REFER TO

U. 4950.
W/ 7-8.

IN YOUR REPLY

DERBY, 20th Feb.,1930.

(CENTRE No. 49.)

To the
LOCOMOTIVE AND ELECTRICAL COMMITTEE.

Gentlemen,

MISHAP TO "ROYAL SCOT" ENGINE NO. 6399, "FURY",
at Carstairs, Monday, 10th February, 1930.

I very much regret to report that one of the water pipes which formed the firebox of the closed circuit of the above locomotive split over about a length of 5" longitudinally in the tube when the engine was just running into Carstairs Station. The engine was making its first breaking-in trip under its own steam from Polmadie to Carstairs and return.

Riding on the engine were Driver Hall, Fireman Blair, Mr. Lewis Schofield, the representative of the Superheater Company, and Mr. Pepper from the C.M.E. Department, Derby. Unfortunately, at the time the pipe burst, Mr. Schofield happened to be standing almost opposite the firehole door which was full open, and received the full force of the escaping steam and fire which was blown out of the firebox, receiving serious scalding and burning injuries. He was first attended to at Carstairs Station by the ambulance staff, and was removed by special train to the Glasgow Royal Infirmary, where he died at mid-day on the 11th instant.

The fireman was standing close to Mr. Schofield at the time of the accident. He immediately jumped head first out of the engine cab, and received minor cuts and bruises about the head. His right forearm was also either scalded or burned. The fireman was detained at the Infirmary, although his injuries, I understand, are not serious.

The driver managed to escape any serious injury with the exception of slight scalding on the right wrist which occurred when he leaned forward to apply the brake as soon as this was possible when the escaping steam had practically died down.

Mr. Pepper escaped by climbing from the cab through the side top opening. His only injury was a slight scalding on the wrist and both ankles.

Yours faithfully,

Hy. Fowler

H.H.

With this terrible accident the ill-starred high pressure experiment on the LMS was over. The Germans had been involved in this field for some time and Fowler by 1928 wrote (profoundly wrongly as it turned out) that high pressure locomotives were The Coming Thing – 'the general tendency in the locomotive world' was how he put it. His eye had been caught by a 4-6-0 running on the German State Railways. It was one of its regular three cylinder express passenger engines, but fitted with a Schmidt-Henschel high pressure boiler. *'There is no doubt'*, Fowler wrote on 11 October 1928, *'that there is a general tendency through the locomotive world to move in the direction of much higher steam pressures, and I am of the opinion that if the proposal is looked upon in the lines of research, it would be advantageous for us to make a trial of some type of high pressure locomotive'.*

After careful consideration of the various types, on 11 October 1928 Fowler recommended to the Locomotive and Electrical Committee that a Schmidt-Henschel high pressure boiler, similar to the one which had been in

6399 FURY outside the North British Hyde Park works; the nameplate (from 6138) when first fitted did not have the little plaque that went with it, but it was added later. There is no precise date as to when FURY came out from NBL; the Engine Record Card has gone but according to a review by Stanier, dated 16 July 1934, it was 'ordered' on 14 December 1928 and passed its steam test on 4 February 1930. Two days later, on 6 February 1930, it was 'handed over' to the LMS. Its fateful run to Carstairs on 10 February was merely a short trip from Polmadie for running in the axleboxes and so on.

service for some two years in Germany, should be fitted to a Royal Scot. This, he suggested, would effect an economy of 20% in coal consumption, equivalent to between £130 and £140 per annum per engine. Fowler explained that the LMS would provide the engine and frames and would share with the Superheater Company, with whom he had already consulted, the cost of the boiler. This was estimated at £3,000, but he had agreed with the Superheater Co. that, however the cost turned out, the maximum amount the LMS would be called upon to pay in this respect would be £1,500. Fowler had considered a variety of high pressure boilers, but considered the Schmidt-Henschel one the most suitable; as a result of long trials in Germany, it was more advanced than any other type.

In view of the fact that the present stock of Royal Scots 'was required for service' (it would be inconvenient for Fowler's experiment if they weren't) he recommended that a wholly new engine be built by North British, an idea that was replicating the work of the Germans. The Royal Scot inside cylinder arrangement would be modified to make the new engine a three cylinder compound type, at an estimated cost of £7,250, which, with the agreed maximum payment of £1,500 towards the cost of the high pressure boiler, gave a total estimated expenditure of £8,750. This was £1,000 more than the earlier conventional NBL Scots but of course the high pressure engine was a 'one off', and a number of new patterns would also be required.

All this was 'Approved, and Ordered' in the rather portentous way of doing such things at the time, and an order was straight away placed with NBL for a Royal Scot suitably made up with the Schmidt-Henschel high pressure boiler.

No.6399 FURY was handed over to the LMS on 6 February 1930 for running in and was to have perhaps the shortest career of any British main line locomotive. In retrospect, it seems inevitably doomed by its own complexity. In an effort to raise the thermal efficiency, this terrifyingly ultra high pressure boiler generated steam at different pressures, the highest an astonishing 1,400lb/sq.in.. There was a single high pressure inside cylinder fed at 900lb/sq.in.; the exhaust from this mixed with steam at 250lb/sq.in. (from a 'normal' part of the boiler) and this went to the two conventional outside cylinders.

As the mournful memo at the head of this section shows, it was only days later that the thing failed, catastrophically. The accident occurred on 10 February 1930, only four days after the engine's reception by the LMS, and on the 26th Fowler was submitting diagrams which supported his opinion that the mishap was due to a defective tube, although very great care had been taken in selecting and testing them. The matter was being fully investigated and 'at the suggestion of the Vice President he was going to

ask Dr. Frank Smith, CB. CBE, Secretary to the Royal Society and Secretary to the Department of Industrial and Scientific Research, to assist in the investigation.'

The generally accepted notion is that FURY was laid aside after this until Stanier came across it at Derby. However, it was repaired after the disaster and put on further trial:

'MISHAP TO HIGH PRESSURE ROYAL SCOT CLASS ENGINE NO.6399 "FURY", CARSTAIRS, 10TH FEBRUARY, 1930.

Submitted report 24th June from the Chief Mechanical Engineer that the matter had been carefully investigated by the Railway Company's Officials; Dr. Lea and Dr. Desch of the University of Sheffield; and the Superheater Company.

The mishap was due to the bursting of a pipe at approximately the centre of the crown of the firebox.

The fracture of the tube itself shewed signs of a flaw, but close micrographic investigation shewed that although a slight flaw undoubtedly existed, there was clear evidence of 'creep' in the metal of the tube. It is thought that this was due to a 'steam pocket' being formed in the

6399 was so infrequently in steam that is small wonder photographs of it 'at work' are few and far between. This is a familiar one, presumably in the works yard at Derby.

tube which burst, and that the fracture would ultimately have taken place fairly early even had the slight flaw not existed. The reason for this steam pocket was probably due to two causes:-

1. The rate of circulation of the water was slowed down owing to the small inclination of the tubes forming the top of the firebox. The inclination of the tubes from the horizontal at the crown of the box was 3 degrees as against 7 degrees in the case of the German locomotive, which has been running for two years. The reason for this small inclination was to allow of the expansion of the tubes it was thought necessary to have in the low pressure boiler.

2. The provision of tubes running from the front of the foundation ring up to the back of the firebox, these being used as supports for the brick arch. These tended to rob the other tubes of water. The high temperature reached by the metal of the tube was apparently due to the long brick arch put in to ensure good mixture of the gases. This led to a restricted space between the top of the arch and the box, and deflected the gases somewhat on to the tubes forming the top of the box, where the tube which burst was situated. To overcome these difficulties, the following steps are being taken:

1. The tubes at the top of the box are receiving an inclination generally of 13 degrees, this being gradually reduced in the last 5 (bifurcated) tubes near the low pressure tubeplate, where the tubes are not so exposed to the direct action of the flames.

2. The brick arch supporting-pipes to be done away with, and a new type of brick arch to be provided. This latter to be shortened and given less inclination and to have rounded corners at the open end to prevent local eddying and high velocity of the flames. Several minor alterations were proposed but it was felt by Dr. Lea, the Superheater

Company and the Chief Mechanical Engineer that the above modifications should make the boiler safe and satisfactory, with which the Vice President agreed, and after consideration the Committee ordered that the experiments be proceeded with, a further report to be submitted in due course.'

So, the real trials of the efficacy of FURY actually took place *after* the explosion, though they ultimately proved only the loco's unsuitedness to the task. By the summer of 1934 Stanier was ready to review events. He had little good news to impart: 'in spite of elaborate and prolonged trials, (it) had not proved successful, the steaming in every case having been unsatisfactory. In spite of continual modification there had been no signs of the boiler becoming an efficient and reliable steam producing unit or suitable for use on ordinary services; in addition, the coal consumption had always been higher than for any similar engine fitted with a standard type of boiler doing the same work.'

There had been extensive redesigning and modification of the high pressure circuit and a stationary steam test finally undertaken once again in July 1931. Steam was subsequently raised on many occasions (you can imagine the trepidation of the blokes in the cab) but every time some defect or other arose, and it was not until the autumn of 1932 that further road tests were carried out. These were repeated at intervals up to 24 March 1934, and in every case the steaming was poor.

As it turned out, the German engine also suffered a burst tube, in 1931, and the record of the other high pressure locos was hardly encouraging. There were three others; of these the French one had shown an improvement in coal consumption but had nonetheless been re-converted, no

figures were available for the Canadian Pacific engine and so far as the New York Central one was concerned, Stanier wrote, 'the last we heard was that it was still in the American Locomotive Company's shops...'

From now on FURY, as the far more prosaically named BRITISH LEGION would continue its semi-detached, somewhat meandering course through the design history of the Royal Scots – after a brief interlude pitting Royal Scots against Pacifics and Kings, see the penultimate section, *A New Engine.*

Legal Footnote

The Superheater Company was the big commercial loser in the FURY episode, and by 1934 it was asking for some contribution to the massive £20,000 or so it had spent in development work. The legal position of the LMS was ironclad, however, for Fowler's original agreement (he was ever a better manager than engineer!) restricted the LMS contribution to a maximum of £1,500, and even then only if the engine 'was found to be satisfactory in its service'. Stanier's review of the FURY years makes it plain that the engine had never given satisfactory service, as the agreement demanded, and furthermore that it was of no practical value whatsoever. But in the light of the Superheater Co.'s efforts, he asked for authority to offer a contribution 'not exceeding £1,500'. The Superheater Co. actually pressed for more than the £1,500, given that it had pursued additional experiments at the behest of the LMS. The Board had some sympathy with the firm's plight, and in July 1934 settled the matter with an *ex-gratia* payment of £3,000.

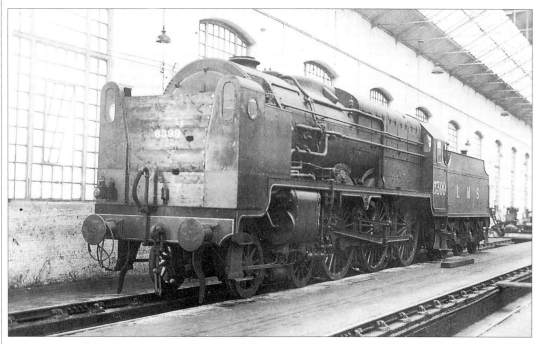

FURY seems to have spent most of its time in the cool and quiet of the Derby Paint Shop, sometimes with indicator shelter, sometimes without. Though it looks grey, it was actually wearing red livery throughout this time.

QUEEN'S WESTMINSTER RIFLEMAN on a pre-test run, in Sonning Cutting with the 8.30am Plymouth-Paddington express. Photograph M.W. Earley.

Down at The Cross. No one seemed to notice that the LM (now the London Midland *Region)* took care to see that 'LMS' was on the tenders of its participating locos! Photograph C.C.B. Herbert.

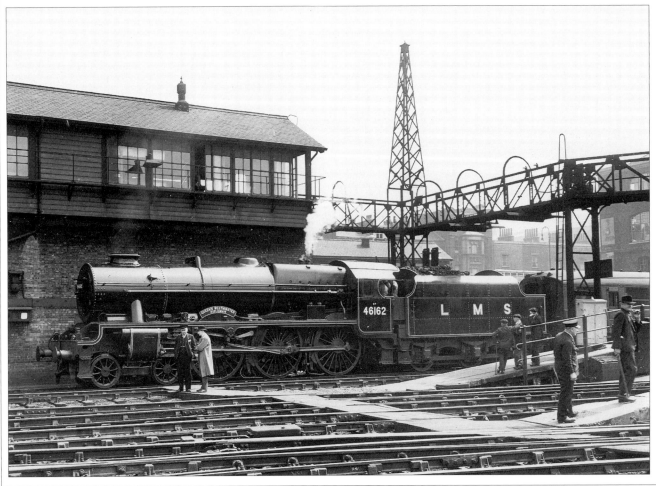

1948 – The Great Exchange

The great BR Interchange Trial came in 1948 and if there was any star of the show, it was probably a Royal Scot. Two were used, 46162 QUEEN'S WESTMINSTER RIFLEMAN and 46154 THE HUSSAR. In the express passenger category they were pitted against Coronation, A4 and Merchant Navy Pacifics and the GW King 4-6-0. On the Southern THE HUSSAR had a 5,000 gallon WD tender (lettered LMS!) fitted to increase the water supply. The story of the 1948 Interchanges is a long and complex one; suffice it to say that the Royal Scots acquitted themselves well. Cecil J. Allen (*The Locomotive Exchanges 1870-1948*, Ian Allan, 1949) could not have more unequivocal: they *'achieved feats of brilliance that I should barely have conceived possible with an engine of such dimensions'*.

The celebrated No.9 platform at Paddington, with 46162 QUEEN'S WESTMINSTER RIFLEMAN. Some of the Western Region runs were the only ones (except for Euston-Carlisle) where the Scot had a reduced load compared to the Pacifics against which it was set. It is easy, because it was so often on trial against Pacifics, to regard the Scot as a 'small' engine, yet it was only a little smaller than the King – its firegrate area for instance, at 31.3sq.ft. was not that far behind the King's 34.3sq.ft.. Photograph C.C.B. Herbert.

WORKING OF EXPRESS PASSENGER ENGINES (CONTD.)

LONDON MIDLAND REGION '6P' CLASS.

Paddington-Plymouth route
25th to 28th May inclusive.

The load for this locomotive was nominally less than for the other express passenger locomotives by 45 tons in the Up direction (Plymouth-Paddington) and in the Down direction by 35 tons Paddington to Newton Abbot, and 45 tons Newton Abbot to Plymouth.

12.1/2% to 15% cut-off with 1st valve of regulator on the easier stretches. Maximum cut-off 45% on Hemerdon Bank on the 2nd valve of the regulator.

King's Cross-Leeds route
27th to 30th April inclusive.

Engine steamed freely, the pressure being maintained between 230 and 235 lbs/sq.in. Normal running was made with a half-open regulator and gradients climbed in the 3/4-open position with an occasional full-open regulator. Cut-off positions were varied from 15% to 30% according to the power required.

There was generally a good body of fire on the grate and very little black smoke was seen, indicating good firebox temperature.

Euston-Carlisle route
4th to 7th May inclusive.

The engine was normally free steaming, pressures varying between 220 and 245 lbs/sq.in., but somewhat inferior on May 6th when priming occurred three times. On this occasion minimum pressure was 190 lbs/sq.in. at Low Gill.

Water level was always well maintained.

Exhaust showed little smoke at any time. Engine free running.

Mainly worked in the following cut-off and regulator positions :-

Cut-off 17%-24% with 1/3-3/4 reg. - rising gradients.
Cut-off 15%-19% with 1/3-1/2 reg. - level.
Cut-off 13%-15% with 1/4-1/3 reg. - falling gradients.

Riding mainly good but some vertical vibration and lateral oscillation felt at speed.

Waterloo-Exeter route
15th to 18th June inclusive.

Engine usually worked in 15% cut-off on 1st valve of the regulator on the easier stretches. Maximum cut-off used - 45% with second valve of the regulator half open.

FURY tamed – 6170 BRITISH LEGION, sparkling new in 1935. Thus transmogrified, the engine provided a template of sorts for the *grand idée,* a fleet of 6P taper boiler 4-6-0s from the bones of the Jubilees, Patriots and Royal Scots. With its No.2 boiler and restricted sphere of movement it remained very much the odd one out. The steam pipes jutted forward in that peculiar way (though they did not last long in this form) because the boiler barrel was 15in. longer than on the other Scots; the top feed was also further back and it was the only taper Scot to run with the old style vacuum pump on the left-hand crosshead. A further distinction was that it was the only taper Scot to run in crimson livery. Photograph National Railway Museum.

A new 6104 SCOTTISH BORDERER, painted up for the official works photograph, in 1946. It has the later design of bush on the leading crank pin, not the split bushes which BRITISH LEGION inherited from FURY. Photograph National Railway Museum.

A New Engine

6170 BRITISH LEGION rose from the ashes of the high pressure experiment, going to traffic in the then unfamiliar form of a taper boiler 6P locomotive from 31 October 1935 (according to its Record Card). Formed from the bare bones of FURY, 6170 was not the 'prototype' of the 'rebuilt' Royal Scots, though it assuredly pointed the way. The taper boiler Scots, rather, sprang from the two reconstituted 5XP Jubilees, 5735 and 5736, of 1942.

FURY, as we have seen, had been promulgated back in 1928 as a 'Royal Scot with a high pressure boiler', but it was plainly not a Royal Scot; rebuilt as 6170 BRITISH LEGION it would look much more like a taper boiler Royal Scot than FURY ever looked liked a conventional Royal Scot, but it was still not the *pattern* for the new class, though the Locomotive and Electrical Engineering Committee in July 1934 (quoted in full in the FURY section) was working along these lines: *'It was therefore recommended that the engine be converted to a 'Royal Scot' type, the alterations including provision of a new boiler of the taper barrel type,* <u>*which it was proposed to fit to the 'Royal Scot' class as a whole,*</u> [My underlining] *as and when present boilers fell due for renewal...'*

So it was in Stanier's mind to upgrade the Royal Scots almost from the first; money, priorities and problems with the 5XP Jubilees meant it took some years to implement. It was in the war, surprisingly, that Derby took two Jubilees, 5735 and 5736, at Stanier's behest (looking to the post-war LMS world, no doubt) and rebuilt them with the larger and higher pressure boiler known as the 2A. The idea was to bring all the 5XP Jubilee 4-6-0s into the 6P Royal Scot power fold. The two engines came out in April (5736) and May (5735) 1942, the 2A boiler being a new 250lb design. 6170, rebuilt from FURY as BRITISH LEGION had shown the way, back in 1935, with its No.2 boiler of similar pressure; the 2A was *'the sloping throatplate version of the similar No.2 boiler'*. (Rowledge and Reed, *The Stanier 4-6-0s of the LMS*, D&C, 1977). It was the two Jubilees, with the new standard 2A boiler, that finally precipitated the 'rebuilding' of the Royal Scots, into one of the most formidable 4-6-0 classes ever to run in Britain.

Despite the Second World War, the decision was not long in coming. On 26 November 1942 the Mechanical and Electrical Engineering Committee received a memorandum from the Chief Operating Manager and the Acting Chief Mechanical Engineer (Stanier was seconded to the Ministry of Production as Scientific Advisor from October that year). This outlined the necessary technical reasons (there was a war on after all) though these had been making themselves felt back in 1934: *'The smokeboxes at present fitted to the 'Royal Scot' engines were of bad design, causing frequent loss of time in service and excessive maintenance at Sheds, and the trouble could not be overcome without major structural alterations, including a new design of cylinders. Further, the engines were prohibited by their weight from working over the Midland Division where the class 5X three cylinder engines at present in use were overloaded. Certain of the engines were now falling due for renewal of boilers, cylinders and frames and it was proposed to alter twenty engines by fitting taper boilers – sufficiently lighter in weight to enable the engines to work over the Midland Division; new cylinders; and new design of smokebox which it was anticipated would result in less shed maintenance and overcome the smokebox trouble. The estimated cost excluding cost of boilers was £57,440. In addition authority was required to increase the expenditure of*

And thereby hangs a tale! 46146 in beautiful BR green and in possession of its taper boiler since 1943, *retains* the accursed split bushes, first condemned nearly twenty years before and to be recondemned in 1945... Photograph National Railway Museum.

£199,860 authorised by Mechanical and Electrical Engineering Minute of 25th July 1940 on the 1941 Boiler Renewal Programme, which included the construction of ten parallel boilers for the 'Royal Scot' engines, by £1,940 representing the additional cost of the taper boilers compared with parallel boilers; the remaining ten taper boilers being included in the 1943 Boiler Renewal Programme. Approved.'

On 29 June 1944 a further £237,000 was approved for the conversion of the remaining fifty Royal Scots with taper boilers, new cylinders and new smokebox, and on 28 September the same year a similar recommendation came for eighteen 'class 5X parallel boiler engines'. The LMS Minutes usually refer to both Jubilees and Patriots as '5X', only occasionally differentiating them by boiler type, parallel or taper.

The new engines were always known as 'rebuilt' but it is something of a moot point whether they were or not. They were hardly 'rebuilt' by most means of measuring it; they were, *in the main,* complete renewals – a new class if you like, with nothing remaining from the original days of 1927-30 except odd bits of metal and the cabs. And yet – some engines had new frames late in their parallel boiler days, keeping them when the taper boilers were fitted. In these cases it is less easy to deny the engines' 'rebuilt' status. It is also very likely that some Royal Scots retained rather more of their forebears than others – each locomotive was assessed during renewal, to no fixed formula.

Smoke Deflectors Again

The new engines did not at first have smoke deflectors, though from 1949 the whole of the class was progressively fitted with the characteristic curving plates, except, peculiarly, 46106 which got Britannia style plates. Whether there were instances of smoke drifting down again, obscuring the Driver's view, or whether the exercise was a simple precaution against such an eventuality, is not clear.

Slipping and Sanding

In addition to the original sandboxes very prominent, upright rectangular sandboxes were added from at least as early as 1945, through to BR days. It was retrospective in some cases, coming two or three years after an engine's conversion; later on, (certainly by 1949) the 'double sandboxes' as they were called were being fitted at the same time as the engine's conversion. Each box was divided in two, feeding sand both to the front of the trailing wheel and to the rear of the middle driving wheel. There had been expensive reasons for this...

The Mechanical and Electrical Engineering Committee heard on 22

6130 THE WEST YORKSHIRE REGIMENT in June 1935. This shows the notorious split brasses of the leading crankpin, so disliked by fitting staff. When engines came back from works with this replaced by the modern version they breathed a sigh of relief. It seems to have been an old Midland idea, and whereas a modern bushed coupling rod could just be pulled off the crankpin once the end 'nut/washer' had been removed, this type required the whole engine to be jacked up. This took the weight off the leading driving wheels, which than had to be rotated a few inches (using a jack) to release the front split brass. Once the cotter and so on had been removed the rear brass could be slid out, but the crankpin was hard against the front brass so the wheel had to be turned again to release it! Usually another jack on a convenient spoke served – but it was fairly primitive stuff...

March 1945 that 'trouble' (an understatement) was being experienced with rebuilt Royal Scots 'due to the bending of their coupling rods'. This was alarming in a new engine and the fact that sand was previously applied to the leading and intermediate driving wheels and not to the trailers, was considered to be partly responsible. *'It was therefore recommended that double sandboxes be provided between the driving and trailing wheels at an estimated cost for the 70 engines concerned of £2,799.'* The new boxes stood on the footplating adjacent to the firebox.

The problem continued; though it was the human dimension that was to blame. The company still called the engines Royal Scots, and given the almost complete absence of technical induction to new types on British railways, drivers had to feel their way. It was hardly surprising that they sought to drive their charges much as they had before... By 27 September 1945 a number of cases had occurred of the converted Royal Scots bending their coupling rods as a result of slipping. While the trouble had practically disappeared as the enginemen became more accustomed to the different characteristics of the new engines, the Mechanical and Electrical Engineering Committee proposed a belt and braces approach: *'as and when the coupling rods required renewal in the ordinary course of maintenance, to provide a stronger design of rod by increasing the cross section* [in the event most Scots emerged from rebuilding only rarely

The two types set up in the sort of comparison so beloved of the official photographer. In wartime black, on the left is 6103 ROYAL SCOTS FUSILIER and on the right in pre-war garb, 6102 BLACK WATCH. The year is presumably 1943, with 6103 newly rebuilt and 6102 in for repair. There was a deliberate policy to station the engines with Scottish names in Scotland; laudable enough but it made life difficult for spotters in the south. Photograph National Railway Museum.

with plain section rods] *and to fit a solid bush at leading crank pin in place of the older design of split bush'*, the estimated cost of which was £14,782.

The old Derby design of split bush at the leading crankpin is difficult to describe but its rectangular shape makes it obvious in photographs – when not obscured by rods. Their replacement had been ordered back in 1935 – see *Split Bushes* in the section *'Fifty Improved 4-6-0 Passenger Tender Engines'* but this seems to have been watered down; at least it fell by the wayside in some fashion. In the end the work was carried out from as early as 1943, through to the early 1950s. On the Record Cards the job is given as '6091' which would also seem to be the reference for fitting the taper boilers. Only close study of photographs will give the true picture; 6135 for instance came out with taper

boiler at the beginning of 1947 yet still had the old pattern of front coupling rod end... The joys of engine picking!

An Easier Life

The LMS was to have an upgraded locomotive fleet based on the 2A boiler (a boiler, incidentally, which was never fitted to any *new* locomotive); it was designed to fit the Scots, Patriots and Jubilees but the prospect of this vast 6P fleet was lost when the BR Standards began appearing and 'new work' on Regional types petered out. BR raised the LMS 6P to 7P under a reformulation of power gradings, in 1951. At the forefront of this 'upgrading drive' (though the Jubilees would have eventually outnumbered them greatly) the Royal Scots and the other renewed 4-6-0s, it was thought, should have the most up to date mechanical aids to ease their running

and ameliorate disposal at the sheds. On 24 July 1946 comes the first mention of upgrading the Scots in this regard: *'With reference to Mechanical and Electrical Engineering Committee Minute 2437 authorising expenditure of £237,000 on the conversion of the Royal Scot locomotives; submitted, with the approval of the Executive Committee, memorandum (July 1946) from the Chief Mechanical Engineer and the Chief Operating Manager recommending that the following additional features and modifications be introduced into the locomotives at additional cost of £14,859:-*
Fitting of self cleaning smokeboxes, self-emptying ashpans and rocking grates to the 35 locomotives still to be rebuilt.
Fitting of modified spring gear and latest type of hornstay to the 35 engines still to be rebuilt and that 35 already

46112 SHERWOOD FORESTER in pristine condition, at Nottingham for the presentation of new plaques – strange that of all the naming ceremonies associated with these locomotives, the two we've managed to come up with concern the same loco! According to the RCTS *LMS Locomotive Names*, the ceremony took place on 18 April 1948, with new plaques presented by Brigadier P.N. White. On the footplate were ex-Foresters Driver Croll and Fireman Follon, both wearing their medals and doubtless bursting with deserved pride.

Close enough to *feel* the metal. ROYAL SCOT on the occasion of its Derby visit, 25 September 1955. See also page 41 Photograph R.C. Riley.

converted and the welding of the frame plates in the case of the latter engines.' The total estimated cost would be increased to £251,859.

Riding

Riding quality was ever a problem with the Royal Scots, 'old' and 'new', though Geoffrey Freeman Allen (in the 1961 *Locospotters' Annual* – Ian Allan) was more precise: 'at times they bucked like a mad steer'. The engines rolled, nosed, rocked and tail-wagged and complaints rose to such a pitch that some slight modifications were ordered to the springing – see the above reference to modified spring gear – but this did not seem to have any great effect. The main cause was thought to be patches of poor track after wartime neglect and by June 1947 E.S. Cox was out riding the Royal Scots on a mission to find the underlying reasons for the poor riding.

They were several and vague, and in part depended on ill chance. The oscillations etc. were worst when a run down engine hit poor track. The bogie side control had been set very high with the first conversions, of the

Powering away in sunshine and rain, 46146 THE RIFLE BRIGADE provides the quintessential 'Scot at Work' image – rolling along with an Up express from Barrow on a Saturday, 19 August 1950. The photograph is taken from the steps of Watford No.2 signal box. The *matériel* over on the right marks the site of the area S&T stores. Photograph E.D. Bruton.

The 'other' odd one out, after 6170 – 46106 GORDON HIGHLANDER with its BR Britannia type smoke deflectors, at Crewe North on 17 April 1957. The story of why and how this change was effected seems never to have emerged. Photograph B. Hilton, B.P. Hoper Collection.

Jubilees 5735 and 5736, and Cox, upon investigation, thought this tended to 'fix' the front end of the engine. An exaggerated movement was thus concentrated at the back end. Some reduction in the bogie side control values was made (the over-emphasis went back to the days of 6131's Weaver Junction derailment) along with a careful rebalancing of the coupled wheels. Stiffer springs with greater internal friction helped but Cox emphasised that it was the fitting of manganese steel liners (already due for fitting to the 5X engines) that would

go to the heart of the problem. He would also liked to have seen roller bearings, *'for which the Class 6 engine would be an ideal type … i.e., it would benefit more than any other from the reduction in side clearance which these bearings make possible'*. The roller bearings of course, were not to be but the manganese linings and so on were duly and promptly decreed:

'MECHANICAL AND ELECTRICAL ENGINEERING COMMITTEE 29th October 1947 to improve the riding and general condition of "Royal Scot"

and 5X locomotives the following 80 locomotives be fitted with manganese steel liners, slightly stronger bearing springs and the latest type of horn stays and cross stays at approximate cost of £42,700 – 30 "Royal Scots" still to be converted. 40 "Royal Scots" already converted, 8 Patriots already converted or in course of conversion and 2 Jubilees.'

Despite this work, the Royal Scots never lost a reputation for being 'rough' and there some quite hair-raising tales regarding their propensity to buck and

With the famous Shap 'twin tree' on the right, 46136 THE BORDER REGIMENT, in BR Brunswick green, approaches Shap Wells with the Down 10.08am Euston-Perth on 26 May 1952. As a class, they seemed to make the wild places their own. Photograph E.D. Bruton.

46109 ROYAL ENGINEER justifiably attracts platform end attention at Leeds City on 3 August 1959, Bank Holiday. The Scot, one of Holbeck's own and now belonging to the North Eastern Region, is waiting to leave with the 10.35am to Glasgow; beyond is 2-6-0 46493. Photograph Michael Mensing.

twist. Yet the problem was much alleviated, especially as track continued to improve in the 1950s. As Cox put it, nothing dangerous remained, though the back end movement in a 4-6-0 was always lurking in the background, waiting a chance to make itself felt. When a rundown Scot approached a stretch of track of ill repute, crews learnt to grab the handrails!

Speed Indicators
The Mechanical and Electrical Engineering Committee turned its attention once more to speed indicators, more than a year after the War's end, on 29 January 1947. So far as the twenty 'express engines' so fitted back in 1937 were concerned, it was revealed that wartime conditions had made it impossible to maintain and service the instruments; they had now therefore been removed and the equipment stored. The fitting of electrical speed indicators on all '998 engines' had also been *discontinued owing to shortage of materials, staff and so on and of the indicators already fitted approximately 400 were removed, the materials being placed in store. Since the cessation of hostilities the question of refitting the speed recorders and indicators had been reconsidered and it was recommended that the speed recorders should not be replaced and the speed indicators should be fitted to 366 locos of the following classes: Class 7 4-6-2, class 6 4-6-0 ('Royal Scot'), class 6 4-6-0 (5X converted), 5x 4-6-0. During the time the speed indicators were fitted certain defects developed*

which were under consideration with Messrs. British Thomson Houston with a view to their elimination before refitting commenced and immediately these defects had been removed a report setting out the modified proposals, together with the cost of the work already carried out would be submitted'.

The first Royal Scot speed indicator appeared with the first rebuild, 6103; it was driven off the left-hand trailing driving wheel crankpin but no others were fitted. A general application of 'speedos' had to await the late 1950s – by that time the Royal Scots only had a year or two of full scale working and by then installation was largely pointless.

Liveries
Whatever livery variation the LMS came up with, in all probability the Royal Scots carried it, or some form of it. Taking a deep breath, here is an attempt at an outline...

1927	6100-6149 (NBL) crimson lake, large numerals on tender, insignia on cab.
1928	6100-6149 crimson lake, LMS on tender, large numerals on cab. Some had smaller 10in. numerals.
1930	6150-6169 (Derby) crimson lake, LMS on tender, large numerals on cab.
1930-1936	Spacing between letters

	begins to vary, but tends to concentrate on 40in.
1936	Quite a few begin to get a non-serif, widely spaced cab number.
1937	The serif, with a flourish of shading, begins to return!
1939-1945	Wartime black, though not all get it, some survive in very bedraggled 'crimson' – 'reddish dirt' a better description. 6103 and other wartime conversions get same 'austerity black'.
1946	The stylish LMS '1946 black' with red and straw lining and block numbers begins to appear, on parallel boiler engines and converted engines.
1948	BRITISH RAILWAYS on tenders and new numbers. A few get mixed traffic lined black. 46139 appears in experimental apple green.
mid-1949	From now on, it's BR Brunswick green with first emblem, though a few get 'LNW black' before orders come down from on high. Some parallel boiler survivors got both 'LNW black' and BR green.
1957	Second BR emblem.

The most complete accounts of liveries have always seemed to be those of Essery and Jenkinson; the sheer amount of livery detail (and more comes to light with every passing year) is confounding, and those interested in how many angels can dance on the lamp iron of an LMS buffer beam (whether a 1930 all vermilion, pre-1928 full vermilion or narrow crimson band *plus* vermilion one – you see what I mean!) should make an attempt on these works – see *Acknowledgements*. A note on emblems is also worthwhile; here is the story, courtesy Eric Youldon, who has probably put more people straight on British locomotive matters than anyone, giving generously of his time in the process:

First Emblem introduced mid-1949. There were right-hand and left-hand versions so that whichever side the loco was viewed, the lion faced 'forwards', towards the loco.

Second Emblem, generally introduced March 1957. Was first seen by way of preview on 70016 in 1956. This emblem followed the 1949 one, being initially produced in right-hand and left-hand versions. BUT, this now apparently did not meet with the approval of the College of Heralds, insofar as the right-hand one was concerned, so only the left-hand one was permitted. The change was effected from September 1958 and from then on only the left-facing lion was applied, which meant that on the right-hand side of the engine the lion faced towards the rear. It's easy when you know.

A Scot at 100 mph

There were instances of Scots at very high speeds but this is the story of a genuine 100mph occasion – from the horse's mouth. Alec Swain writes:

'In a recent edition of *The Railway Magazine* there was an article on steam locomotive classes which were known to have reached the speed of 100 mph and it mentioned the Kentish Town Driver Harry Edwards, who was evidently well known to the train timing fraternity as a 'fast runner'. I can confirm that Harry did indeed reach that magic speed on at least one occasion as I happened to be on the footplate as an unofficial observer...

'At that time, with Scots and Britannias on the Midland fitted with hitherto unseen (to Midland men anyway) speedometers there was a good deal of banter in the messrooms as to who had really achieved 100 mph. They knew steam traction was on the way out and Harry, in particular, was adamant that he had reached that magic figure. The problem was that few would believe him, so he needed a 'witness'.

'So it came about that one Sunday morning I joined Harry at St. Pancras armed with a stop watch. He had prepared well for the attempt, having discussed with the Kentish Town Mechanical Foreman which was the best of the 14B Scots – the last through works, recent boiler washout and so on. Through the Running Foreman he had it allocated to this service that Sunday morning. Now Harry was a most meticulous Driver

and always planned his trips taking into account known permanent way checks as listed in the Weekly Notices, and knew where he could get a few minutes in hand to allow for these. On the chosen Sunday there was no work listed on the Down Fast line between London and Bedford and, with few trains about anyway, the chances of delay were remote. He had his regular Fireman had arrived at Kentish Town well before their booking-on time and prepared the locomotive very thoroughly. Harry had spoken to the Foreman Boilersmith as well, so our steed (its identity long lost in the mists) was in the best of condition, or 'good nick' in footplate terms.

'Thus we set off and my first task was to check the accuracy of the speedometer using ¼ mile posts in the approved manner but with help from Harry, who brought the speed up to 60 mph and held it there whilst I did the necessary checks and pronounced the reading accurate. I would add that Sunday schedules were very easy and the train was lightweight compared with those on the 'North Western'.

'The object was to reach and maintain 100 mph plus on the falling gradients beyond Leagrave towards Bedford and this we achieved with ease with a light train. Perhaps at this stage I had better explain why I have no record of that day – although I had a footplate pass I was NOT on duty and, strictly speaking, should not have been there. I had agreed to act as 'witness' as I had known Harry for some time, respecting him as a locomotive man, but only on the

46113 CAMERONIAN in ear-splitting form at Dumfries, with an afternoon Glasgow-St Enoch train, 16 April 1960. Photograph B.P. Hoper Collection.

Left. Glory days. 46117 WELSH GUARDSMAN at Carlisle Citadel with the Thames-Clyde Express. Alec Swain accused me of neglecting the Midland lines in this volume and if readers find this is so, I apologise. The Royal Scots for long did fine work north of Leeds but it could be overlooked in the light of their storming performances on the West Coast route. I look at HST sets powering up and down the Midland today with something like 5,000hp under their belts for eight coaches or whatever it is, and always fall to pondering those Royal Scots, half the horsepower and a dozen coaches maybe. Higson *(London Midland Fireman,* Ian Allan, 1972) is unequivocal in his praise of these locomotives, which ranged the length of the country for so long. Next to the Duchess Pacifics, he considered them the 'most competent express passenger engines on the LMR' with a boiler power that was quite simply 'enormous'. And didn't they look it! Photograph J. Robertson, B.P. Hoper Collection.

Sublime to Ridiculous – A 2-Cylinder Scot

One day, courtesy Alec Swain, Crewe Works received for repair a *two* cylinder Scot which had arrived under its own steam from Leicester. This is the background...

'One night the Down St. Pancras-Glasgow sleeper failed at Market Harborough with a hot middle big end. With the regulator open and the middle piston cushioned to some extent, the Driver had not noticed anything amiss until he had shut off steam for the descent and curve through Market Harborough. Then it became apparent that all was not well and he wisely stopped and took the locomotive on shed – fortunately help was at hand. Thus the following morning, as Mechanical Foreman at Leicester Midland, I had a 'Scot' at Market Harborough which had to be brought to Leicester to see what we could do with it – that is, how serious was the damage?

'I sent my Chargehand together with a fitter and his mate to examine her to she if she was fit to travel 'dead' to Leicester. This they did and a telephone call later confirmed they'd dismantled the inside motion and all was ready. Through the Control Officer a Down light engine was diverted to the shed to pick up the 'Scot' and bring her to Leicester.

'On arrival it was put in the Repair Shop over the Wheel Drop, just outside my Office in fact, and I went beneath. I confirmed what my Chargehand had said on his return – the journal was badly damaged and the strap of the big end of the inside connecting rod badly distorted. The front and back cylinder covers looked OK but... The Derby Motive Power Office was 'got on the phone' and the news broken. One of their Mechanical

understanding that there was to be no publicity and it was just to enable Harry to achieve a personal ambition.

'Thus all three of us saw the speedometer creep just past the 100 mark, at which point Harry eased the regulator, quite content. We entered Ampthill Tunnel and emerged only to immediately see the colour light distant signal for Millbrook at caution – YELLOW! Now the basic semaphore signalling was never intended for 100 mph running; in fact, when the 'Blue Pullmans' began to run, 'double block' working had to be introduced because their attainable speeds did not match the 'steam age' signal spacing, particularly the distances between distants and stops.

'This was the first occasion I had experienced a steam locomotive being 'poled' in footplate jargon i.e. put into reverse and steam applied to slow it down! Harry had acted instantly on seeing the distant 'ON', snapping the regulator shut, winding her into reverse and then opening the regulator. As we approached Millbrook Box we could see permanent way men all over the track in front of us, so Harry gave

the time-honoured 'distress' signal on the Stanier whistle – a series of short blasts. They got the message as we approached and scattered as we shot past the semaphore signal we should have stopped at – towards them. Fortunately they had not removed a rail or crossing nose and we shuddered to a halt some distance beyond the signal box. Harry was sanguine, donning his jacket and walking back to the box. Meanwhile, I realised that should this 'signal passed at danger' incident result in a local inquiry (I chaired many later in my career) I would have some explaining to do!

'In due course Harry returned, put his jacket in the locker, exchanged hand signals with the Guard and off we went. He turned to me and said 'It's all right guv'nor, I've squared it with the Signalman, we'll hear no more about it'. And we never did.

'The remainder of the journey to Derby was normal, on time of course as we'd made up so much by our fast running – the Sunday schedule had absorbed all that we'd lost at Millbrook.'

And Dog Days. 46126 ROYAL ARMY SERVICE CORPS, miraculously keeping hold of its nameplate, at Cricklewood shed on 27 July 1963. This was one of the Scots put on the hopeless last years of the Great Central as BR's closure plans progressed. An inspired wheeze was to close Neasden shed and send locos round the North Circular for servicing at Cricklewood. Photograph Peter Groom.

Inspectors came down, took one look and together we filled in the standard Shopping Proposal form, which in fact he took back to Derby with him the same day – he was an old colleague.

Thus the 'Scot' awaited the call to Crewe Works and I was determined not to waste resources by having her dragged there 'dead' – requiring another locomotive and crew plus, in those days, a 'rider' on the dead locomotive. Locomotives and men were always in demand and there was no reason why she could not get there under her own steam working on two cylinders only.

'So, the middle piston valve was disconnected and fixed in mid-position and made safe, the inside crosshead secured to prevent movement and the connecting rod lashed securely to the side footplating, with other parts loaded on the tender back. To ensure that nobody 'pinched' her to work a train en-route (from the outside she looked in fine fettle) I painted 'working on two cylinders only – light engine only' on the regulator handle and prepared a Repair Card suitably endorsed that would travel with the locomotive, and be handed from Driver to Driver on the way. The Control

Office too were made fully aware of the restrictions. It left during the night, with our Leicester men as far as Derby, so I was unable to hear what she sounded like. I did ask our Driver when I next saw him and he said he hardly noticed the difference once on the move, although she sounded 'a bit odd' getting under way…

'Thus a 2-cylinder rebuilt 'Scot' did work on BR, albeit light engine only. It was just another working day so, unfortunately, I kept no record of the date nor the locomotive number.'

And It Got Worse. 46143, its CIVIL SERVICE RIFLEMAN plates gone, heads, of all things, an empty iron ore train with Colwick O4/8 2-8-0 63675, on 27 April 1963. The unlikely setting is the cutting south of Bagthorpe Junction, on the GC main line north of Nottingham. 46163 had been at Holyhead, working away in time-honoured Royal Scot fashion, until 1962 when the end was heralded by a transfer to Willesden. The engine retains a crude painted Willesden '1A' where the shedplate should be, some months after transfer to Annesley – of all places, and a coal carrying outfit – in January 1963. The end, as always, was more of a whimper than a bang – but treat yourself in the following pages to the Royal Scots in proper glory mode… Photograph Malcolm Castledine.

ROYAL SCOT on The Ulster Express, waiting to leave Euston on 28 September 1957. A year or so later it was one of the Royal Scots to go to the Midland Division. When the plans to turn all the passenger 4-6-0s into 6Ps (BR's equivalent grade was 7P) were evolving, It was one of Stanier's ordinances that they should be suitable for the Midland lines. Not enough 6P conversions were made of course and the Jubilees remained in charge out of St Pancras, but the idea paid off when Royal Scots were taken off West Coast work, as dieselisation advanced. Photograph A.G. Ellis, B.P. Hoper Collection.

The Record – Some Notes

**Anything But Not
Always Everything**

The LMS Record Cards are a *guide* to what happened to the engines, a good one but not a perfect, faultless chronology of what went on – always fascinating, sometimes frustrating. The information within them forms a precious 'life story', occasionally misleading or opaque but very often accurate to a few days. There are vagaries of course; the Record Cards might well tell you that 6103 got 'Driver's Leg Guards' (whatever they were) at 15/6d and 'Additional Tool Boxes' at £2.1s.0d, together with its improved piston valves at £7.0.0 but the date will be uncertain and they will tell you absolutely nothing, for example, regarding changing liveries – something which some of us might consider far more important.

When a Date is not a Date

The joys of 'carding' are almost endless – to begin at the beginning for instance, the 6100 Record Card shows it with a 'date built' of 14 August 1927, though it was ready well before that. On 27 July Sir Henry Fowler informed the Board that it was available for inspection by the Directors that very day, on No.15 platform at Euston. Or did the Directors inspect the 'impersonator' 6125? It's gripping stuff!

All the LMS Royal Scot cards in fact give a 'date built' that is at variance with the delivery from North British – usually by a fortnight or so. These latter dates for instance, are the ones given by Reed in his *Loco Profile*, and we can only speculate on the discrepancies. A reason might be that, between leaving NBL and arriving at Crewe, the engines spent some time having parts checked and tightened at Polmadie; the boilers were filled and refilled, fires dropped and so on. The 'date built' usually corresponds to the 'date tender fitted', though both events, absurdly, clearly took place some days – weeks even – before. Probably, so far as the LMS was concerned, the 'date built' represents the date the engines arrived in the Crewe North shed yard, when the card could be 'commenced'. The LMS Cards must be unusual in showing their subjects allocated to their first sheds two weeks or more *before* they were built!

A Tangled Web

It won't do to highlight, overly, the shortcomings of the Record Cards; in most matters they are very precise indeed, though they require interpretation. Take the fitting of taper boilers. Sometimes these are denoted by a straggling line of spidery writing, though even this first-hand evidence cannot be regarded as unequivocal; in some cases, such as 46105, its 'conversion to taper boiler' is written twice, at 15/5/48 *and* 27/5/48. A clerk could get it wrong, his pen could slip, he might have selected the wrong card from the filing cabinet – it doesn't bear thinking about... On other occasions the job is noted by a tiny CONV against one of the repair episodes, or it might appear just as the job reference, lumped with others for convenience. The key is in the boiler listings, when parallel finally gives way to the unmistakable '102A'. So after one or two false starts, we can get the record right...

'102A'

The Cards record the taper boilers as 102A rather than the more familiar 2A used in every account since, including this one, though this does not seem significant.

'Engine in Store'

Some engines spent periods in store, though these have not been recorded here – the entries seem so lackadaisical that to reproduce them might give an unrepresentative picture. There is no hint of the wartime 'emergency' storage of the Scots, as we saw in the Pacifics in the earlier volume, *The Book of the Coronation Pacifics*.

Sheds...

Only one or two Scots did *not* spend some period working out of Crewe North shed and where the reference is simply 'Crewe' (usually early on in the record) this is clearly Crewe North, and had been emended so. Once or twice however, Crewe *South* is specified and the veracity of this I leave to the reader's judgement. I still have doubts about 46161's spell at *Bidston* of all places... Very few Scots had anything like a 'home shed', for their 'home' was the West Coast line, full stop. Most of them changed shed very frequently indeed – 6137 for example moved well over thirty times in its thirty-five year life and in this was not particularly unusual.

One or two engines show an allocation to two sheds at the same time and what this clerical peculiarity might mean – who knows? The Editor of *British Railway Illustrated* tells me he will be happy to hear from any reader who has plotted the movements of *all* the Scots from the monthly *Railway Observer* records over all those years, and might even publish it!

Mileages

Mileages were ever an art rather than a science; everything was compiled by hand, from a sea of paper of course, and argument as to the accuracy of the figures (from all railways) will outlive all of us. Thirty or more years ago Norman McKillop ('Toram Beg') in his *Enginemen Elite* spoke darkly of the LMS methodology: *'according to the 'book' the mileage expected from a Gresley was 80-82,000 miles between shop overhauls. (This was under the LNER system, and should not be confused with the LMSR system, which produced apparently impressive figures until you analysed just how they were compiled).'* He does not elaborate, unfortunately.

Works Codes

Though none were built there, all the work on the Scots was done at Crewe, and while some repairs must surely have taken place at the Polmadie, Rugby or Willesden shops, these jobs are not recorded. It is also inconceivable that a Royal Scot *never* visited St Rollox or Derby for repair, but on this too the Cards are silent – they do not speak even of the odd 'non-classified' repair, where a buffer beam needed to be bashed out or whatever. Crewe of course, was where the parts were – witness Alec Swain's Scot puffing away from Leicester on its two cylinders.

Classification of works jobs also varied over the years and the best we have come up with is: **HG** Heavy General; **NC** Non-Classified; **LS** Light Service and **HS** Heavy Service. These last two evolved by BR times into **LI** Light Intermediate and **HI** Heavy Intermediate. One extra since the days of *The Book of the Coronation Pacifics* is the **(Rect)** which simply means 'rectification' and typically took place a day or two after a major repair – that is, tightening up bits that had come loose and loosening bits that were too tight. They seldom took very long – some only a day. **(EO)** was 'Engine Order', under which some jobs seem to have ordered out of the normal run of things.

***

As with all BR steam locomotives, the record fades from about 1959-60 as the people involved realised their charges were on the way out. No one bothered to record the last sorry perambulations of Scots on empty iron ore trains and so on, and who could blame them? Yet the Cards still represent an unmatched body of endlessly fascinating data, and if the reader gets half as much fun perusing the information as I have had in compiling it, I'll be content.

46100 ROYAL SCOT

Built North British, cost £7,740.
LM 'date built' 14/8/27
(engine actually entered service a month earlier)
Named 7/27
Taper boiler fitted 10/6/50
Original smoke deflectors 30/1/32
BR smoke deflectors fitted period ending 17/6/50
Renumbered 6100 to 46100 week ending 19/6/48

REPAIRS

12/4/28-14/5/28**LO**	22/2/44-11/3/44**LS**
29/6/29-9/7/29**LO**	1/9/44-23/9/44**LO**
12/3/29-15/4/29**HG**	5/2/45-23/2/45**HG**
14/1/30-22/2/30**HG**	4/4/46-17/5/46**LO**
1/10/31-12/11/31**HS**	3/9/46-21/9/46**LO**
19/1/31-14/2/31**HG**	8/11/46-23/11/46**LS**
2/5/32-24/5/32**HG**	28/7/47-30/8/47**LS**
4/1/33-2/3/33**HG**	13/4/48-17/6/48**HG**
22/9/34-17/10/34**HS**	10/11/48-11/12/48**LO**
29/12/34-4/1/35**LO**	1/4/49-26/4/49**LI**
19/3/35-8/4/35**LS**	13/5/49-21/5/49**NC**
22/8/35-13/9/35**LS**	10/4/50-10/6/50**HG**
5/11/35-13/11/35**HG**	24/7/50-8/8/50**NC**
10/2/36-12/3/36**H**	11/7/51-13/8/51**LI**
5/8/36-18/8/36**LO**	28/6/52-2/8/52**LI**
4/1/37-18/1/37**HS**	11/12/52-10/1/53**LC(EO)**
25/5/37-9/6/37**LS**	4/9/53-30/9/53**HG**
23/2/38-17/3/38**HG**	10/8/54-8/9/54**LI**
14/10/38-8/11/38**LS**	11/8/55-10/9/55**HG**
11/7/39-10/8/39**HG**	7/12/56-10/1/57**HI**
22/4/40-9/5/40**LS**	1/2/57-9/2/57**NC(Rect)(EO)**
27/11/40-17/12/40**LS**	28/5/57-18/6/57**LC(EO)**
20/10/41-8/11/41**LS**	17/10/57-7/12/57**HG**
29/4/42-23/5/42**HG**	6/7/58-15/8/58**LC(EO)**
11/11/42-1/12/42**LO**	2/4/59-1/5/59**LI**
31/5/43-12/6/43**LS**	17/8/60-23/9/60**LI**
28/9/43-12/10/43**LO**	18/8/61-28/9/61**HI**

BOILERS

Fitted	No.	From
26/3/29	-	6139
7/2/30	-	6121
27/1/31	-	new
4/5/32	-	6137
20/2/33	-	new
1/10/34	-	6124
27/2/36	-	6169
2/3/38	9883	new
10/8/39	5824	6110
23/5/42	7230	6146
23/2/45	11037	6129
17/6/48	10185	6137
Taper 102A		
10/6/50	13242	new
30/9/53	13240	-
10/9/55	12535	-
7/12/57	13998	-

MILEAGES

1927	22,380	1947	53,361
1928	50,959	1948	52,116
1929	63,025	1949	63,250
1930	56,988	1950	53,979
1931	69,371	1951	68,766
1932	72,298	1952	55,521
1933	3,253(Britain)	1953	71,176
1933	11,194(America)	1954	74,465
1934	61,304	1955	59,158
1935	71,982	1956	51,962
1936	86,735	1957	48,057
1937	83,846	1958	56,673
1938	83,190	1959	64,051
1939	76,134	1960	47,799
1940	71,946	1961	34,801
1941	75,424	**Mileage at 31/12/50 1,508,800**	
1942	73,620	**Mileage at 31/12/61 2,141,229**	
1943	71,773	**Withdrawn week**	
1944	56,978	**ending 13/10/62**	
1945	56,392	**Preserved**	
1946	67,302		

SHEDS

Crewe 6/8/27
Camden 28/8/27
Edge Hill 25/5/46(loan)
Camden 8/6/46
Nottingham 7/11/59
Derby 17/6/61
Nottingham 12/8/61

TENDERS

No.	Fitted
3896	14/8/27
3931	-
3902	-
9338	18/8/36

'ROYAL SCOT", in the later part of the 1930s (the Black 5 alongside, 5269, was built in 1936) after its return from America, still carrying its bell and fitted with Stanier tender, down among the preparation pits at Camden. Photograph B.P. Hoper Collection.

46101 ROYAL SCOTS GREY

Built North British, cost £7,744.
LM 'date built' 11/9/27
Named by 4/28
Taper boiler fitted 16/11/45
Original smoke deflectors 9/12/31
BR smoke deflectors fitted period ending 10/9/49
Renumbered 6101 to 46101 week ending 1/5/48

TENDERS

No.	Fitted
LMS	11/9/27
3919	26/12/31
9016	12/2/36

REPAIRS

22/3/29-11/5/29**HG**	4/10/41-18/10/41**LO**
28/10/29-1/11/29**LO**	16/3/42-1/4/42**LS**
22/3/30-12/4/30**HG**	16/2/43-5/3/43**LS**
28/10/30-12/11/30**LS**	28/12/43-22/1/44**LS**
1/4/31-21/4/31**LS**	18/9/44-7/10/44**HG**
14/11/31-9/12/31**HC**	9/3/45-12/4/45**LO**
15/6/32-1/7/32**LS**	8/9/45-16/11/45**HG**
7/11/32-28/11/32**HS**	14/1/47-5/2/47**LS**
1/5/33-17/5/33**LS**	6/2/48-4/3/48**LS**
5/9/33-16/11/33**HS**	1/4/48-28/4/48**LO**
2/5/34-18/6/34**HG**	2/9/48-28/10/48**HO**
17/11/34-5/12/34**LS**	28/6/49-16/8/49**HG**
1/2/35-22/2/35**LO**	21/10/49-11/11/49**LC**
26/6/35-22/7/35**LS**	8/1/51-26/1/51**HI**
9/1/36-12/2/36**HI**	6/9/51-25/10/51**HG**
19/10/36-4/11/36**LS**	3/1/53-5/2/53**HI**
7/4/37-20/4/37**LS**	10/3/54-29/3/54**LI**
15/11/37-10/12/37**HG**	12/3/55-10/5/55**HG**
25/12/37-24/1/38**HO**	16/12/55-12/1/56**LC(EO)**
16/4/38-11/5/38**LO**	24/11/56-22/12/56**HI**
16/1/39-1/2/39**HS**	26/11/57-4/1/58**HG**
21/8/39-30/9/39**HG**	17/1/59-20/2/59**LI**
21/5/40-3/6/40**LS**	14/9/59-24/10/59**LC(EO)**
27/6/40-19/7/40**LO**	26/2/60-2/4/60**HI**
31/3/41-19/4/41**HS**	18/2/61-28/3/61**LC(EO)**

BOILERS

Fitted	No.	From
11/4/29	-	6106
28/3/30	-	new
17/11/31	-	6125
14/11/32	-	6105
1/6/34	-	6134
28/1/36	-	6144
23/11/37	7255	6143
13/1/38	7234	6103
30/9/39	7226	6164
1/4/42	8134	6152
7/10/44	7215	6123
Taper 102A		
16/11/45	12202	new
16/8/49	12030	6133
25/10/51	12203	-
10/5/55	12205	-
4/1/58	12207	-
27/3/62	12665	-

MILEAGES

1927	18,510	1947	72,615
1928	56,450	1948	46,510
1929	53,615	1949	61,709
1930	58,340	1950	65,510
1931	52,121	1951	46,269
1932	70,893	1952	67,345
1933	65,138	1953	51,154
1934	70,054	1954	61,506
1935	74,230	1955	50,193
1936	82,994	1956	50,997
1937	66,986	1957	53,127
1938	69,266	1958	57,655
1939	59,497	1959	56,911
1940	70,821	1960	48,327
1941	68,665	**Mileage at 31/12/50 1,524,288**	
1942	75,091	**Mileage at 31/12/60 2,067,772**	
1943	82,987	**Withdrawn week ending 31/8/63**	
1944	60,630	**Scrapped Slag Reduction,**	
1945	49,533	**Rotherham, 4/64**	
1946	72,123		

SHEDS

Crewe 19/8/27	Crewe North 25/10/52
Carlisle Upperby 16/9/27	Camden 13/6/53
Camden 17/12/27	Crewe 19/9/53
Longsight (loan) 13/11/48	Camden 14/8/54
Edge Hill (loan) 11/12/48	Crewe North 18/9/54
Longsight (loan) 15/1/49	Longsight 25/9/54
Camden 12/2/49	Crewe North 9/10/54
Crewe North 30/9/50	Camden 23/10/54
Holyhead (loan) 16/2/52	Crewe North 1/1/55
Crewe North 25/4/52	Camden 20/6/59
Camden 5/7/52	Willesden 10/6/61
Crewe North 20/9/52	Llandudno Junction 23/9/61
Carlisle Upperby (loan) 4/10/52	Willesden 23/6/62
	Annesley 5/1/63

46102 BLACK WATCH

Built North British, cost £7,744.
LM 'date built' 11/9/27
Named 3/28
Taper boiler fitted 12/5/45
Original smoke deflectors – not listed
BR smoke deflectors fitted period ending 13/10/49
Renumbered 6102 to 46102 week ending 4/9/49
Early details missing.

SHEDS
-

Camden 10/4/37
Crewe (loan) 4/12/37
Holyhead (loan) 22/1/38
Camden 29/1/38
Perth (loan) 2/7/38
Perth 13/8/38
Carlisle Kingmoor 2/3/40
Polmadie 11/4/42

MILEAGES
-

1937	53,591
1938	84,117
1939	71,838
1940	59,762
1941	58,262
1942	56,222
1943	53,251
1944	46,161
1945	56,143
1946	60,804
1947	49,279
1948	43,610
1949	34,854
1950	51,465
1951	52,785
1952	61,722
1953	56,313
1954	52,691
1955	39,518
1956	55,616
1957	53,683

Mileage to 31/12/50 1,319,731
Mileage to 31/12/57 1,692,057
Withdrawn week ending 29/12/62
Scrapped J. McWilliam, Shettleston 5/64

REPAIRS
-

25/3/36-7/5/36**LS**
9/9/36-19/10/36**HS**
3/5/37-19/5/37**LO**
16/8/37-14/9/37**LO**
27/10/37-22/11/37**HG**
5/4/38-9/5/38**LO**
10/2/39-25/2/39**LS**
8/1/40-22/2/40**HG**
23/10/40-16/11/40**LS**
5/7/41-2/8/41**LS**
21/11/41-6/12/41**LO**
19/10/42-7/11/42**HS**
13/5/43-19/6/43**HG**
9/2/44-25/2/44**LO**
22/11/44-7/12/44**HS**
26/11/45-29/12/45**LS**
25/1/47-26/2/47**HG**
2/8/48-30/8/48**LS**
25/1/49-19/2/49**LC**
22/7/49-13/10/49**G**
14/8/50-2/9/50**LC(EO)**
10/9/51-13/10/51**HI**
12/5/52-7/6/52**LC**
16/2/53-25/4/53**HG**
10/3/54-5/4/54**LI**
11/8/55-11/11/55**HG**
3/12/56-16/1/57**LI**
14/8/58-17/9/58**HI**
29/9/59-27/11/59**HC**
19/6/61-4/8/61**HI(EO)**

BOILERS

Fitted	No.	From
-		
9/10/36	-	6158
3/11/37	7238	6168
22/2/40	8137	6160
19/6/43	7220	6134
26/2/47	11031	6139
Taper 102A		
13/10/49	13238	new
25/4/53		12658	-
11/11/55	12197	-
29/11/59	12672	-

TENDERS

No.	Fitted
9336	7/5/36
9009	21/3/51
9336	9/3/54

46103 ROYAL SCOTS FUSILIER

Built North British, cost £7,744.
LM 'date built' 11/9/27
Named by 4/28
Taper boiler fitted 26/6/43
Original smoke deflectors – not listed
BR smoke deflectors fitted period ending –
not listed
Renumbered 6103 to 46103 week ending 23/10/48

TENDERS

No.	Fitted
3899	11/9/27
3918	26/12/31
3927	31/12/33
9150	25/6/37

MILEAGES

1927	17,963	1948	61,281
1928	54,762	1949	49,075
1929	48,960	1950	68,599
1930	64,672	1951	67,817
1931	61,339	1952	71,172
1932	58,694	1953	64,629
1933	68,899	1954	66,801
1934	70,786	1955	58,127
1935	57,285	1956	67,242
1936	58,168	1957	71,690
1937	58,346	1958	72,781
1938	85,315	1959	60,445
1939	78,778	1960	46,966
1940	67,989		
1941	66,759		
1942	75,573		
1943	42,058		
1944	59,092		
1945	55,179		
1946	64,024		
1947	64,957		

Mileage at 31/12/50 1,459,323
Mileage to 31/12/60 2,106,993
Withdrawn week ending 22/12/62
Scrapped Crewe Works 9/63

BOILERS

Fitted	No.	From
10/28	-	new
13/1/30	-	6144
18/6/31	-	6136
24/5/33	-	6138
6/3/35	-	6117
16/11/37	9884	new
28/9/39	9880	6147
29/8/41	7249	6127
Taper 102A		
26/6/43	11725	new
5/9/47	11734	6117
13/10/51	12089	-
18/8/53	12035	-
5/11/55	11727	-
9/1/58	12202	-

REPAIRS

8/10/28-13/11/28**HG**	10/5/39-23/5/39**LO**	17/8/45-6/10/45**LO**	8/7/54-10/8/54**HI**
31/12/29-31/1/30**HG**	6/9/39-28/9/39**HG**	30/3/46-16/4/46**LS**	14/9/54-1/10/54**LC(EO)**
6/1/31-10/2/31**LS**	8/1/40-20/1/40**LO**	12/11/46-14/12/46**LO**	25/2/55-5/4/55**LC**
6/6/31-3/7/31**HG**	24/4/40-15/5/40**LS**	3/7/47-5/9/47**HG**	24/9/55-5/11/55**HG**
8/6/32-9/7/32**LS**	28/12/40-11/1/41**LS**	20/2/48-16/3/48**LO**	13/5/56-23/6/56**HI**
11/5/33-15/6/33**HG**	27/3/41-10/4/41**LO**	27/9/48-22/10/48**LS**	12/11/56-7/12/56**LI**
3/10/33-27/10/33**LO**	13/8/41-29/8/41**HG**	23/2/49-25/3/49**HC**	27/4/57-7/6/57**LC(EO)**
16/4/34-26/5/34**HS**	24/11/41-6/12/41**LO**	24/8/49-6/10/49**LC**	30/11/57-9/1/58**HG**
21/2/35-25/3/35**HG**	10/6/42-27/6/42**LS**	14/6/50-3/7/50**HI**	11/3/58-16/4/58**HC(EO)**
11/1/37-16/2/37**LS**	23/10/42-7/11/42**LO**	17/2/51-22/3/51**LC**	16/2/59-23/3/59**LI**
11/6/37-25/6/37**LO**	17/4/43-26/6/43**HG**	7/9/51-13/10/51**HG**	7/4/59-16/4/59**NC(EO)**
6/8/37-18/8/37**LO**	3/8/43-17/8/43**LO**	2/5/52-28/5/52**HI**	8/5/59-21/5/59**NC(Rect)(EO)**
5/11/37-3/12/37**HG**	24/10/43-25/11/43**LO**	12/11/52-6/12/52**HI**	8/2/60-18/3/60**HI**
1/10/38-27/10/38**LS**	23/6/44-29/7/44**HS**	14/7/53-18/8/53**HG**	22/3/60-1/4/60**LC(EO)**
	14/5/45-16/6/45**LS**	8/11/53-28/11/53**LC(EO)**	1/12/60-24/1/61**LI**

SHEDS

Carlisle 3/9/27
Camden 17/12/27
Polmadie 15/3/31
Crewe North 17/4/37
Carnforth 3/7/37
Camden 26/2/38
Edge Hill 2/1/43
Camden 3/4/43
Leeds (loan) 28/8/43
Leeds 2/10/43
Kentish Town 11/10/58
Trafford Park 1/11/58
Kentish Town 29/11/58
Saltley 17/6/61
Carlisle Upperby 30/6/62

46104 SCOTTISH BORDERER

Built North British, cost £7,744.
LM 'date built' 11/9/27
Named by 4/28
Taper boiler fitted 30/3/46
Original smoke deflectors – not listed
BR smoke deflectors fitted period ending 11/8/51
Renumbered 6104 to 46104 week ending 7/8/48

BOILERS

Fitted	No.	From
8/1/29	-	6144
22/2/30	-	6139
20/1/31	-	6120
6/5/32	-	6159
21/11/33	-	6104
20/11/34	-	6142
10/5/38	10184	new
4/6/41	7241	6143
14/8/43	7232	6125
Taper 102A		
30/3/46	12206	new
4/8/51	11729	46108
26/1/55	13594	-
8/5/58	12032	-

TENDERS

No.	Fitted
3900	11/9/27
3921	21/7/28
3915	26/12/31
9032	20/2/37
4620	24/9/37
4648	11/10/55
9041	21/3/61

SHEDS

Carlisle 3/9/27
Camden 17/12/27
Polmadie 15/3/31
Corkerhill 7/10/39
Carlisle Kingmoor 25/11/39
Polmadie 11/4/42

REPAIRS

30/6/28-24/7/28**LO**	27/2/45-4/4/45**LO**
3/1/29-12/3/29**HG**	13/12/45-30/3/46**HG**
1/6/29-29/6/29**LO**	5/2/47-31/3/47**HS**
7/2/30-12/3/30**HG**	17/6/48-2/8/48**LS**
10/1/31-11/2/31**H**	7/4/50-3/5/50**HI**
17/10/31-16/11/31**H**	31/10/50-20/11/50**LC**
4/5/32-28/5/32**HO**	8/1/51-6/2/51**LC**
8/3/33-23/3/33**LS**	31/5/51-4/8/51**HG**
9/6/33-23/6/33**LS**	12/5/52-25/6/52**HI**
11/11/33-12/12/33**HG**	11/7/52-16/8/52**LC**
7/11/34-27/11/34**HS**	29/4/53-28/5/53**LI**
9/12/35-27/12/35**LS**	4/7/53-5/8/53**HS**
11/1/37-1/2/37**HS**	3/12/53-5/1/54**HC(EO)**
28/4/38-26/5/38**HG**	18/3/54-27/3/54**LO(EO)**
25/3/39-25/4/39**HS**	11/5/54-3/6/54**LC**
4/4/40-29/4/40**LS**	7/6/54-8/6/54**NC**
3/5/41-4/6/41**HG**	13/12/54-26/1/55**HG**
29/11/41-20/12/41**LO**	30/9/55-11/10/55**LC**
11/7/42-6/8/42**LS**	24/5/56-10/4/56**LI**
14/12/42-13/2/43**LO**	8/2/57-16/3/57**LI**
30/6/43-14/8/43**HG**	23/12/57-8/2/58**HG**
7/2/44-23/2/44**LO**	15/7/58-29/8/58**LC(EO)**
29/6/44-11/8/44**LO**	29/6/59-1/8/59**LI**
4/12/44-30/12/44**LS**	6/1/60-26/2/60**HI**
	20/3/61-27/4/61**LI(EO)**

MILEAGES

1927	22,474	1946	53,841
1928	48,654	1947	49,115
1929	48,071	1948	51,725
1930	61,202	1949	38,584
1931	63,137	1950	53,596
1932	60,410	1951	49,809
1933	62,095	1952	omitted
1934	69,546	1953	47,413
1935	64,128	1954	47,800
1936	41,038	1955	54,973
1937	58,467	1956	51,254
1938	67,811	1957	50,790
1939	60,688		
1940	59,643		
1941	54,640		
1942	57,551		
1943	42,454		
1944	37,281		
1945	46,819		

Mileage at 31/12/50 1,272,960
Withdrawn week
ending 29/12/62
Scrapped J. McWilliam,
Shettleston, 5/64

'Rebuilt' Royal Scot in its pomp, 46100 ROYAL SCOT at (unusually) Derby shed alongside 45610 GHANA, on 25 September 1955, after working a railtour from St Pancras. The big 'No.4' roundhouse is in the background, with 43027 inside. ROYAL SCOT and GHANA are standing on the roads of the outside turntable; this was installed with a new roundhouse in mind, though in the end it was never proceeded with. Note the recesses for the locking pins of the turntable within the well. Photograph R.C. Riley.

One of the Scottish Royal Scots, 46104 SCOTTISH BORDERER in customary spick and span condition, at its home shed of Polmadie, 24 November 1951. Photograph A.G. Ellis, B.P. Hoper Collection.

46105 at Polmadie; by now (see page ii/iii) the new smokebox plates have been issued and fitted. Photograph A.G. Ellis, B.P. Hoper Collection.

The strange GORDON HIGHLANDER, a Crewe North engine in Scotland, at Dalry Road shed, Edinburgh. It was the only one to have 'BR' style deflectors and always looked odd as a consequence. It got these plates in July 1954, replacing the curved type carried since rebuilding in 1949. Photograph W. Hermiston, B.P. Hoper Collection.

46105 CAMERON HIGHLANDER

Built North British, cost £7,744.
LM 'date built' 11/9/27
Taper boiler fitted 27/4/48
Named 1928
Original smoke deflectors – 6/1/32
BR smoke deflectors fitted period ending 27/12/52
Renumbered 6105 to 46105 week ending 1/5/48

BOILERS

Fitted	No.	From
5/2/29	-	6116
12/11/29	-	6119
18/2/31	-	6139
24/5/32	-	6106
24/11/33	-	6120
6/2/36	-	6164
2/6/38	10187	new
27/12/40	7247	6118
3/8/43	8137	6102
14/4/45	8138	6110
Taper 102A		
27/4/48	12660	new
23/12/52	13894	-
29/8/56	12530	-
26/2/59	12657	-
21/2/61	12028	-

SHEDS
Crewe North 27/8/27
Rugby 3/9/27
Camden 18/9/28
Polmadie 13/11/32
Carlisle Kingmoor 14/10/39
Perth 11/1/41
Polmadie 13/2/43

TENDERS

No.	Fitted
3901	11/9/27
3900	26/12/31
9009	25/2/36
9020	13/7/43

REPAIRS

17/7/28-16/8/28**LS**
22/1/29-9/3/29**HG**
29/4/29-1/6/29**LO**
22/10/29-28/11/29**HG**
18/7/30-1/8/30**LS**
16/2/31-7/3/31**HG**
24/5/32-17/6/32**HG**
7/12/31-6/1/32**HS**
25/5/33-16/6/33**LS**
15/11/33-19/12/33**HG**
10/12/34-5/1/35**LS**
27/1/36-25/2/36**HG**
25/11/36-31/12/36**LS**
9/3/37-17/3/37**LO**
5/1/38-1/2/38**HS**
15/3/38-30/3/38**LO**
24/5/38-13/6/38**HO**
1/5/39-23/5/39**LS**
13/11/39-20/12/39**LS**
13/5/40-29/5/40**LO**
14/11/40-27/12/40**HG**
22/9/41-18/10/41**LS**
31/3/42-23/4/42**LO**
18/6/42-2/7/42**LO**
31/12/42-6/2/43**LS**
25/6/43-3/8/43**HG**
15/1/44-3/2/44**LO**
19/12/44-12/1/45**LS**
10/3/45-14/4/45**HO**
23/8/45-11/9/45**LO**
21/12/45-26/1/46**HS**
13/1/47-15/2/47**LS**
12/1/48-27/4/48**HG**
9/12/49-5/1/50**HI**
26/4/50-5/5/50**LC**
5/5/51-2/6/51**HI**
3/12/51-18/1/52**LC(EO)**
29/10/52-23/12/52**HG**
31/10/53-3/12/53**HI**
3/8/54-9/9/54**LC(EO)**
4/4/55-10/5/55**HI**
16/7/56-29/8/56**HG**
31/5/57-25/7/57**LC(EO)**
21/1/58-7/2/58**HI**
30/12/58-26/2/59**HG**
21/3/60-6/5/60**LI**
7/12/60-21/2/61**HG**

MILEAGES

1927	15,800	1945	48,831
1928	55,604	1946	56,710
1929	43,042	1947	44,149
1930	54,703	1948	50,591
1931	75,294	1949	48,950
1932	68,054	1950	62,734
1933	58,634	1951	55,762
1934	67,221	1953	66,208
1935	57,020	1954	57,196
1936	52,628	1955	48,663
1937	52,458	1956	44,266
1938	55,623	1957	49,634
1939	51,985	**Mileage to 31/12/50 1,322,597**	
1940	49,149	**Mileage to 31/12/57 1,644,326**	
1941	77,954	**Withdrawn week**	
1942	64,301	**ending 29/12/62**	
1943	54,411	**Scrapped J. McWilliam,**	
1944	56,751	**Shettleston, 5/64**	

46106 GORDON HIGHLANDER

Built North British, cost £7,744.
LM 'date built' 11/9/27
Taper boiler fitted 21/9/49
BR smoke deflectors fitted period ending 8/10/49
'Britannia' type plates fitted 7/54
Renumbered 6106 to 46106 week ending 12/6/48

BOILERS

Fitted	No.	From
4/4/29	-	6110
3/12/29	-	6114
20/1/31	-	6108
26/4/32	-	6108
1/3/34	-	6105
28/5/36	-	6143
11/4/38	-	6143
11/4/38	7220	6129
22/6/40	7242	6129
16/1/43	8130	6149
27/1/45	8123	6165
Taper 102A		
21/9/49	13239	new
22/5/54	13590	-
14/11/56	12529	-
7/11/58	14000	-

SHEDS
Crewe North 3/9/27*
Rugby 3/9/27*
Camden 1/10/27
Polmadie 15/3/31
Crewe 17/4/37
Carnforth (loan) 14/8/37
Crewe North 21/8/37
Bangor 2/7/38
Holyhead 8/4/39
Crewe North 7/10/39
Camden 10/8/40
Edge Hill 22/5/43
Crewe North 20/9/52
Edge Hill 23/5/53
Crewe North 19/9/53
Camden 22/6/57
Carlisle Upperby 21/9/57
Longsight 14/6/58
Newton Heath 30/4/60
Crewe North 17/9/60
Newton Heath 17/1/60
Crewe North 31/12/60
Trafford Park 31/12/60
Derby 17/6/61
Trafford Park 2/9/61*
Saltley 2/9/61*
Leicester (GC) 12/5/62
Saltley 30/6/62
Carlisle Upperby 30/6/62
*same dates

TENDERS

No.	Fitted
3902	11/9/27
3909	26/12/31
9343	11/6/36
9352	31/10/57

REPAIRS

2/3/28-5/4/28**LS**
16/3/29-23/4/29**HG**
9/11/29-18/12/29**HG**
23/9/31-12/10/31**HO**
16/1/31-13/2/31**HG**
21/4/32-18/5/32**HG**
1/5/33-17/5/33**LS**
3/7/33-6/7/33**LO**
14/12/33-13/1/34**HG**
9/2/34-16/3/34**HG**
14/11/34-7/12/34**LS**
22/1/35-14/2/35**HO**
4/9/35-26/9/35**LS**
21/5/36-11/6/36**HG**
28/6/37-22/7/37**HS**
28/3/38-2/5/38**HG**
7/1/39-23/1/39**LS**
18/9/39-4/10/39**LS**
1/6/40-22/6/40**HG**
13/7/40-14/8/40**LO**
17/2/41-4/3/41**HI**
23/5/41-7/6/41**LO**
7/10/41-25/10/41**LO**
16/1/42-10/2/42**LS**
17/6/42-18/7/42**LO**
29/12/42-16/1/43**HG**
4/5/43-17/5/43**LO**
29/1/44-19/2/44**HS**
6/1/45-27/1/45**HG**
3/12/45-2/1/46**LS**
21/7/46-22/8/46**LS**
25/1/47-18/2/47**LO**
1/7/47-11/8/47**HS**
26/11/47-17/1/48**LO**
20/5/48-12/6/48**LS**
29/11/48-22/12/48**LO**
30/5/49-21/9/49**HG**
20/5/51-20/6/51**HI**
14/5/52-14/6/52**LI**
24/3/53-25/4/53**LI**
9/9/53-10/10/53**LC(EO)**
23/4/54-22/5/54**HG**
14/9/55-4/10/55**HI**
28/12/55-12/1/56**LC(EO)**
2/10/56-14/11/56**HG**
2/10/57-31/10/57**HI**
4/10/58-7/11/58**HG**
28/8/59-15/10/59**HI**
6/4/61-5/5/61**HI**

MILEAGES

1927	16,057	1941	65,972	1956	53,112
1928	60,803	1942	75,436	1957	56,380
1929	47,714	1943	68,469	1958	66,256
1930	64,231	1944	57,286	1959	66,817
1931	69,863	1945	51,319	1960	52,738
1932	60,971	1946	64,762	1961	33,378
1933	65,909	1947	46,665	1962	27,465
1934	58,152	1948	49,253	**Mileage to 31/12/50 1,428,500**	
1935	61,747	1949	49,618	**Mileage to end of life 2,058,872**	
1936	57,012	1950	64,176	**Withdrawn week ending 8/12/62**	
1937	71,332	1951	65,968	**but reinstated for short while**	
1938	78,994	1952	55,427	**the following year**	
1939	65,689	1953	48,509	**Scrapped Crewe Works 4/63**	
1940	67,050	1954	52,968		
		1955	51,354		

46106 in straitened circumstances, far off and years later and by now AWS fitted, at Cricklewood in the 'Great Freeze' of early 1963. It had been withdrawn the previous December but pressed back into service as locos – particularly new diesels – got into trouble across the system. By now without nameplates of course, the engine was working the GC, but with the closure of Neasden, Cricklewood, with the lunatic logic of the time, was serving as the London shed for these workings. Photograph Peter Groom.

A rousing exit from Princes Street, Edinburgh, by 46107 ARGYLL AND SUTHERLAND HIGHLANDER, 29 August 1953, the Driver exchanging a brief pleasantry with a colleague on the footplate of 2-6-4T 42162, over on the right by the turntable. The peculiar Caledonian 'semaphore' route indicator is still in use – perched on No.7's buffer beam. Crewe North (with some justification, it must be said) regarded itself as occupying the pinnacle of West Coast workings and, with the railway habit of, at best, near-pity towards those condemned to work out of other sheds, regarded the Polmadie engines as far rougher than any others, even the cockney ones. Photograph B.P. Hoper Collection.

46107 ARGYLL AND SUTHERLAND HIGHLANDER

Built North British, cost £7,744
LM 'date built' 11/9/27
Named 1928
Taper boiler fitted 20/2/50
Original smoke deflectors 4/12/31
BR smoke deflectors fitted period ending 25/2/50
Renumbered 6107 to 46107 week ending 3/4/48

SHEDS
Crewe North 3/9/27
Camden 17/12/27
Polmadie 21/7/32
Aberdeen 5/10/35
Carlisle Kingmoor 18/7/36
Polmadie 17/4/37
Carlisle Kingmoor 2/12/39
Polmadie 11/4/42

TENDERS

No.	Fitted
3903	11/9/27
3933	24/12/31
3899	31/12/32
9020	13/2/36
9009	13/7/43
9336	21/3/51
9009	9/3/54

MILEAGES

Year	Miles	Year	Miles
1927	19,517	1944	54,272
1928	61,202	1945	50,738
1929	55,075	1946	48,646
1930	51,041	1947	54,037
1931	65,071	1948	42,599
1932	63,988	1949	32,561
1933	69,643	1950	50,382
1934	55,014	1951	57,016
1935	58,662	1953	51,212
1936	40,997	1954	45,995
1937	42,585	1955	45,218
1938	51,040	1956	55,657
1939	67,352	1957	56,459
1940	43,877		
1941	46,647		
1942	59,921		
1943	55,082		

Mileage at 31/12/50 1,239,949
Mileage to 31/12/57 1,561,506
Withdrawn week ending 29/12/62
Scrapped J. McWilliam, Shettleston, 5/64

BOILERS

Fitted	No.	From
30/4/30	-	6101
17/9/30	-	6104
9/11/31	-	6138
24/4/33	-	6135
21/3/34	-	6151
29/1/36	-	6124
2/11/38	8131	6159
20/2/41	10187	6105
21/10/44	5573	6111
3/10/47	8124	6158
Taper 102A		
20/2/50	3243	new
27/8/54	13241	-
9/7/57	11729	-
13/5/60	12674	-

REPAIRS

5/5/28-21/6/28LS	20/9/44-21/10/44HG
21/3/29-20/4/29HG	21/6/45-19/7/45LO
23/4/30-15/5/30HG	27/11/45-10/1/46LS
5/9/30-24/9/30HO	19/11/46-27/12/46LS
4/4/31-29/4/31LS	1/9/47-3/10/47HG
6/11/31-4/12/31HG	16/3/48-2/4/48LO
5/4/32-11/5/32LS	6/12/48-4/1/49LI
13/6/32-1/8/32HO	1/8/49-9/9/49LC
3/4/33-13/5/33HG	26/11/49-20/2/50HG
6/1/34-20/1/34LO	24/5/50-21/6/50LC
9/2/34-3/4/34HS	27/7/50-12/9/50LI
7/4/35-7/5/35LS	18/6/51-2/8/51HI
1/8/35-28/8/35LS	27/8/52-26/9/52HI
20/1/36-13/2/36HG	19/1/53-19/2/53LI
7/12/37-28/12/37HS	19/1/54-24/2/54LC
11/1/38-15/1/38LO	19/7/54-27/8/54HG
17/2/38-21/2/38LO	25/2/55-15/3/55LC(EO)
9/3/38-18/3/38LO	10/1/56-20/1/56LC(EO)
16/9/38-2/11/38HG	26/3/56-2/5/56HI
3/1/40-8/2/40LS	13/12/56-15/12/56NC
18/1/41-20/2/41HG	28/5/57-9/7/57HG
2/4/41-29/5/41LS	1/5/58-5/6/58LI
25/9/41-16/10/41LO	24/8/59-25/9/59LI
8/9/42-26/9/42LS	14/3/60-13/5/60HG
29/9/43-21/10/43HS	11/4/61NC(EO)

46108 SEAFORTH HIGHLANDER

Built North British, cost £7,744
LM 'date built' 11/9/27
Named 1927/8
Taper boiler fitted 21/8/43
Original smoke deflectors 14/12/31
BR smoke deflectors fitted period ending 25/2/51
Renumbered 6108 to 46108 week ending 8/5/48

BOILERS

Fitted	No.	From
7/3/30	-	6116
31/10/30	-	6128
17/9/31	-	6140
27/2/33	-	6121
17/9/34	-	6126
1/6/37	-	6114
17/9/34	-	6126
1/6/37	-	6114
15/7/38	8128	6164
7/1/41	7239	6169
Taper 102A		
21/8/43	11728	new
22/8/47	11729	6172
3/2/51	12531	6135
3/9/53	12198	-
13/4/57	12036	-
23/10/61	13892	-

SHEDS
Crewe North 3/9/27
Edge Hill 15/10/27
Camden 17/12/27
Polmadie 31/1/32
Perth 4/7/36
Crewe North 17/4/37
Polmadie (loan) 19/11/38
Polmadie 3/12/38
Carlisle Kingmoor 2/12/39
Polmadie 11/4/42
Leeds (loan) 4/9/43
Leeds 2/10/43
Longsight 6/12/52
Preston 28/11/59
Longsight 23/1/60
Crewe North 10/9/60
Carlisle 5/11/60

REPAIRS

17/1/28-7/3/28LO	12/6/45-30/6/45LO
21/3/29-7/5/29HG	22/8/45-27/10/45HS
1/3/30-26/3/30HG	11/8/46-31/8/46LS
6/10/30-7/11/30HO	9/6/47-22/8/47HG
10/3/31-27/3/31LS	12/3/48-7/5/48HG
4/9/31-6/10/31HG	2/11/48-2/12/48LS
13/6/32-30/6/32LS	1/4/49-6/5/49LC
18/2/33-30/3/33HG	8/7/49-23/8/49LC
7/3/34-29/3/34LS	3/12/49-18/1/50HI
8/9/34-4/10/34HG	27/12/50-3/2/51HG
1/5/36-15/6/36HS	26/2/52-24/4/52HI
24/5/37-18/6/37HG	23/12/52-10/2/53HI
1/5/36-15/6/36HS	3/8/53-3/9/53HG
24/5/37-18/6/37HG	19/8/54-10/9/54LI
25/4/38-11/5/38HS	6/5/55-9/6/55HI
28/6/38-27/7/38HO	13/10/55-5/11/55LC(EO)
22/3/39-4/4/39LS	4/6/56-30/6/56HI
15/4/40-26/4/40LS	17/7/56-23/7/
3/12/40-7/1/41HG	56NC(Rect)(EO)
28/10/41-15/11/41LS	16/2/57-13/4/57HG
28/9/42-24/10/42LS	28/4/58-22/5/58HI
20/5/43-21/8/43HG	3/1/59-30/1/59LI
16/9/44-3/10/44LS	15/1/60-19/2/60LI
	30/8/61-23/10/61HG

MILEAGES

Year	Miles	Year	Miles
1927	16,114	1947	57,971
1928	47,931	1948	49,482
1929	46,879	1949	44,222
1930	48,433	1950	69,096
1931	61,613	1951	61,405
1932	70,850	1952	61,610
1933	72,223	1953	64,330
1934	64,044	1954	69,082
1935	66,346	1955	58,197
1936	43,946	1956	54,527
1937	55,702	1957	74,431
1938	74,099	1958	64,394
1939	60,588	1959	66,468
1940	58,113	1960	44,139
1941	69,531	1961	39,117
1942	59,533	1962	41,847
1943	24,096		
1944	57,461		
1945	48,966		
1946	72,087		

Mileage to 31/12/50 1,339,426
Mileage to 31/12/62 2,038,973
Withdrawn week ending 26/1/63
Scrapped Crewe Works 5/63

TENDERS

No.	Fitted
3904	11/9/27
3906	26/12/31
9048	18/6/37

46109 ROYAL ENGINEER

Built North British, cost £7,744
LM 'date built' 11/9/27
Named 4/28
Taper boiler fitted 21/7/43
Original smoke deflectors – not listed
BR smoke deflectors fitted period ending 28/1/50
Renumbered 6109 to 46109 week ending 1/5/48

TENDERS

No.	Fitted
3905	11/9/27
3897	26/12/34
3945	22/5/35
9335	23/4/36
9035	26/7/37
9047	11/2/57

SHEDS

Crewe North 10/9/27
Camden 3/10/28
Preston 29/4/39
Edge Hill 15/2/41
Camden 7/8/43
Leeds (loan) 21/8/43
Leeds 2/10/43

REPAIRS

19/12/27-23/12/27**L**	2/10/44-20/10/44**LS**
5/9/28-27/9/28**LS**	5/7/45-17/8/45**LS**
21/3/29-18/4/29**HG**	21/2/46-3/4/46**HO**
28/4/30-20/5/30**HG**	9/10/46-1/11/46**HG**
17/4/31-16/5/31**HG**	21/8/47-18/9/47**HS**
25/2/32-14/3/32**HS**	14/3/48-26/3/48**LO**
13/6/32-25/7/32**HG**	8/4/48-28/4/48**LO**
18/5/33-2/6/33**LO**	27/9/48-19/10/48**LS**
12/7/33-4/8/33**LS**	20/8/49-8/9/49**LC**
22/1/34-9/2/34**LS**	5/11/49-16/1/50**HG**
28/5/34-27/6/34**HG**	6/6/50-23/6/50**HG**
19/11/34-5/12/34**LS**	4/1/51-18/1/51**LC**
23/5/35-12/6/35**LS**	6/2/51-8/3/51**HI**
23/10/35-8/11/35**LS**	26/7/51-31/8/51**HC(EO)**
4/4/36-23/4/36**HS**	9/6/52-5/8/52**HG**
27/1/37-17/2/37**HG**	28/3/53-29/4/53**LI**
9/7/37-26/7/37**LO**	14/10/53-14/11/53**LC**
12/2/38-24/2/38**HS**	4/3/54-10/4/54**HI**
13/10/38-16/11/38**HG**	17/2/55-28/3/55**HG**
31/3/39-18/4/39**LO**	15/8/55-3/9/55**LC(EO)**
4/10/39-27/10/39**LS**	23/12/55-7/2/56**LI**
23/10/40-20/11/40**HG**	4/2/57-22/3/57**HI**
20/1/42-21/2/42**HS**	21/9/57-2/11/57**LC(EO)**
20/5/42-5/6/42**LO**	6/9/58-20/10/58**HG**
8/5/43-21/7/43**HG**	omitted-2/7/59**HI**
5/1/44-3/2/44**LO**	11/7/60-31/8/60**HI**
	1/9/60-23/9/60**HC(EO)**

MILEAGES

1927	14,748	1944	66,398
1928	57,280	1945	67,150
1929	61,742	1946	66,834
1930	63,148	1947	76,822
1931	67,622	1948	64,228
1932	73,868	1949	50,989
1933	60,967	1950	62,189
1934	72,439	1951	57,825
1935	72,904	1952	71,351
1936	86,700	1953	69,970
1937	79,325	1954	75,098
1938	61,439	1955	66,025
1939	72,741	1956	76,019
1940	44,979	1957	63,552
1941	64,634	Mileage to 31/12/50 1,511,015
1942	46,721	Mileage to 31/12/57 1,990,855
1943	55,148	Withdrawn week ending 29/12/62
		Scrapped Crewe Works 12/63

BOILERS

Fitted	No.	From			
5/5/30	-	6131	21/2/42	9878	
22/4/31	-	6143		6135	
20/6/32	-	6140	*Taper 102A*		
15/6/34	-	6133	21/7/43	11726	new
4/2/37	-	6149	1/11/46	11727	6125
16/11/38	7243	6125	16/1/50	12537	5521
20/11/40	11034	6125	5/8/52	12537	-
			28/3/55	12031	-
			20/10/58	13892	-

46108 SEAFORTH HIGHLANDER waits to head north at Crewe, August 1956. O.S. Nock (*The Royal Scots and Patriots of the LMS,* D&C, 1978) recounts the naming hiccup involving 6108 and 6125; they were among the early conversions and 6108 emerged bearing 6125's name 3RD CARABINIER instead of its own SEAFORTH HIGHLANDER, a contretemps which had to be rapidly sorted out. Photograph B.P. Hoper Collection.

A scruffy 46109 ROYAL ENGINEER at Low Moor shed, Bradford, in 1961. The chalked inscriptions seem to read '8/10 Lightcliffe' – her next duty? and 'CD/CF' which might be local code for 'coaled, clean fire'. Photograph B.P. Hoper Collection.

46110 GRENADIER GUARDSMAN

Built North British, cost £7,744
LM 'date built' 11/9/27
Named 3/28
Taper boiler fitted 21/1/53
Original smoke deflectors 30/1/32
BR smoke deflectors fitted period ending 21/2/53
Renumbered 6110 to 46110 week ending 15/5/48

TENDERS

No.	Fitted
3906	11/9/27
3896	26/12/31
4239	9/5/33
3896	28/6/33
9007	13/1/36

MILEAGES

Year	Mileage	Year	Mileage
1927	11,915	1946	55,510
1928	55,938	1947	50,367
1929	49,279	1948	49,734
1930	62,730	1949	34,900
1931	66,487	1950	47,220
1932	66,408	1951	36,817
1933	59,452	1952	41,203
1934	69,256	1953	71,948
1935	61,265	1954	59,730
1936	62,898	1955	59,725
1937	68,596	1956	53,968
1938	72,050	1957	63,413
1939	54,085	1958	53,578
1940	53,698	1959	52,080
1941	55,677	1960	45,649
1942	51,795		
1943	49,423		
1944	48,191		
1945	60,173		

Mileage at 31/12/50 1,317,038
Mileage at 31/12/60 1,844,649
Withdrawn week ending 22/2/64
Scrapped J. McWilliam, Shettleston, 12/64

SHEDS

Crewe North	10/9/27
Rugby	24/9/27
Camden	7/5/30
Edge Hill	19/5/34
Speke Junction	16/9/39
Longsight	30/9/39
Carlisle	7/10/39
Crewe North	17/1/42
Polmadie (loan)	11/4/42
Polmadie	9/5/42
Crewe North	13/5/44
Crewe	17/6/44
Carlisle	17/6/44
Bushbury	30/9/50
Carlisle Upperby	7/7/51
Crewe North	12/4/52
Holyhead	18/4/53
Edge Hill	27/3/54
Camden	23/6/56
Crewe North	15/9/56
Kentish Town	19/10/57
Camden	7/6/58
Crewe	20/9/58
Edge hill	28/10/61
Longsight	16/12/61
Edge Hill	30/12/61
Springs Branch	29/6/63
Rugby	6/7/63

REPAIRS

3/10/28-5/11/28**LO**	1/2/44-17/2/44**LO**
14/3/29-19/4/29**HG**	13/7/44-29/7/44**LO**
29/10/29-17/11/29**LO**	15/1/45-3/2/45**HG**
10/6/30-2/7/30**HG**	7/12/45-18/1/46**LS**
23/8/30-29/8/30**HO**	17/12/46-21/1/47**HG**
7/4/31-23/4/31**LS**	22/10/47-9/12/47**LO**
13/10/31-5/11/31**HG**	4/3/48-8/4/48**LS**
12/7/32-2/8/32**LS**	9/3/49-29/3/49**LI**
18/1/33-14/2/33**HS**	14/4/49-5/5/49**LC**
26/5/33-1/6/33**LO**	24/5/49-31/5/49**NC**
6/9/33-29/9/33**HS**	3/8/49-22/9/49**HC**
20/3/34-3/5/34**HG**	24/1/50-20/2/50**LC**
12/6/34-19/6/34**LO**	4/2/51-23/2/51**HI**
4/2/35-26/2/35**LS**	28/9/51-7/11/51**LC(EO)**
10/7/35-25/7/35**LO**	29/11/51-10/1/52**LC**
22/11/35-31/12/35**HG**	30/1/52-26/2/52**NC**
17/10/36-13/11/36**HS**	11/12/52-31/1/53**HG**
7/4/37-23/4/37**LO**	10/2/53-13/2/53**NC(Rect)(EO)**
6/8/37-13/9/37**HG**	26/4/54-19/5/54**HI**
28/12/38-23/1/39**HS**	28/9/54-5/11/54**LC(EO)**
19/1/40-3/2/40**HS**	14/6/55-22/7/55**HI**
12/8/40-30/8/40**LO**	9/1/56-8/2/56**HG**
1/2/41-15/2/41**LS**	26/6/57-3/8/57**LI**
28/5/41-13/6/41**LO**	31/3/58-2/5/58**LI**
22/1/42-13/2/42**HG**	6/5/59-26/6/59**HG**
16/1/43-13/2/43**LS**	24/3/60-12/5/60**LI**
23/8/43-21/9/43**LO**	19/7/60-31/8/60**HC(EO)**
2/12/43-8/1/44**HS**	31/5/61-24/7/61**LI**

BOILERS

Fitted	No.	From			
30/4/29	-	6142	23/1/39	7235	6163
16/6/30	-	6109	13/2/42	8138	6157
26/8/30	-	6133	3/2/45	8134	6101
14/10/31	-	6126	21/1/47	11032	6141
24/1/33	-	6154	22/9/49	11033	6143
18/4/34	-	6115	*Taper 102A*		
4/12/35	-	6102	31/1/53	13895	-
4/11/36	-	6157	8/2/56	12673	-
26/8/37	5824	6121	26/6/59	13240	-

46111 ROYAL FUSILIER

Built North British, cost £7,744
LM 'date built' 9/10/27
Taper boiler fitted 1/10/47
Original smoke deflectors 26/11/31
BR smoke deflectors fitted period ending 11/8/51
Renumbered 6111 to 46111 week ending 20/11/48

MILEAGES

Year	Mileage	Year	Mileage
1927	13,670	1946	69,749
1928	54,382	1947	41,035
1929	61,085	1948	68,364
1930	49,016	1949	62,000
1931	62,301	1950	56,472
1932	66,851	1951	62,897
1933	75,855	1952	54,075
1934	69,870	1953	58,268
1935	78,720	1954	46,549
1936	75,703	1955	63,822
1937	67,516	1956	57,475
1938	73,997	1957	71,799
1939	56,568	1958	63,030
1940	63,400	1959	56,192
1941	65,198	1960	36,523
1942	58,835		
1943	61,678		
1944	59,933		
1945	59,363		

Mileage at 31/12/50 1,471,561
Mileage at 31/12/60 2,042,191
Withdrawn week ending 28/9/63
Scrapped Crewe Works 11/63

TENDERS

No.	Fitted
3907	9/10/27
3928	26/12/31
3945	31/12/32
3897	22/5/35
?	23/1/36
9039	31/12/36
9042	26/7/52

REPAIRS

20/7/28-28/7/28**LO**	16/6/43-30/6/43**HG**
3/12/28-17/12/28**LO**	9/10/43-22/10/43**LO**
20/3/29-16/4/29**HG**	30/5/44-16/6/44**HG**
7/4/30-6/6/30**HG**	13/11/44-1/12/44**LO**
17/10/31-26/11/31**LO**	24/4/45-11/5/45**LS**
4/5/31-19/5/31**LS**	7/8/45-22/9/45**HO**
12/2/32-16/3/32**HG**	28/12/45-19/1/46**LO**
29/8/32-26/9/32**LO**	4/5/46-28/5/46**HS**
21/3/33-20/4/33**HS**	7/4/47-1/10/47**HG**
6/1/34-7/2/34**HG**	18/10/48-15/11/48**HS**
30/5/34-12/6/34**LS**	20/1/49-8/2/49**LC**
27/8/34-10/9/34**HG**	25/1/50-14/2/50**LI**
10/12/34-31/12/34**HS**	3/11/50-24/11/50**LG**
17/6/35-11/7/35**LS**	25/5/51-26/7/51**HG**
4/1/36-23/1/36**HG**	18/7/52-22/8/52**LI**
27/2/36-9/3/36**LO**	22/7/53-17/8/53**LI**
3/7/36-23/7/36**LO**	11/11/54-20/12/54**HG**
26/11/36-21/12/36**LS**	13/2/56-7/3/56**LI**
9/3/37-22/3/37**LO**	15/11/56-20/12/56**HG**
5/6/37-18/6/37**LO**	14/8/57-18/9/57**LC**
22/11/37-17/12/37**HG**	25/8/58-26/9/58**HG**
15/8/38-12/9/38**LS**	6/1/59-23/1/59**LC(EO)**
21/2/39-13/3/39**HS**	23/2/59-23/2/59**NC**
2/3/40-2/4/40**HG**	1/4/59-14/4/59**NC(EO)**
22/2/41-13/3/41**LS**	21/3/60-27/5/60**HI**
22/12/41-8/1/42**HS**	17/6/60-8/7/60**LC(EO)**
29/8/42-17/9/42**HG**	29/10/60-26/11/60**LC(EO)**

SHEDS

Rugby	17/9/27
Camden	7/5/30
Longsight	25/9/37
Preston (loan)	28/5/38
Longsight	25/6/38
Crewe North (loan)	28/10/39
Camden	10/2/40
Carlisle (loan)	4/8/40
Carlisle	19/10/40
Crewe	10/1/42
Edge Hill	21/2/42
Leeds (loan)	15/1/44
Edge Hill	5/2/44
Crewe North	20/9/52
Longsight	13/6/53
Holyhead	22/8/53
Longsight	26/9/53
Holyhead	25/5/57
Longsight	26/6/57
Crewe North	10/9/60
Willesden	10/6/61
Annesley	12/1/63

BOILERS

Fitted	No.	From			
14/4/30	-	new	17/9/42	15573	6137
16/2/32	-	6143	16/6/44	10182	6164
3/4/33	-	6141	22/9/45	9879	6157
16/1/34	-	6163	*Taper 102A*		
4/9/34	-	6168	1/10/47	12542	new
13/1/36	-	6153	26/7/51	13594	new
2/12/37	5574	6139	20/12/54	13594	-
13/3/39	7222	6146	20/12/56	12663	-
2/4/40	8127	6161	20/12/56	12204	-
			26/9/58	12541	-

Royal Scot in original condition, 6110 GRENADIER GUARDSMAN with a short train approaching Bushey troughs on the Up Fast about 1928. Number on tender, coat of arms on cabside, and buffer beam lining. Ominously, smoke is clinging to the top of the boiler. Photograph B.P. Hoper Collection.

46112 SHERWOOD FORESTER

Built North British, cost £7.744
LM 'date built' 9/10/27
Named 4/28
Taper boiler fitted 14/9/43
Original smoke deflectors 27/2/32
BR smoke deflectors fitted period ending 8/10/49
Renumbered 6112 to 46112 week ending 11/9/48

REPAIRS	
21/3/29-29/4/29**HG**	12/3/45-21/4/45**HS**
12/2/30-6/3/30**LO**	27/2/46-19/3/46**LS**
23/4/30-24/5/30**HG**	5/9/46-28/9/46**LO**
31/3/31-1/5/31**HG**	15/4/47-27/5/47**HG**
15/3/32-4/4/32**HS**	31/7/48-7/9/48**LS**
12/10/32-27/10/32**LS**	16/12/48-7/1/4**LC**
18/4/33-22/5/33**HG**	19/8/49-6/10/49**HG**
2/3/34-19/3/34**HS**	11/11/49-24/11/49**NC**
4/10/34-23/10/34**LO**	7/7/50-3/8/50**LC**
7/12/34-14/1/35**HG**	5/12/50-23/12/50**LI**
17/6/35-10/7/35**HS**	11/10/51-10/11/51**HG**
25/4/36-12/5/36**LS**	10/3/52-9/4/52**HC(EO)**
1/11/36-4/12/36**HG**	18/10/52-6/11/52**LI**
17/12/37-3/1/38**HS**	25/11/52-28/11/52**NC(Rect)(EO)**
14/3/38-29/3/38**HO**	29/7/53-19/8/53**LI**
11/7/38-28/7/38**LO**	20/5/54-11/6/54**HI**
13/10/38-27/10/38**LO**	28/2/55-21/4/55**HG**
2/12/38-20/12/38**LO**	15/12/55-20/1/56**LI**
27/2/39-27/3/39**HG**	5/3/56-3/4/56**LC(EO)**
9/2/40-27/2/40**LS**	24/9/56-27/10/56**LC**
12/4/40-24/4/40**LO**	31/12/56-6/2/57**HG**
29/3/41-26/4/41**HG**	21/8/57-26/9/57**LO**
4/11/41-21/11/41**LS**	21/6/58-30/7/58**HI**
11/6/42-17/7/42**LS**	21/4/59-30/5/59**HI**
23/6/43-14/9/43**HG**	18/9/59-19/11/59**HC(EO)**
15/8/44-31/8/44**HS**	27/11/59**NC(Rect)(EO)**
	10/5/60-13/6/60**HG**

SHEDS	
Crewe North	24/9/27
Carlisle	15/10/27
Rugby	17/12/27
Camden	7/5/30
Edge Hill	26/1/35
Speke Jct	16/9/39
Crewe	30/9/39
Preston (loan)	26/10/40
Crewe North	16/11/40
Holyhead	27/12/41
Crewe North	11/4/42
Holyhead	4/12/43
Crewe North	23/2/46
Holyhead	6/4/46
Crewe North	24/5/47
Holyhead	21/6/47
Crewe North	7/8/48
Holyhead	2/10/48
Leeds	21/2/53
Nottingham	19/12/59
Trafford Park	17/12/60
Annesley	29/2/62

BOILERS		
Fitted	**No.**	**From**
8/5/30	-	6145
8/4/31	-	new
26/4/33	-	6149
27/12/34	-	6145
19/11/36	5821	6122
18/3/38	5823	6165
27/3/39	7215	6109
26/4/41	7257	6155
Taper 102A		
14/9/43	11729	new
27/5/47	12031	5735
6/10/49	10753	5736
10/11/51	12208	-
21/4/55	12537	-
6/3/57	10753	-
13/6/60	12209	-

MILEAGES	
1927	13,774
1928	58,917
1929	59,657
1930	54,045
1931	66,112
1932	61,551
1933	77,563
1934	68,400
1935	71,263
1936	76,011
1937	77,728
1938	59,282
1939	55,082
1940	59,316
1941	55,535
1942	58,602
1943	52,019
1944	67,353
1945	54,545
1946	60,843
1947	63,588
1948	55,258
1949	57,029
1950	59,670
1951	68,072
1952	62,405
1953	79,614
1954	74,228
1955	59,184
1956	65,003
1957	69,465
1958	71,812
1959	52,722
1960	55,809

Mileage at 31/12/50 1,443,143
Mileage at 31/12/60 2,101,457
Withdrawn week ending 9/5/64
Scrapped J. Cashmore Ltd, Great Bridge, 9/64

TENDERS	
No.	**Fitted**
3908	9/10/27
3902	26/12/31
4237	29/8/35
9034	12/5/36
9352	14/12/45
9052	10/12/52

46112 SHERWOOD FORESTER on the Polmadie turntable, 9 May 1953. It had never been a Scottish engine and for much of the 1950s was on the Holbeck complement, before (appropriately) moving on to Nottingham. The plaque on the splasher under the nameplate records the numerous occasions the engine was specially turned out for movements of the Regiment. *'Can we have our engine, please?'* was a frequent request when regiments were on the move. Photograph J. Robertson, B.P. Hoper Collection.

CAMERONIAN getting on for its final BR form (only second emblem, speedo and AWS to go!) at Corkerhill shed on 26 April 1952. Photograph J. Robertson, B.P. Hoper Collection.

46113 CAMERONIAN

Built North British, cost £7,744
LM 'date built' 9/10/27
Named 3/28
Taper boiler fitted 15/12/50
Original smoke deflectors 29/1/32
BR smoke deflectors fitted period ending 30/12/50
Renumbered 6113 to 46113 week ending 14/5/49

REPAIRS	
12/9/28-8/11/28**HG**	27/4/44-15/5/44**LS**
4/1/29-25/2/29**L**	1/11/44-30/11/44**LO**
9/9/29-27/9/29**LO**	5/9/45-5/10/45**LS**
8/3/30-5/4/30**HG**	19/11/46-6/12/46**HS**
17/11/30-4/12/30**LS**	6/10/47-15/11/47**HG**
15/7/31-31/7/31**HS**	13/4/49-12/5/49**LI**
31/12/31-29/1/32**HG**	27/11/49-17/12/49**LC**
16/8/32-8/9/32**LS**	2/11/50-15/12/50**HG**
17/2/33-10/3/33**HS**	29/2/52-24/3/52**HI**
5/9/33-26/9/33**LS**	7/11/52-10/12/52**HI(EO)**
3/4/34-16/5/34**HG**	20/1/54-15/2/54**HC**
24/10/35-13/11/35**HS**	6/8/54-4/9/54**HC**
2/12/36-26/12/36**LS**	7/1/55-3/2/55**HI**
20/4/37-1/6/37**HG**	13/7/55-10/8/55**LC**
11/4/38-3/5/38**LS**	6/9/55-29/9/55**LC**
10/10/38-26/10/38**HO**	23/12/55-31/1/56**HI**
13/3/39-2/5/39**HG**	7/3/57-6/4/57**HG**
16/12/39-3/1/40**HS**	8/8/57-30/8/57**LC(EO)**
21/8/40-7/9/40**HS**	4/10/57-12/10/57**NC(Rect)**
15/3/41-29/3/41**LS**	30/8/58-3/10/58**HI**
12/10/41-8/11/41**HG**	16/1/59-27/2/59**LC**
18/6/42-4/7/42**HS**	16/12/59-1/4/60**HI**
25/1/43-18/2/43**LS**	19/9/60**NC(EO)**
27/5/43-22/6/43**LS**	24/1/61-25/2/61**LI**

SHEDS	
Crewe	8/10/27
Rugby	17/12/27
Camden	7/4/28
Holyhead	13/7/32
Carlisle	20/5/34
Polmadie	-
Carlisle Kingmoor	11/4/36
Crewe	17/4/37
Bangor	2/7/38
Crewe	28/1/39
Camden	1/7/39
Crewe South	29/9/45
Edge Hill (loan)	24/1/48
Crewe North	28/2/48
Holyhead (loan)	10/4/48
Crewe North	1/5/48
Leeds (loan)	17/2/51

MILEAGES			
1927	16,200	1944	53,168
1928	47,821	1945	63,628
1929	48,065	1946	56,297
1930	52,863	1947	52,373
1931	78,269	1948	64,159
1932	62,816	1949	40,584
1933	67,009	1950	44,081
1934	53,140	1951	73,172
1935	59,826	1952	67,463
1936	48,260	1953	70,486
1937	64,189	1954	69,267
1938	71,779	1955	60,116
1939	61,354	1956	64,261
1940	67,988	1957	64,668
1941	59,845	Mileage at 31/12/50 1,386,275	
1942	76,294	Mileage at 31/12/60 1,855,708	
1943	76,267	**Withdrawn week ending 22/12/62**	
		Scrapped Crewe Works 6/63	

TENDERS	
No.	Fitted
3909	9/10/27
2805	6/11/28
3904	26/12/31
9052	1/6/37
9352	10/12/52
9331	12/10/57

BOILERS		
Fitted	No.	From
10/28	-	new
3/30	-	new
4/1/32	-	6149
7/5/34	-	6143
17/5/37	-	new
2/5/39	7217	6131
8/11/41	7240	6123
22/6/43	7233	6167
15/11/47	11036	6142
Taper 102A		
15/12/50	13244	new
15/2/54	13242	-
6/4/57	13525	-

46114 COLDSTREAM GUARDSMAN

Built North British, cost £7,744
LM 'date built' 9/10/27
Taper boiler fitted 28/6/46
Original smoke deflectors 12/1/32
BR smoke deflectors fitted period ending 9/9/50
Renumbered 6114 to 46114 week ending 28/9/63

REPAIRS	
24/10/28-3/12/28**HG**	17/10/41-7/11/41**HG**
28/4/29-16/5/29**LO**	22/8/42-5/9/42**HS**
4/6/29-18/6/29**LO**	21/8/43-11/9/43**HG**
23/10/29-14/12/29**HG**	14/6/44-1/7/44**LS**
24/12/30-21/1/31**HG**	26/1/45-2/3/45**LO**
28/3/31-22/4/31**HG**	3/7/45-11/8/45**LS**
16/12/31-12/9/32**HG**	1/5/46-28/6/46**HG**
23/7/32-22/8/32**HG**	27/3/47-5/5/47**HS**
11/1/33-26/1/33**LS**	4/6/48-25/6/48**HS**
5/6/33-22/6/33**LS**	27/10/48-23/11/48**LO**
19/9/33-24/9/33**LO**	9/6/49-24/6/49**LI**
21/11/33-11/12/33**HS**	19/12/49-12/1/50**LC**
7/5/34-11/6/34**HG**	26/6/50-7/9/50**HG**
16/11/34-4/12/34**LS**	9/5/51-7/6/51**HC**
22/4/35-13/5/35**HS**	26/5/52-14/6/52**LI**
7/10/35-23/10/35**LS**	26/2/53-30/3/53**HG**
12/8/36-26/8/36**LS**	18/5/53-3/6/53**NC(EO)**
27/2/37-25/3/37**HG**	8/3/54-7/4/54**LC(EO)**
20/11/37-15/12/37**HS**	17/2/55-18/3/55**HI**
26/4/38-18/5/38**LO**	4/1/56-3/2/56**HG**
9/8/38-26/8/38**LO**	3/4/56-27/4/56**LC(EO)**
4/1/39-16/2/39**HG**	6/9/56-10/10/56**LI**
19/9/39-13/10/39**LS**	11/8/57-11/10/57**HG**
19/10/39-3/11/39**LO**	8/9/58-7/10/58**LI**
17/1/40-31/1/40**LO**	28/3/59-24/4/59**LC**
22/5/40-6/6/40**LO**	6/5/59-30/5/59**LC**
19/11/40-13/12/40**LS**	12/2/60-25/3/60**HI**
	20/9/61-18/10/61**LI**

SHEDS	
Crewe	24/9/27
Camden	7/4/28
Crewe	17/9/30
Camden	12/11/30
Longsight	12/10/46
Camden	18/6/55
Edge Hill	24/9/55
Longsight	11/2/56
Edge Hill	25/2/56
Willesden	14/1/61
Bushbury	4/3/61
Llandudno Junction	10/6/61
Holyhead	9/9/61
Willesden	22/6/63

BOILERS		
Fitted	No.	From
11/28	-	6113
29/11/29	-	6137
30/12/30	-	6118
1/4/31	-	6137
26/7/32	-	6168
30/5/34	-	6127
1/5/35	-	6122
12/3/37	-	6166
16/2/39	7258	6126
7/11/41	7246	6133
11/9/43	7257	6112
Taper 102A		
28/6/46	12205	new
7/9/50	12035	6129
30/3/53	12033	-
3/2/56	12207	-
11/10/57	12035	-

MILEAGES			
1927	9,813	1946	61,008
1928	52,427	1947	61,328
1929	43,226	1948	55,908
1930	61,809	1949	68,049
1931	60,580	1950	59,090
1932	58,312	1951	64,244
1933	72,779	1952	69,772
1934	71,270	1953	48,476
1935	72,254	1954	50,820
1936	79,232	1955	48,859
1937	66,994	1956	59,474
1938	87,447	1957	58,255
1939	66,906	1958	63,186
1940	64,589	1959	57,582
1941	71,415	1960	47,426
1942	90,401	Mileage at 31/12/50 1,526,387	
1943	72,147	Mileage at 31/12/60 2,094,481	
1944	58,652	**Withdrawn week ending 28/9/63**	
1945	60,751	**Scrapped Slag Reduction, Rotherham, 4/64**	

TENDERS	
No.	Fitted
3910	9/10/27
3905	26/12/31
9352	24/8/34
9049	16/10/39
9129	20/3/59

46115 SCOTS GUARDSMAN

Built North British, cost £7,744
LM 'date built' 9/10/27
Taper boiler fitted 20/8/47
Original smoke deflectors 4/2/32
BR smoke deflectors fitted period ending – not recorded
Renumbered 6115 to 46115 week ending 22/1/49

SHEDS

Crewe 8/10/27	Crewe North (loan) 28/9/40
Rugby 15/10/27	Crewe 26/10/40
Crewe North 17/12/27	Carlisle Upperby 18/10/41
Camden 7/4/28	Camden 22/11/41
Crewe North 19/9/30	Crewe North 12/10/46
Camden 12/11/30	Carlisle Upperby (loan) 5/3/49
Polmadie 20/11/32	Longsight 1/10/49
'Carlisle' no date	Crewe North 10/9/60
Polmadie 2/10/37	Carlisle Upperby 6/5/61
Carlisle Jingmoor 7/10/39	Longsight 15/7/61

REPAIRS

21/3/29-20/4/29**HG**	7/6/44-19/7/44**LS**
25/11/29-21/12/29**LS**	26/2/45-29/3/45**LS**
28/4/30-30/5/30**HG**	19/11/45-5/12/45**HS**
4/5/31-3/6/31**HG**	27/3/47-20/8/47**HG**
14/1/32-4/2/32**HO**	10/9/47-16/10/47**HO**
20/5/32-9/6/32**HG**	11/12/48-19/1/49**LI**
20/2/33-3/3/33**LS**	17/4/50-26/5/50**HG**
28/3/33-5/4/33**LO**	20/9/50-28/10/50**LC**
26/6/33-24/7/33**HO**	26/7/51-15/8/51**HI**
17/4/34-29/5/34**HG**	12/8/52-12/9/52**HG**
3/5/35-25/5/35**LS**	5/11/53-5/12/53**HI**
26/5/36**LS**	1/1/55-26/1/55**HG**
13/1/37-9/2/37**HG**	7/2/56-27/2/56**HI**
21/7/38-9/8/38**HS**	28/6/56-8/8/56**HC(EO)**
17/8/39-28/9/39**HG**	25/9/56-25/10/56**LC(EO)**
9/3/40-6/4/40**LO**	27/7/57-24/8/57**HG**
11/10/40-26/10/40**LS**	26/11/57-10/12/57**LC(EO)**
2/8/41-9/9/41**LS**	12/5/58-4/6/58**LI**
26/3/42-15/4/42**LS**	28/10/58-3/12/58**LC(EO)**
31/10/42-27/11/42**HS**	13/8/59-25/9/59**HI**
15/7/43-28/8/43**HG**	21/9/60-28/10/60**HI**
23/3/44-11/4/44**LO**	

MILEAGES

Year	Miles	Year	Miles
1927	15,098	1946	61,421
1928	57,613	1947	30,028
1929	62,169	1948	58,683
1930	95,887	1949	60,269
1931	62,919	1950	52,111
1932	64,498	1951	66,533
1933	72,076	1952	66,513
1934	65,472	1953	69,413
1935	58,747	1954	63,572
1936	44,222	1955	69,328
1937	66,888	1956	56,145
1938	59,086	1957	66,483
1939	62,614	1958	65,219
1940	56,053	1959	67,814
1941	60,153	1960	59,516
1942	70,199		
1943	79,486		
1944	59,638		
1945	59,920		

Mileage at 31/12/50 1,395,250
Mileage at 31/12/60 2,045,786
Withdrawn week ending 1/1/66
Preserved

TENDERS

No.	Fitted
3911	9/10/27
3939	26/12/31
9021	21/5/36

BOILERS

Fitted	No.	From
15/5/30	-	6111
13/5/31	-	6130
23/5/32	-	6123
10/7/33	-	6134
21/5/34	-	6120
20/1/37	-	6116
28/9/39	7237	6134
28/8/43	8121	6128
Taper 102A		
20/8/47	12532	new
26/5/50	12197	6122
12/9/52	12662	-
26/1/55	12661	-
24/8/57	12659	-

46116 IRISH GUARDSMAN

Built North British, cost £7,744
LM 'date built' 9/10/27
Named 1928
Taper boiler fitted 10/5/44
Original smoke deflectors – not listed
BR smoke deflectors fitted period ending 4/11/50
Renumbered 6116 to 46116 week ending 25/9/48

TENDERS

No.	Fitted
3912	9/10/27
3937	26/12/31
9346	22/6/36

REPAIRS

6/3/28-13/3/28**LO**	1/1/43-16/1/43**LS**
14/1/29-9/3/29**HG**	3/9/43-21/9/43**LS**
8/6/29-22/6/29**LO**	1/2/44-10/5/44**HG**
27/7/29-4/8/29**LO**	19/5/45-2/6/45**HS**
22/1/30-26/2/30**HG**	23/5/46-7/6/46**HS**
11/2/31-27/2/31**LS**	7/1/47-20/1/47**TRO**
13/5/31-17/6/31**HG**	16/5/47-21/6/47**HG**
20/5/32-23/6/32**HG**	5/9/47-10/10/47**HO**
16/2/33-7/3/33**LS**	9/3/48-25/3/48**LO**
16/8/33-8/9/33**LS**	24/8/48-21/9/48**LS**
9/2/34-28/3/34**HG**	21/8/49-15/9/49**LI**
13/10/34-30/10/34**HS**	8/11/49-5/12/49**LC**
18/2/35-7/3/35**HS**	18/9/50-1/11/50**HG**
17/7/35-2/8/35**LS**	13/2/52-7/3/52**HI**
23/11/35-10/12/35**LO**	19/5/52-7/6/52**LC**
3/6/36-22/6/36**LS**	2/4/53-16/5/53**HG**
24/11/36-16/12/36**HG**	30/10/53-25/11/53**LC(EO)**
27/5/37-11/6/37**LO**	10/2/54-11/3/54**HI**
9/11/37-25/11/37**LS**	26/1/55-12/3/55**HG**
28/4/38-15/6/38**HG**	11/6/56-27/7/56**HI**
8/8/38-29/8/38**LO**	26/7/57-31/8/57**HG**
17/4/39-1/5/39**LS**	28/4/58-28/5/58**HI**
2/3/40-28/3/40**HG**	11/6/59-9/7/59**HI**
20/2/41-15/3/41**HS**	9/3/60-23/4/60**HI**
29/11/41-20/12/41**LS**	30/11/60-31/1/61**LC(EO)**
2/7/42-25/7/42**LO**	4/5/61-9/6/61**LI**

SHEDS

Crewe North 8/10/27
Camden 7/4/28
Crewe North 17/9/30
Camden 12/11/30
Holyhead 12/10/35
Llandudno Junction 5/12/36
Longsight (loan) 9/10/37
Holyhead 30/10/37
Crewe North 26/2/38
Camden 1/7/39
Holyhead (loan) 8/7/39
Crewe North (loan) 7/10/39
Edge Hill 6/4/40
Camden 1/6/40
Carlisle Upperby 25/9/54
Holyhead 28/4/56
Carlisle Upperby 16/6/56
Kentish Town 19/10/57
Trafford Park 5/7/58
Camden (loan) 19/7/58
Camden 2/8/58
Crewe 20/9/58
Edge Hill 28/10/61
Carlisle Kingmoor 3/11/62

MILEAGES

Year	Miles	Year	Miles
		1946	80,881
1927	9,704	1947	60,609
1928	55,272	1948	73,696
1929	53,975	1949	59,681
1930	60,898	1950	56,686
1931	42,930	1951	61,499
1932	61,620	1952	62,597
1933	73,953	1953	64,292
1934	60,291	1954	64,724
1935	78,177	1955	56,509
1936	60,480	1956	61,432
1937	74,429	1957	56,673
1938	71,982	1958	61,604
1939	79,193	1959	56,158
1940	70,458	1960	48,930
1941	50,949		
1942	73,694		
1943	74,135		
1944	31,056		
1945	72,825		

Mileage at 31/12/50 1,487,574
Mileage at 31/12/60 2,081,992
Withdrawn week ending 17/8/63
Scrapped Crewe Works 9/63

BOILERS

Fitted	No.	From
18/1/29	-	6104
11/2/30	-	6102
21/5/31	-	6132
27/5/32	-	6162
13/3/34	-	6137
25/2/35	-	6104
2/12/36	-	6138
27/5/38	7214	6102
28/3/40	7229	6117
15/3/41	9877	6142
Taper 102A		
10/5/44	12028	new
21/6/47	12526	new
1/11/50	12527	6131
16/5/53	12205	-
12/3/55	12202	-
31/8/57	12533	-
7/6/62	12036	-

46114 COLDSTREAM GUARDSMAN in 1955, a splendid picture without, unfortunately, any details as to place – though it could well be Shrewsbury. However the two types are regarded – parallel boiler versus taper boiler – that proud double chimney always, to my mind, wins the day. The squat original just wasn't in it. 6114 was the engine in the Leighton Buzzard derailment, with a suggestion that smoke may have obscured the Driver's view. While this didn't actually lead to the application of smoke deflectors (trials had begun well before) it certainly hastened their application. The idea that Leighton Buzzard alone prompted the fitting of smoke deflectors, and impaired look-out was *the* reason for the accident has gained strength over the years, erroneously. The Inspecting Officer was quite adamant that, as in previous accidents, what was really needed was some system of Automatic Train Control. Photograph B.P. Hoper Collection.

Longsight's 46115 SCOTS GUARDSMAN, which was eventually preserved, at Dalry Road in February 1955. The taper boiler Scots could be used on the Midland Division but they were kept for the harder work north of Leeds, until more became available at the end of the 1950s. The great bulk were always on the Western Division, but from the advent of the Pacifics they were seen less often north of Carlisle. No.15 was a Longsight engine for many years, and a favourite on the London trains via Stoke-on-Trent. Photograph W. Hermiston, B.P. Hoper Collection.

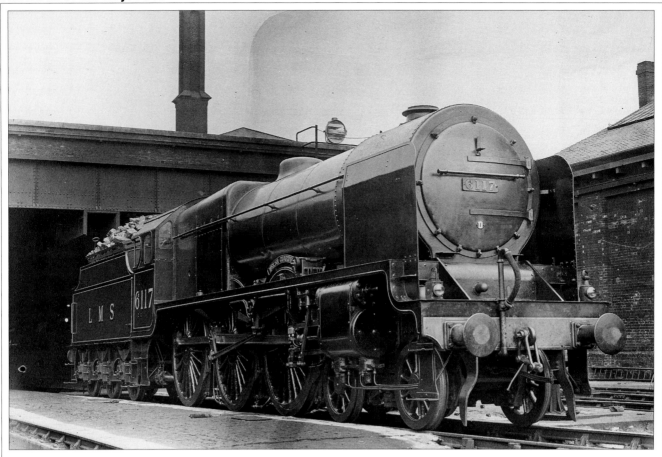

An exquisite 6117 WELSH GUARDSMAN outside its home shed, Camden, ready for the next job north, early in the 1930s, in the second style of painting, with LMS (rather than the engine number) on the tender and the number in its 'proper' place, at the cabside. Note the multiplicity of 'dogs' to keep the smokebox door 'tight' and the ill-matched headlamps – an LMS (square) example on the left and a round (LNW?) one on the right. Also lack of rainstrip at join of cab side and the roof. For once the exhaust pipes from the middle cylinder are visible, attached to a bracket on the left-hand rail guard. That big lamp, set on the ancient blackened roof of the shed, must have been the most modern then in use anywhere on the Western Division! Photograph B.P. Hoper Collection.

6119 LANCASHIRE FUSILIER, with the earlier angled smoke deflectors, at Crewe North, 30 May 1937. Note *circa*-1936 style of numerals and insignia. Photograph J.A. Whaley, B.P. Hoper Collection.

46117 WELSH GUARDSMAN

Built North British, cost £7,744
LM 'date built' 6/11/27
Named 4/28
Taper boiler fitted 9/12/43
Original smoke deflectors 30/1/32
BR smoke deflectors fitted period ending 4/11/50
Renumbered 6117 to 46117 week ending 29/5/48

SHEDS	
Crewe North	15/10/27
Camden	7/4/28
Carlisle	2/7/30
Crewe North	17/9/30
Camden	12/11/30
Crewe North	22/4/31
Camden	24/6/31
Carlisle Upperby	15/7/31
Camden	6/5/33
Llandudno	12/10/35
Crewe North	21/10/39
Edge Hill	6/4/40
Camden	1/6/40
Leeds (loan)	11/3/44
Leeds	1/4/44

BOILERS

Fitted	No.	From
16/4/30	-	6124
4/9/30	-	6149
29/5/31	-	6144
11/4/33	-	6108
5/12/34	-	6111
22/10/36	-	6137
20/4/38	7229	6111
10/1/40	7234	6101
25/6/41	7248	6167
Taper 102A		
9/12/43	11734	-
25/6/47	11732	6124
9/10/50	11727	6109
10/6/52	12202	-
18/12/54	11734	-
5/2/57	12029	-
10/10/59	10752	-

REPAIRS	
22/3/29-2/5/29**HG**	16/1/45-8/2/45**HS**
12/12/29-21/12/29**LO**	16/10/45-15/11/45**LO**
7/4/30-7/5/30**HG**	18/3/46-12/4/46**LS**
27/8/30-10/9/30**HO**	20/8/46-3/10/46**HO**
29/12/30-20/1/31**LS**	28/11/46-16/1/47**LO**
25/5/31-2/7/31**HS**	28/4/47-25/6/47**HG**
23/3/32-7/4/32**HS**	4/9/47-9/10/47**LO**
3/4/33-5/5/33**HG**	24/3/48-27/5/48**HS**
26/9/33-13/10/33**HS**	6/12/48-10/2/49**HC**
17/2/34-6/3/34**LS**	11/3/49-6/4/49**HC**
9/7/34-27/7/34**LS**	19/9/49-6/10/49**LI**
26/11/34-19/12/34**HG**	28/8/50-9/10/50**HG**
6/7/35**TRO**	25/7/51-30/8/51**HI**
5/12/35-23/12/35**LS**	6/10/51-9/11/51**LC(EO)**
16/10/36-11/11/36**HG**	25/12/51-25/1/52**LI(EO)**
2/1/37-4/1/37**LO**	19/4/52-10/6/52**HG**
23/7/37-11/8/37**LS**	16/2/53-14/3/53**HI**
11/4/38-10/5/38**HS**	12/12/53-7/1/54**HI**
22/11/38-7/12/38**HS**	18/1/54-22/1/54**NC(Rect)(EO)**
25/4/39-9/5/39**LO**	15/11/54-18/12/54**HG**
9/8/39-23/8/39**LO**	17/10/55-15/11/55**LI**
15/12/39-10/1/40**HG**	29/12/56-5/2/57**HG**
6/8/40-23/8/40**LS**	26/2/57**NC(Rect)(EO)**
9/6/41-25/6/41**HS**	7/7/57-10/8/57**LI**
26/11/41-11/12/41**LO**	1/5/58-31/5/58**HI**
15/5/42-30/5/42**LS**	5/11/58-18/12/58**LC(EO)**
21/9/42-14/10/42**LO**	17/8/59-10/10/59**HG**
5/4/43-17/4/43**LS**	28/10/59**NC(Rect)(EO)**
24/5/43-29/5/43**TRO**	10/10/60-10/11/60**HI**
16/10/43-9/12/43**HG**	15/5/61-14/6/61**HI(EO)**

TENDERS	
No.	Fitted
3913	6/11/27
3941	26/12/31
9047	11/11/36
9357	6/10/56

MILEAGES			
1927	1,016	1945	55,419
1928	53,214	1946	45,655
1929	44,227	1947	51,785
1930	56,695	1948	56,555
1931	62,172	1949	52,259
1932	53,056	1950	61,550
1933	74,891	1951	65,064
1934	75,989	1952	66,762
1935	67,387	1953	71,327
1936	77,115	1954	69,517
1937	81,655	1955	78,215
1938	69,940	1956	61,456
1939	60,300	1957	65,111
1940	69,992	Mileage at 31/12/50	1,416,145
1941	64,942	Mileage at 31/12/57	1,893,597
1942	75,270	Withdrawn week ending 1/12/62	
1943	37,657	Scrapped Crewe Works 12/63	

46118 ROYAL WELCH FUSILIER

Built North British, cost £7,744
LM 'date built' 6/11/27
Named 1928
Taper boiler fitted 17/12/46
Original smoke deflectors 15/12/31
BR smoke deflectors fitted period ending 22/4/50
Renumbered 6118 to 46118 week ending 12/2/49

MILEAGES			
1927	10,378	1948	67,031
1928	52,819	1949	52,695
1929	44,347	1950	67,098
1930	65,413	1951	51,039
1931	45,334	1952	48,275
1932	56,660	1953	56,710
1933	61,562	1954	61,725
1934	57,646	1955	52,011
1935	62,402	1956	47,330
1936	83,176	1957	54,073
1937	87,522	1958	48,446
1938	73,901	1959	44,411
1939	67,891	1960	61,388
1940	61,852	1961	41,055
1941	83,286	1962	34,431
1942	62,430	1963	39,494
1943	64,097	Mileage at 31/12/50 1,449,342	
1944	57,840	Mileage at 31/12/63 2,092,730	
1945	51,039	Withdrawn week ending 13/6/64	
1946	46,370	Scrapped J.N. Connell, Coatbridge, 11/64	
1947	66,553		

TENDERS	
No.	Fitted
3914	6/11/27
3817	26/12/31
9333	9/4/36

REPAIRS	
29/3/28-30/4/28**L**	30/10/42-21/11/42**HG**
21/3/29-26/4/29**HG**	21/8/43-23/9/43**HS**
22/11/29-21/12/29**HG**	16/6/44-12/7/44**HG**
30/9/30-24/10/30**HG**	25/10/44-25/11/44**LO**
11/7/31-4/8/31**HS**	13/10/45-7/11/45**LS**
10/11/31-15/12/31**HG**	27/8/46-17/12/46**HG**
3/4/33-21/4/33**LS**	1/2/47-19/12/47**LS**
9/11/33-30/11/33**LS**	10/1/49-7/2/49**HI**
2/5/34-20/6/34**HG**	4/3/50-12/4/50**HG**
15/5/35-4/6/35**HS**	17/5/51-8/6/51**LI**
20/8/35-30/8/35**HO**	12/12/51-12/1/52**LC**
15/10/35-29/10/35**LO**	18/6/52-28/7/52**LI**
20/3/36-9/4/36**LS**	30/7/52-11/8/52**NC(Rect)(EO)**
26/8/36-28/9/36**HG**	20/11/52-22/12/52**HC(EO)**
7/6/37-21/6/37**LS**	31/10/53-12/12/53**HG**
25/10/37-8/11/37**LO**	26/5/55-20/6/55**HI**
16/3/38-11/4/38**HG**	23/7/55-18/8/55**LC(EO)**
13/9/38-28/9/38**LO**	27/4/56-10/5/56**NC(EO)**
15/2/39-8/3/39**LO**	1/8/56-17/9/56**HG**
19/6/39-1/7/39**LS**	8/5/58-7/6/58**LI**
10/6/40-4/7/40**HG**	9/7/58-14/7/58**NC(Rect)(EO)**
30/6/41-19/7/41**LS**	6/10/59-28/11/59**LI**
26/1/42-14/2/42**LO**	28/7/60-16/9/60**HG**

SHEDS			
Crewe North	15/10/27	Edge Hill (loan)	7/6/47
Camden	7/4/28	Edge Hill	21/6/47
Carlisle	26/6/29	Holyhead	23/8/47
Camden	18/9/29	Edge Hill	6/9/47
Crewe North	7/5/30	Camden	11/10/47
Camden	12/11/30	Crewe North	30/9/50
Holyhead	26/11/30	Holyhead (loan)	21/2/53
Crewe North	24/10/30	Crewe North	18/4/53
Holyhead	4/8/31	Camden	21/8/54
Crewe North	31/8/35	Crewe North	25/9/54
Holyhead	26/2/38	Nottingham	2/1/60
Crewe North	8/3/38	Derby	17/6/61
Holyhead	15/7/39	Nottingham	26/8/61*
Crewe North	21/10/39	Saltley	26/8/61*
Edge Hill	6/4/40	Leicester (GC)	19/5/62
Holyhead	9/11/40	Saltley	30/6/62*
Crewe North	11/4/42	Carlisle	30/6/62*
Edge Hill	24/3/45	Carlisle	20/7/62
Holyhead	17/5/47	*same dates- reason not known	

BOILERS

Fitted	No.	From
8/4/29	-	6100
5/12/29	-	6105
3/10/30	-	6134
17/11/31	-	6148
7/6/34	-	6101
27/8/35	-	6125
16/9/36	-	6142
25/3/38	7247	6135
4/7/40	8125	6132
21/11/42	5822	6165
12/7/44	10186	6154
Taper 102A		
17/12/46	12530	new
12/4/50	12665	6154
12/12/53	12529	-
17/9/56	11730	-
16/9/60	12663	-

46119 LANCASHIRE FUSILIER

Built North British, cost £7,744
LM 'date built' 6/11/27
Taper boiler fitted 2/9/44
Original smoke deflectors 22/1/32
BR smoke deflectors fitted period ending 10/9/49
Renumbered 6119 to 46119 week ending 31/7/48

TENDERS

No.	Fitted
3915	6/11/27
3900	29/6/28
3944	26/12/31
9349	4/7/36

MILEAGES

1927	7,975	1947	50,127
1928	60,146	1948	39,321
1929	56,275	1949	56,600
1930	71,194	1950	48,945
1931	68,031	1951	52,539
1932	64,210	1952	58,510
1933	63,951	1953	61,791
1934	76,384	1954	52,294
1935	70,982	1955	55,359
1936	83,989	1956	70,852
1937	91,475	1957	59,440
1938	78,407	1958	54,979
1939	67,029	1959	53,522
1940	55,858	1960	47,463
1941	56,438	1961	32,558
1942	77,046	1962	27,082
1943	67,590	1963	10,989
1944	57,762	Mileage at 31/12/50 1,505,248	
1945	76,070	Mileage at 28/9/63 2,142,626	
1946	53,443	Withdrawn week ending 16/11/63	
		Scrapped Crewe Works 11/63	

REPAIRS

23/5/28-30/6/28	LO
8/1/29-13/3/29	HG
3/6/29-11/6/29	LO
14/10/29-7/11/29	HG
13/6/30-4/7/40	LS
12/10/31-26/10/31	HS
29/1/31-24/2/31	HG
23/5/32-16/6/32	HG
14/11/32-30/11/32	LS
4/5/33-29/5/33	HS
26/12/33-12/1/34	LS
23/5/34-19/6/34	HG
24/11/34-12/12/34	LS
6/4/35-25/4/35	HO
23/8/35-12/9/35	HS
14/2/36-4/3/36	LS
22/6/36-4/7/36	HS
3/11/36-28/11/36	HG
3/4/37-15/4/37	LO
23/8/37-9/9/37	LS
26/1/38-10/2/38	LO
14/7/38-8/8/38	HG
7/9/38-19/9/38	LO
26/6/39-20/7/39	HS
20/7/40-13/8/40	HG
29/3/41-17/4/41	LO
27/9/41-15/10/41	LS
19/3/42-3/4/42	LO
28/8/42-23/9/42	LS
29/1/43-26/2/43	LO
11/10/43-30/10/43	LS
15/6/44-2/9/44	HG
28/6/45-28/7/45	HS
12/9/46-31/10/46	LS
11/3/47-15/4/47	HO
10/10/47-4/11/47	HS
30/12/47-27/1/48	LO
1/5/48-27/7/48	HO
18/11/48-5/1/49	LC
25/7/49-31/8/49	HG
11/7/50-10/8/50	LI
28/8/50-14/11/50	HI
9/3/51-29/3/51	LC
23/10/51-1/12/51	HG
4/12/51-12/12/51	NC(Rect)(EO)
24/6/52-6/8/52	HI
29/11/52-20/12/52	LC(EO)
10/8/53-11/9/53	LI
24/8/54-15/10/54	HG
18/10/55-19/11/55	HI
21/1/57-27/2/57	HG
1/3/58-11/3/58	LI
19/5/59-26/6/59	HG
18/7/59-14/8/59	LC(EO)
16/1/60-20/2/60	HI
11/5/60-19/5/60	NC(EO)
7/8/61-7/9/61	HI

SHEDS

Crewe North	22/10/27
Holyhead (loan)	20/11/37
Crewe North	18/12/37
Holyhead (loan)	6/5/39
Crewe North	13/5/39
Longsight	29/7/39
Bushbury	21/10/39
Carlisle Upperby	4/10/41
Camden	22/11/41
Crewe North	12/10/46
Leeds (loan)	7/12/46
Crewe North	11/1/47
Willesden (loan)	12/7/47
Holyhead (loan)	16/8/47
Crewe North	23/8/47
Longsight (loan)	13/11/48
Crewe North	27/11/48
Holyhead	29/4/50
Crewe North	18/4/53
Camden	25/4/53
Crewe North	6/6/53
Holyhead	17/4/54
Camden	12/6/54
Crewe North	18/9/54
Camden	25/6/55
Crewe North	24/9/55
Camden	14/6/58
Crewe	20/9/58
Edge Hill	18/10/58

BOILERS

Fitted	No.	From			
21/10/29	-	6128	13/8/40	11038	new
5/2/31	-	6147	*Taper 102A*		
24/5/32	-	6124	2/9/44	12032	new
12/5/33	-	6117	31/8/49	12200	6122
5/6/34	-	6125	1/12/51	13892	-
3/9/35	-	6157	15/10/54	12036	-
12/11/36	-	6151	27/3/57	13999	-
8/8/38	10186	new	26/6/59	12030	-

46120 ROYAL INNISKILLING FUSILIER

Built North British, cost £7,744
LM 'date built' 4/12/27
Named by 4/28
Taper boiler fitted 7/11/44
Original smoke deflectors 8/1/32
BR smoke deflectors fitted period ending 14/7/51
Renumbered 6120 to 46120 week ending 12/6/48

TENDERS

No.	Fitted
-	4/12/27
3910	26/12/31
3934	28/9/36

MILEAGES

		1946	66,815
1927	6,823	1947	55,275
1928	41,763	1948	49,683
1929	38,730	1949	37,605
1930	68,868	1950	51,910
1931	68,472	1951	61,202
1932	73,865	1952	55,852
1933	72,770	1953	65,373
1934	73,330	1954	62,186
1935	73,979	1955	34,573
1936	72,139	1956	50,255
1937	65,263	1957	48,792
1938	69,596	1958	51,131
1939	74,754	1959	46,108
1940	66,877	1960	49,256
1941	76,347	Mileage at 31/12/50 1,470,416	
1942	64,472	Mileage at 31/12/60 1,995,144	
1943	69,718	Withdrawn week ending 6/7/63	
1944	57,818	Scrapped Crewe Works 10/63	
1945	73,544		

SHEDS

Crewe North	12/11/27
Bangor	12/10/35
Holyhead	5/12/36
Preston (loan)	30/1/37
Holyhead	13/2/37
Crewe North	5/2/38
Edge Hill (loan)	12/3/38
Crewe North	2/4/38
Perth (loan)	23/4/38
Perth	14/5/38
Camden (loan)	2/7/38
Camden	13/8/38
Longsight	12/10/46
Derby	3/7/48
Longsight	24/7/48
Derby (loan)	23/10/48
Longsight	11/12/48
Derby (loan)	12/2/49
Longsight	7/5/49
Derby (loan)	21/5/49
Longsight	11/6/49
Derby (loan)	18/6/49
Leeds (loan)	3/12/49
Longsight	28/1/50
Holyhead	26/6/54
Longsight	24/7/54
Crewe North	23/10/54
MEE Derby	8/10/55
Derby	19/11/55
Longsight	18/2/56
Crewe North	2/6/56
Camden	14/6/58
Crewe	20/9/58
Longsight	11/6/60
Camden	10/9/60
Willesden	21/1/61
Llandudno Junction	23/9/61
Crewe North	22/6/63

BOILERS

Fitted	No.	From			
10/28	-	new	22/2/39	7212	6137
15/11/29	-	6123	16/1/41	11033	new
17/11/30	-	6110	*Taper 102A*		
8/3/32	-	6153	31/10/44	12035	new
12/6/33	-	6132	7/6/48	11725	6103
4/4/34	-	6141	3/7/51	12034	45736
21/5/35	-	6143	15/10/53	11725	-
1/3/37	-	6102	3/7/56	13237	-
			15/8/59	12532	-

REPAIRS

7/5/28-30/5/28	L
18/10/28-29/11/28	HG
26/4/29-5/6/29	LO
4/10/29-4/12/29	HG
13/11/30-4/12/30	HG
11/9/31-9/10/31	HS
5/3/32-5/4/32	HG
28/12/32-19/1/33	LS
6/6/33-15/7/33	HG
20/2/34-16/4/34	HS
21/8/34-11/9/34	LS
10/1/35-31/1/35	LS
7/5/35-3/6/35	HG
21/11/35-9/12/35	LS
12/9/36-28/9/36	LS
19/2/37-12/3/37	HG
30/10/37-23/11/37	HS
16/9/38-4/10/38	LS
28/1/39-22/2/39	HG
30/1/40-13/2/40	HS
14/6/40-2/7/40	LO
17/8/40-31/8/40	LO
24/12/40-16/1/41	HG
3/1/42-23/1/42	LS
10/10/42-31/10/42	LS
19/12/42-7/1/43	LO
11/5/43-27/5/43	LO
13/10/43-30/10/43	LS
16/9/44-31/10/44	HG
15/2/46-8/3/46	LS
17/8/46-12/9/46	LO
16/1/47-4/2/47	HS
5/8/47-6/9/47	LO
18/11/47-13/12/47	LO
19/4/48-7/6/48	HG
6/12/48-3/1/49	HI
13/3/49-31/3/49	NC
13/4/49-16/5/49	HC
10/10/49-12/10/49	NC
14/11/49-15/11/49	NC
21/11/49-22/11/49	NC
13/6/50-21/7/50	HI
10/11/50-8/12/50	LC
2/6/51-3/7/51	HG
27/10/52-4/12/52	HI
7/9/53-15/10/53	HG
28/9/54-22/10/54	HI
25/6/55-2/8/55	LC(EO)
7/9/55-6/10/55	NC(EO)
9/1/56-10/1/56	NC(EO)
26/5/56-3/7/56	HG
25/2/57-30/3/57	HI
6/12/57-25/1/58	LI
5/9/58-9/10/58	LC(EO)
17/6/59-15/8/59	HG
7/12/59-29/1/60	LC(EO)
11/2/60-30/3/60	NC(Rect)(EO)
6/11/60-20/12/60	HI

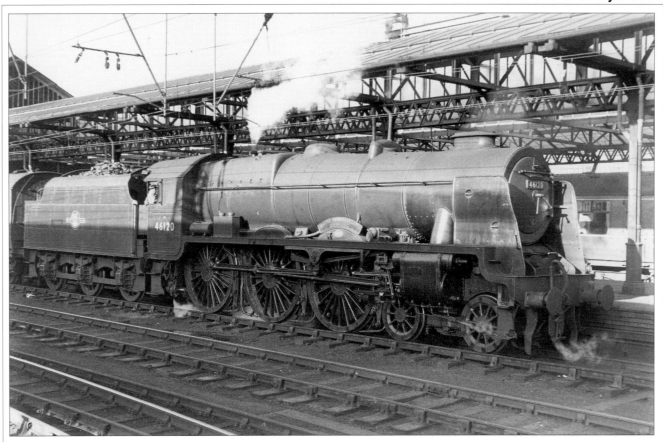

46120 ROYAL INNISKILLING FUSILIER, a beautiful sight in the sun and shadow, under the wires at Crewe about 1961. ATC (note the protective plate behind the coupling and the reservoir in front of the cab) had been fitted at the end of 1959. Despite the shadow below the footplate, the steam blowing down shows up the pipes from the 'double sanding box' to good effect. Photograph B.P. Hoper Collection.

6122 ROYAL ULSTER RIFLEMAN, with the 1936 style of lettering, at Crewe North on 24 April 1937. The Royal Scots saw the first application in Britain of three separate sets of Walschaerts motion to a three cylinder locomotive and although the long travel valve events owed much to modern practice (as seen at the time on the 2-6-4Ts being built at Derby) it was not a period when everyday servicing needs were much to the fore, and the inside motion was notoriously difficult to reach. Prominent here is the arm at the end of the crosshead, connected by a rod to the soon to be removed vacuum pump. Photograph B.P. Hoper Collection.

46121 HIGHLAND LIGHT INFANTRY, CITY OF GLASGOW REGIMENT

Built North British, cost £7,744
LM 'date built' 6/11/27
Taper boiler fitted 13/8/46
Originally named H.L.I (1928), renamed 15/1/49
Original smoke deflectors 18/12/31
BR smoke deflectors fitted period ending 20/4/51
Renumbered 6121 to 46121 week ending 9/10/48

REPAIRS	
17/3/28-24/5/28LS	23/8/43-18/9/43LS
11/12/28-12/12/28LO	1/4/44-27/4/44HG
16/2/29-12/3/29HG	23/10/44-18/11/44LS
20/3/29-25/3/29LO	18/6/45-26/7/45LS
30/10/29-14/11/29LO	1/6/46-13/8/46HG
6/1/30-8/2/30HG	1/12/47-20/12/47HS
11/3/30-5/4/30LO	17/8/48-4/10/48HG
21/8/30-27/8/30HO	23/12/48-7/1/49LC
29/1/31-18/2/31LS	21/3/49-6/4/49LC
8/6/31-3/7/31HG	13/3/50-14/3/50TRO
27/5/32-16/6/32LS	22/5/50-21/6/50HI
7/11/32-13/12/32HG	15/11/50-22/12/50LC
27/6/33-20/7/33LS	23/2/51-20/4/51HG
21/5/34-25/6/34HG	21/1/52-15/2/52HI
22/5/35-26/6/35LS	8/10/52-7/11/52HI
1/7/36-23/7/36LS	12/3/53-6/5/53HG
20/4/37-28/5/37HG	28/5/54-23/6/54HI
12/3/38-28/3/38HS	25/5/55-25/5/55NC
10/10/38-31/10/38LS	2/8/55-28/9/55HG
27/2/39-16/3/39LO	23/3/57-3/5/57HI
9/10/39-28/10/39HG	1/2/58-14/3/58HI
29/4/40-18/5/40LO	16/3/59-25/4/59HG
13/12/40-28/12/40LS	4/5/59NC(Rect)(EO)
13/1/42-3/2/42LO	14/5/59NC(Rect)(EO)
27/3/42-16/4/42LO	5/11/59-18/12/59LC(EO)
17/6/42-3/7/42LO	2/2/60-18/12/59LC(EO)
30/10/42-21/11/42HS	19/9/60-24/11/60LI

SHEDS
Crewe North 11/27
Polmadie 7/1/34
Crewe North 17/4/37
Holyhead (loan)23/10/37
Crewe North 30/10/37
Camden 14/5/38
Preston 29/4/39
Carlisle Upperby 16/9/39
Camden 6/1/40
Longsight 19/10/46
Polmadie (loan) 18/6/49
Polmadie 23/7/49

TENDERS
No.	Fitted
3917	6/11/27
3899	26/12/31
3933	1932
9351	23/7/36

MILEAGES			
		1944	60,710
1927	9,567	1945	71,428
1928	57,132	1946	50,445
1929	63,593	1947	55,661
1930	59,365	1948	65,340
1931	61,154	1949	53,769
1932	67,163	1950	54,367
1933	72,018	1951	68,551
1934	73,494	1953	60,437
1935	67,705	1954	58,682
1936	44,516	1955	45,610
1937	65,388	1956	58,214
1938	82,968	1957	52,120
1939	66,005	Mileage at 31/12/50 1,489,720	
1940	70,245	Mileage at 31/12/57 1,833,334	
1941	77,825	Withdrawn week ending 29/12/62	
1942	62,918	Scrapped J. McWilliam, Shettleston, 5/64	
1943	76,941		

BOILERS					
Fitted	No.	From	3/2/42	7260	6121
21/2/29	-	6135	27/4/44	7237	6115
27/1/30	-	6148	*Taper 102A*		
25/8/30	-	6122	13/8/46	12209	new
10/6/31	-	6122	4/10/48	12091	6169
14/11/32	-	6119	20/4/51	12198	6150
13/6/34	-	6128	6/5/53	10532	-
11/5/37	-	6144	28/9/55	10752	-
21/3/38	7260	6101	25/4/59	12538	-
9/10/39	8126	6123			

46122 ROYAL ULSTER RIFLEMAN

Built North British, cost £7,744
LM 'date built' 6/11/27
Named by 4/28
Taper boiler fitted 22/9/45
Original smoke deflectors 1/1/32
BR smoke deflectors fitted period ending 25/3/50
Renumbered 6122 to 46122 week ending 17/4/48

REPAIRS	
3/1/29-5/3/29HG	21/5/42-6/6/42HG
7/5/29-31/5/29LO	18/11/42-5/12/42LO
30/12/29-18/1/30HG	2/6/43-19/6/43LS
3/6/30-6/6/30HO	12/4/43-14/4/43TRO
18/3/31-15/4/31HG	24/11/43-11/12/43LO
8/12/31-1/1/32HG	8/6/44-24/6/44LS
11/7/32-4/8/32HG	6/10/44-8/11/44LO
6/2/33-21/2/33LS	23/7/45-22/9/45HG
22/7/33-17/8/33HS	28/8/46-30/9/46LS
1/1/34-23/1/34HG	24/12/47-24/1/48LS
8/11/34-16/11/34LO	24/3/48-15/4/48LO
17/12/34-14/1/35HS	29/12/48-17/2/49HG
4/6/35-20/6/35LS	22/9/49-17/10/49LC
22/10/35-5/11/35LO	20/2/50-20/3/50HG
10/3/36-25/3/36LS	8/12/50-13/1/51HI
4/8/36-26/8/36HG	25/2/52-21/3/52LI
15/1/37-28/1/37LO	2/10/52-1/11/52HG
10/4/37-16/4/37LO	12/10/53-6/11/53LI
17/7/37-2/8/37LS	22/11/54-18/12/54HG
22/1/38-8/2/38LS	4/1/56-15/2/56HI
19/7/38-18/8/38HG	8/11/56-22/12/56HG
10/7/39-26/7/39HS	22/11/57-14/12/57LI
23/4/40-11/5/40HG	9/10/58-7/11/58LI
26/10/40-13/11/40HS	18/11/58-5/12/58NC(Rect)(EO)
5/5/41-22/5/41LS	17/9/59-23/10/59LC(EO)
10/10/41-29/10/41LO	22/7/60-27/8/60HI

SHEDS
Crewe North 29/10/27
Carnforth (loan) 30/10/37
Crewe North 25/12/37
Carnforth 26/2/38
Preston 20/8/38
Carlisle 30/9/39
Camden 6/1/40
Longsight 12/10/46
Trafford Park 25/4/59
Longsight 13/6/59
Bushbury 7/11/59
Willesden 3/12/60
Trafford Park 17/12/61
Trafford Park 4/2/61
Saltley 17/6/61
Carlisle Upperby 30/6/62
'Carlisle' Kingmoor? 21/7/62

TENDERS
No.	Fitted
3918	6/11/27
3901	26/12/31
9355	26/8/36

MILEAGES			
		1946	62,338
1927	9,327	1947	60,579
1928	63,857	1948	58,202
1929	54,098	1949	59,212
1930	68,272	1950	63,040
1931	59,020	1951	69,762
1932	70,160	1952	63,914
1933	80,593	1953	62,296
1934	62,182	1954	62,101
1935	86,959	1955	69,652
1936	82,142	1956	52,645
1937	71,734	1957	71,040
1938	70,500	1958	62,938
1939	61,522	1959	53,883
1940	67,917	1960	57,964
1941	73,138	Mileage at 31/12/50 1,536,351	
1942	59,391	Mileage at 31/12/60 2,162,546	
1943	68,956	Withdrawn week ending 17/10/64	
1944	65,743	Scrapped A. Draper Ltd, Hull, 2/65	
1945	57,469		

BOILERS					
Fitted	No.	From	11/5/40	7251	6130
8/1/29	-	6137	6/6/42	7251	6122
3/1/30	-	6118	*Taper 102A*		
5/6/30	-	6112	22/9/45	12200	new
19/3/31	-	new	17/2/49	12197	6144
13/7/32	-	6127	20/3/50	12199	6152
8/1/34	-	6157	1/11/52	12031	-
3/1/35	-	6151	18/12/54	12201	-
13/8/36	-	6100	22/12/56	11725	-
18/8/38	7252	6130	4/5/62	12199	-

46123 ROYAL IRISH FUSILIER

Built North British, cost £7,744
LM 'date built' 6/11/27
Taper boiler fitted 5/5/49
Named by 4/28
Original smoke deflectors 27/11/31
BR smoke deflectors fitted period ending 13/6/53
Renumbered 6123 to 46123 week ending 26/6/48

TENDERS

No.	Fitted
3919	6/11/27
3930	26/12/31
9037	31/12/35
9765	30/4/53
9039	30/11/57

SHEDS

Crewe North 29/10/27
Holyhead (loan) 3/4/37
Crewe North 10/4/37
Carnforth 3/7/37
Camden 20/8/38
Crewe North 27/8/38
Camden 1/7/39
Edge Hill 13/3/48
Holyhead 31/5/58
Edge Hill 14/6/58
Kentish Town 26/9/59
Saltley 17/6/61
Carlisle Upperby 30/6/62
'Carlisle' Kingmoor? 21/7/62

MILEAGES

1927	9,070
1928	66,000
1929	59,522
1930	58,878
1931	49,467
1932	72,476
1933	72,285
1934	60,988
1935	74,180
1936	76,146
1937	85,270
1938	73,854
1939	75,187
1940	67,402
1941	63,347
1942	60,278
1943	76,087
1944	73,705
1945	56,793
1946	71,585
1947	60,723
1948	64,199
1949	57,286
1950	60,140
1951	54,034
1952	61,964
1953	52,912
1954	64,781
1955	52,612
1956	51,118
1957	56,159
1958	58,261
1959	55,840
1960	46,650

Mileage at 31/12/50 1,544,868
Mileage at 31/12/60 2,198,599
Withdrawn week ending 3/11/62
Scrapped Crewe Works 4/63

REPAIRS

10/7/28-7/8/28**L**	19/8/44-2/9/44**LS**
25/2/29-26/3/29**HG**	31/5/45-24/7/45**LS**
10/10/29-14/11/29**HG**	16/10/45-17/11/45**LO**
12/9/30-18/10/30**HG**	15/2/46-8/3/46**HG**
28/10/31-27/11/31**HS**	14/1/47-4/2/47**LS**
14/4/32-13/5/32**HG**	29/10/47-5/12/47**HS**
10/10/32-24/10/32**LS**	27/5/48-26/6/48**LO**
27/3/33-18/4/33**LS**	23/1/49-5/5/49**HG**
5/9/33-27/9/33**HS**	28/7/50-26/8/50**HI**
12/2/34-8/4/34**HG**	11/4/51-5/5/51**LC**
28/9/34-14/10/34**LS**	13/11/51-13/12/51**HI**
15/3/35-2/4/35**LS**	18/9/52-18/10/52**HC**
23/11/35-23/12/35**HG**	21/4/53-30/5/53**HG**
14/3/36-27/3/36**LO**	20/7/53-11/8/53**LC(EO)**
13/6/36-30/6/36**LS**	30/10/53-19/11/53**LC(EO)**
10/11/36-10/12/36**HS**	12/1/54-30/1/54**LC(EO)**
31/5/37-14/6/37**LS**	27/8/54-20/9/5**LI**
31/12/37-24/1/38**HG**	27/7/55-3/9/55**HG**
15/8/38-6/9/38**LO**	26/12/55-28/1/56**LC**
15/2/39-14/3/39**HS**	27/6/56-16/8/56**HI**
12/2/40-1/3/40**LS**	6/5/57-1/6/57**LC(EO)**
1/8/40-20/8/40**LS**	4/6/57-8/6/57**NC(Rect)(EO)**
1/1/41-25/1/41**LO**	17/10/57-30/11/57**HI**
2/9/41-20/9/41**HG**	15/4/58-16/5/58**HC(EO)**
26/3/42-24/12/42**LS**	9/1/59-5/2/59**LI**
7/8/42-21/8/41**LO**	13/4/60-24/5/60**LI**
25/11/42-24/12/42**LS**	3/6/60-9/6/60**NC(Rect)(EO)**
15/7/43-29/7/43**LO**	3/10/60-11/11/60**HC**
1/1/44-20/1/44**HG**	24/7/61-16/9/61**HI**

BOILERS

Fitted	No.	From
11/3/29	-	6121
22/10/29	-	6101
29/9/30	-	6143
20/4/32	-	6160
16/3/34	-	6106
10/12/35	-	6162
7/1/38	8126	6150
14/3/39	7240	6120
20/9/41	7215	6112
20/1/44	11035	6153
8/3/46	9883	6169
Taper 102A		
5/5/49	12673	new
30/5/53	13238	-
3/9/55	12541	-
16/5/58	13594	-

6123 in original condition, with coat of arms on the cabside, number on the tender and blank nameplate, not long after delivery from NBL Queens Park (note the diamond works plate; it was the oval Hyde Park plate which betrayed '6100' as an imposter in the first official photograph). The building in the background is Crewe North shed. Photograph B.P. Hoper Collection.

46124 LONDON SCOTTISH

Built North British, cost £7,743
LM 'date built' 6/11/27
Taper boiler fitted 31/12/43
Named by 4/28
Original smoke deflectors 30/1/32
BR smoke deflectors fitted period ending 31/12/49
Renumbered 6124 to 46124 week ending 10/4/48

SHEDS	
Crewe North 5/11/27	
Carlisle 9/1/37	
Camden 3/7/37	
Crewe North 27/11/37	
Camden (loan) 18/12/37	
Crewe North 1/1/38	
Edge Hill (loan) 21/3/42	
Crewe North 25/7/42	
Edge Hill 24/3/45	
Camden (loan) 18/10/47	
Edge Hill 13/12/47	
Carlisle Kingmoor 3/11/62	

BOILERS		
Fitted	No.	From
23/4/29	-	6118
21/3/30	-	6141
24/11/30	-	6121
22/4/32	-	6167
3/5/33	-	6125
1/5/34	-	6111
22/8/35	-	6149
26/11/36	-	6135
19/8/38	-	6135
4/9/40	10185	6145
Taper 102A		
31/12/43	11732	new
14/5/47	12033	6127
23/12/49	12202	6101
17/1/52	12037	-
29/6/54	12531	-
1/2/58	11090	-

TENDERS	
No.	Fitted
3920	6/11/27
3911	26/12/31
9132	2/7/36
9033	14/4/51

MILEAGES			
1927	6,155	1946	55,585
1928	48,355	1947	67,250
1929	69,587	1948	59,803
1930	64,212	1949	58,043
1931	53,703	1950	69,461
1932	71,391	1951	54,604
1933	66,681	1952	64,544
1934	84,536	1953	59,831
1935	84,045	1954	57,132
1936	68,250	1955	59,452
1937	72,103	1956	63,232
1938	69,361	1957	60,423
1939	64,876	1958	58,874
1940	57,454	1959	53,765
1941	68,503	1960	53,080
1942	54,117	**Mileage at 31/12/50 1,482,137**	
1943	58,516	**Mileage at 31/12/60 1,867,074**	
1944	56,715	**Withdrawn week ending 29/12/62**	
1945	53,435	**Scrapped Crewe Works 4/63**	

REPAIRS	
29/10/28-18/12/28LS	2/11/42-28/11/42HS
18/4/29-7/5/29HG	8/11/43-31/12/43HG
17/3/30-8/4/30HG	19/2/45-13/3/45LS
18/11/30-13/12/30HG	2/6/45-28/6/45LO
21/10/31-16/11/31HS	19/9/45-13/10/45LO
14/4/32-18/5/32H	2/4/46-2/5/46LS
17/10/32-31/10/32LS	31/3/47-14/5/47HG
27/4/33-16/5/33HS	9/2/48-10/4/48HS
24/10/33-13/11/33HG	24/11/48-14/12/48LS
19/4/34-15/5/34HG	3/11/49-23/12/49HG
17/9/34-9/10/34LS	20/11/50-19/12/50LI
18/2/35-5/3/35LS	13/11/51-17/1/52HG
13/8/35-29/8/35HS	6/10/52-1/11/52LI
17/1/36-5/2/36HS	22/6/53-4/8/53LI
29/6/36-2/7/36LS	25/5/54-29/6/54HG
14/11/36-8/12/36HG	2/12/54-11/1/55LC(EO)
28/4/37-11/5/37LO	17/8/55-17/9/55LI
27/10/37-10/11/37LS	19/6/56-4/8/56HI
15/7/38-19/8/38HG	7/1/57-7/2/57HC
23/3/39-12/4/39HS	28/12/57-1/2/58HG
14/9/39-23/10/39LO	11/4/59-7/5/59HI
13/8/40-4/9/40HG	20/4/60-26/5/60LI
19/5/41-4/6/41LS	1/6/60-2/6/60NC(Rect)(EO)
14/2/42-28/2/42LS	27/2/61-7/4/61HI

46125 3RD CARABINIER

Built North British, cost £7,744
LM 'date built' 11/9/27
Taper boiler fitted 7/8/43
First named LANCASHIRE WITCH (3/28), renamed 1935-36
Original smoke deflectors – not listed
BR smoke deflectors fitted period ending 5/11/49
Renumbered 6125 to 46125 week ending 11/9/48

TENDERS	
No.	Fitted
3921	11/9/27
3915	28/6/28
3908	26/12/31
9129	24/7/36
9039	21/4/53
9133	9/11/57

SHEDS	
Crewe North 20/8/27	Leeds (loan) 19/3/49
Edge Hill 29/12/29	Crewe North 23/4/49
Crewe North 11/5/34	Leeds (loan) 7/5/49
Holyhead 27/2/37	Crewe North 20/8/49
Bangor 17/4/37	Camden 5/7/52
Crewe North 15/5/37	Crewe North 20/9/52
Camden 30/4/38	Holyhead (loan) 21/2/53
Crewe North 14/5/38	Crewe North 7/3/58
Holyhead 4/12/43	Camden 13/6/53
Crewe North 26/8/44	Crewe North 19/9/53
Holyhead 17/3/45	Carnforth 23/1/54
Crewe North 7/4/45	Carlisle 6/2/54
Holyhead (loan) 30/6/45	Carlisle Upperby 5/5/62
Crewe North 7/7/45	Crewe North 26/5/62
Holyhead (loan) 26/7/47	Holyhead 22/9/62
Crewe North 16/8/47	Crewe North 16/3/63
Leeds (loan) 2/10/48	Holyhead 20/4/63
Crewe North 12/2/49	Willesden 22/6/63

REPAIRS	
12/12/27-21/12/27LC	13/5/43-7/8/43HG
8/6/28-30/6/26LS	19/1/45-3/2/45LS
21/1/29-15/2/29HG	11/4/45-25/5/45HO
19/4/29-13/5/29LO	14/2/46-14/3/46HG
20/11/29-10/12/29LO	25/1/47-25/2/47HS
4/2/30-11/3/30HG	14/8/47-24/9/47LO
23/2/31-7/3/31LS	16/10/47-27/10/47LO
14/8/31-28/9/31HG	17/8/49-13/10/49HG
28/10/31-1/12/31LO	23/7/50-24/10/50LI
15/8/32-29/8/32LS	4/7/51-8/8/51LC
20/3/33-24/4/33HG	13/8/51-15/9/51HC(EO)
3/10/33-17/10/33LS	7/11/51-18/12/51HG
7/4/34-11/5/34HS	29/7/52-28/8/52HI
1/10/34-23/10/34LS	23/9/52-16/10/52LC(EO)
25/3/35-24/4/35HG	18/3/53-21/4/53LC(EO)
25/9/35-10/10/35HS	12/11/53-10/12/53HI
30/1/36-13/2/36HS	20/7/54-14/8/54LC(EO)
2/7/36-24/7/36LC	11/4/55-7/6/55HG
3/11/36-6/11/36LO	26/3/56-27/4/56LI
14/4/37-15/5/37HG	17/11/56-29/12/56HI
28/2/38-16/3/38LS	8/4/57-6/5/57NC(EO)
6/8/38-7/9/38HG	8/11/57-9/11/57NC(EO)
28/7/39-15/8/39LS	27/3/58-9/5/58HG
31/5/40-19/6/40HG	26/8/59-2/10/59HI
30/1/41-21/2/41LS	25/1/60-5/3/60LC(EO)
30/10/41-19/11/41HS	1/4/60-23/5/60LC(EO)
14/2/42-28/2/42LS	5/5/61-5/6/61HI
24/12/42-16/1/43LS	

BOILERS						
Fitted	No.	From	*Taper 102A*			
24/1/29	-	6122	7/8/43	11727		
1/3/30	-	new	new			
26/8/31	-	6142	14/3/46	12207		
27/3/33	-	6110	new			
4/5/34	-	6123	13/10/49	10752		
4/4/35	-	6112	5735			
30/4/37	-	6103	18/12/51	12542	-
7/9/38	8124	6119	7/6/55	11728	-
9/6/40	7232	6162	9/5/58	11727	-

MILEAGES	
1927	21,248
1928	57,807
1929	51,221
1930	47,828
1931	46,881
1932	62,975
1933	71,519
1934	75,044
1935	82,050
1936	78,624
1937	74,374
1938	82,879
1939	65,054
1940	62,927
1941	69,893
1942	57,017
1943	54,976
1944	49,884
1945	53,157
1946	57,067
1947	49,532
1948	59,193
1949	55,241
1950	57,277
1951	37,411
1952	58,134
1953	56,724
1954	58,441
1955	53,929
1956	54,371
1957	56,725
1958	45,699
1959	54,560
1960	47,715
Mileage at 31/12/50 1,443,668	
Mileage at 31/12/60 1,967,377	
Withdrawn week ending 3/10/64	
Scrapped J. Cashmore Ltd, Great Bridge, 1/65	

46125 3ʳᴰ CARABINIER late in the day, but still looking spritely despite the loss of its crest, at Willesden shed on 30 July 1963. Speedo very prominent. According to Nock (*The Royal Scots and Patriots of the LMS, D&C, 1978*) an 'amusing contretemps' occurred when the early conversions were appearing in some numbers; in August 1943 both 6108 and 6125 emerged from Crewe in taper boiler form, with the names transposed (or could it have been the numbers?). They went straight back in and the mistakes were rectified. Photograph Peter Groom.

46128 THE LOVAT SCOUTS – a lovely side-on view which illustrates very well the degree to which enormous power was got from a relatively modest size. Even in a more enlightened age, three cylinders on a frame such as this put the task of oiling back into the dark age of locomotive matters, hardly better than the parallel boiler predecessors. A Royal Scot (preferably) had to be parked with the inside big end at the bottom and a man had to worm his way up to a perch on the inside connecting rod. From there it was possible to oil all the required inside parts. This was bad enough in perfect conditions, let alone the more usual ones of dark, frost, cross-wind or worse – and it was a long way down, often to the bottom of a filthy, oily waterlogged pit – if oil can or a cork dropped, to an accompaniment of scuffed knuckles and loud cursing. For the fitters, working often on the very same pits, it was even worse. Polmadie, 8 September 1956. Photograph J.L. Stevenson.

46126 ROYAL ARMY SERVICE CORPS

Built North British, cost £7,744
LM 'date built' 11/9/27
Taper boiler fitted 30/6/45
First named SANSPAREIL (by 4/28), renamed 6/36
Original smoke deflectors 26/12/31
BR smoke deflectors fitted period ending 6/10/51
Renumbered 6126 to 46126 week ending 4/12/48

BOILERS

Fitted	No.	From
14/1/29	-	6136
21/11/29	-	6146
5/6/31	-	6135
15/6/33	-	6124
11/5/34	-	6110
30/8/35	-	6114
26/5/37	-	6146
6/10/38	5576	6128
19/6/40	11032	new
21/11/42	9881	6138
Taper 102A		
30/6/45	12198	new
1/12/48	12208	-
18/9/51	12090	-
10/12/54	13892	-
4/7/58	11733	-

TENDERS

No.	Fitted
3922	11/9/27
3920	26/12/31
9038	23/4/36

MILEAGES

1927	20,851
1928	52,404
1929	49,101
1930	55,063
1931	55,867
1932	64,650
1933	71,745
1934	83,149
1935	80,259
1936	82,566
1937	79,248
1938	71,815
1939	74,324
1940	63,086
1941	55,767
1942	63,121
1943	57,085
1944	61,728
1945	52,476
1946	62,465
1947	55,723
1948	52,235
1949	73,578
1950	62,134
1951	52,431
1952	62,613
1953	56,361
1954	47,751
1955	52,448
1956	60,075
1957	28,132
1958	59,326
1959	59,480
1960	50,137

Mileage at 31/12/50 1,500,430
Mileage at 31/12/60 2,029,184
Withdrawn week ending 5/10/63
Scrapped Crewe Works 11/63

SHEDS

Crewe North 20/8/27
Holyhead 27/2/37
Crewe North 15/5/37
Leeds (loan) 30/3/46
Crewe North 4/5/46
Holyhead (loan) 24/5/46
Crewe North 19/7/47
Camden 10/7/48
Edge Hill (loan) 11/12/48
Leeds (loan) 10/9/49
Camden 15/10/49
Crewe North 20/9/52
Camden 10/1/53
Carlisle 25/9/54
Leeds 5/3/55
Carlisle 9/4/55
Holyhead 11/1/58
Carlisle Upperby 8/2/58
Preston 7/11/59
Edge Hill 17/9/60
Willesden 14/1/61
Annesley 1/12/62

REPAIRS

22/3/28-1/5/28**L**	12/8/43-11/9/43**LS**
8/1/29-9/3/29**HG**	8/6/44-29/6/44**LS**
20/3/29-25/3/29**LO**	7/5/45-30/6/45**HG**
13/11/29-10/12/29**HG**	6/8/46-30/8/46**LS**
26/3/30-11/4/30**LO**	15/10/47-11/11/47**LS**
3/6/31-3/7/31**HG**	22/10/48-1/12/48**HG**
9/7/32-25/7/32**LS**	10/6/49-25/7/49**LC**
9/1/33-26/1/33**LS**	10/6/50-1/7/50**HI**
10/6/33-21/7/33**HG**	27/6/51-18/9/51**HG**
28/4/34-21/5/34**HS**	11/9/52-10/10/52**LI**
22/8/35-16/9/35**HG**	23/3/53-21/5/53**HI**
24/9/35-11/10/34**LS**	25/2/54-27/3/54**HI**
25/3/35-15/4/35**LS**	9/11/54-10/12/54**HG**
3/4/36-23/4/36**LS**	5/8/55-27/8/55**LC(EO)**
4/9/36-29/9/36**HS**	12/1/56-8/2/56**HI**
9/1/37-25/1/37**LO**	31/7/56-1/9/56**LI**
18/5/37-15/6/37**HG**	12/3/57-23/3/57**LC(EO)**
6/3/38-29/3/38**LS**	9/5/57-10/8/57**LC(EO)**
5/9/38-6/10/38**HG**	25/10/57-16/11/57**LC(EO)**
22/8/39-8/9/39**LS**	24/5/58-4/7/58**HG**
31/5/40-19/6/40**HG**	7/7/58-10/7/58**NC(Rect)(EO)**
1/2/41-15/2/41**LS**	18/10/58-25/11/58**HC**
16/8/41-3/9/41**LO**	24/9/59-12/11/59**HI**
29/12/41-16/1/42**LS**	7/11/60-16/12/60**HI**
5/11/42-21/11/42**HG**	17/12/60-17/2/61**LC(EO)**
28/4/43-5/6/43**LO**	10/7/61-21/8/61**HC(EO)**

The classic Camden bank picture – 46126 ROYAL ARMY SERVICE CORPS comes confidently up the grade on 21 September 1958. Photograph R.C. Riley.

Holbeck's THE GREEN HOWARDS at Corkerhill, 17 September 1949. 46133 was renewed with taper boiler in 1944 and did not get its LM smoke deflectors until 1951. Like every skoolboy, I pored endlessly over the various class lists in the Ian Allan spotters' books, especially the Royal Scots for, living alternately by the Midland and the GN, there were precious few marked off. I had stumbled on some great mystery, it seemed, known to no other, when it emerged that 46126–46148 were named after the regiments, yet the others (largely) were *soldiers* in regiments. The oddity lay in the renaming of NOVELTY, VESTA and the rest of course. It seems the LMS sought to follow the established order, for 6127 (formerly NOVELTY) appeared in April 1936 with plates reading THE OLD CONTEMPTIBLE. This would make it at one with ROYAL ENGINEER and the rest. (I was never quite sure about BLACK WATCH – the best locomotive name ever, mysterious and brooding). Later, new plates appeared with a plaque and the name OLD CONTEMPTIBLES. The new way of doing it, apparently, had more to do with the publicity to be had, when the regimental band attended the naming ceremony. So the class ended up being named in two distinct ways, after regiments and soldiers. Such pointless rumination of course, is the stuff of enthusiast life. Photograph A.G. Ellis, B.P. Hoper Collection.

46127 OLD CONTEMPTIBLES
1914 AUG.5 to NOV.22

Built North British, cost £7,744
LM 'date built' 11/9/27
Taper boiler fitted 2/8/44
First named NOVELTY (by 4/28); named
THE OLD CONTEMPTIBLE for a short while in 1936; renamed
OLD CONTEMPTIBLES 1914 AUG.5 TO NOV.22 (11/36)
Original smoke deflectors 1/12/31
BR smoke deflectors fitted period ending 11/8/51
Renumbered 6127 to 46127 week ending 1/5/48

TENDERS

No.	Fitted
3923	11/9/28
2863	26/12/31
3913	28/6/34
2863	11/8/34
9142	31/12/35
9043	18/3/54

BOILERS

Fitted	No.	From
14/4/32	-	6150
28/5/34	-	6113
17/5/35	-	6116
29/10/36	8133	6145
28/7/37	7221	6142
10/11/38	7249	6122
20/5/41	11040	new
Taper 102A		
2/8/44	12033	new
10/3/47	11726	6109
24/6/49	12203	6150
26/7/51	12036	46145
29/8/53	12528	-
22/1/55	12199	-
28/9/57	12037	-

REPAIRS

	18/5/43-4/6/43**LS**
4/5/29-13/6/29**HG**	17/5/44-2/8/44**HG**
14/5/30-12/7/30**HG**	14/6/45-30/6/45**LS**
19/10/31-1/12/31**LO**	30/3/46-17/4/46**LS**
9/4/32-5/5/32**HG**	2/2/47-10/3/47**HG**
20/4/33-11/5/33**LS**	6/4/48-27/4/48**LS**
17/10/33-6/11/33**HS**	15/9/48-19/10/48**LO**
21/4/34-7/6/34**HG**	23/12/48-26/1/49**LC**
10/11/34-3/12/34**LS**	23/5/49-24/6/49**HG**
9/5/35-29/5/35**HS**	7/10/49-9/11/49**HC**
1/5/36-15/5/36**LO**	2/5/50-3/6/50**HI**
14/11/35-10/12/35**HS**	30/5/51-26/7/51**HG**
16/6/36-1/7/36**LS**	23/8/52-19/9/52**HI**
21/10/36-7/11/36**HG**	1/8/53-29/8/53**HG**
20/11/36-26/11/36**LO**	3/9/53-10/9/53**NC(Rect)(EO)**
19/7/37-4/8/37**HS**	17/12/54-22/1/55**HG**
3/3/38-21/3/38**LS**	20/6/56-9/8/56**LI**
20/10/38-10/11/38**HG**	18/7/57-28/9/57**HG**
10/7/39-27/7/39**HS**	6/9/58-13/10/58**HI**
6/9/40-20/9/40**HS**	26/11/59-1/1/60**HI**
23/4/41-20/5/41**HG**	4/4/60-17/5/60**LC(EO)**
19/8/42-8/9/42**LS**	19/4/61-5/6/61**LI**

SHEDS

Polmadie 18/8/27
Camden 20/11/32
Holyhead 26/2/38
Crewe North 21/10/39
Edge Hill (loan)12/10/40
Crewe North 16/11/40
Holyhead 28/11/42
Crewe North 4/12/43
Leeds (loan) 18/1/44
Crewe North 15/1/44
Holyhead (loan) 26/8/44
Crewe North 6/4/46
Edge Hill 24/5/47
Holyhead 21/6/47
Crewe North 3/2/51
Holyhead 24/3/51
Crewe North 2/10/54
Camden 25/6/55
Crewe North 24/9/55
Camden 22/7/57
Crewe North 21/9/57
Kentish Town 19/10/57
Holyhead (loan) 5/7/58
Holyhead 12/7/58
Crewe North 30/4/60
Longsight 11/6/60
Crewe North 10/9/60
Carlisle Upperby 5/5/62

MILEAGES

1927	12,285	1946	73,556
1928	59,565	1947	75,737
1929	62,585	1948	65,526
1930	54,498	1949	56,457
1931	45,820	1950	67,033
1932	56,890	1951	60,847
1933	72,480	1952	68,073
1934	61,904	1953	66,563
1935	70,164	1954	66,464
1936	73,856	1955	58,604
1937	89,220	1956	56,190
1938	81,804	1957	46,690
1939	66,798	1958	49,915
1940	57,909	1959	57,123
1941	67,028	1960	51,250
1942	66,152	**Mileage at 31/12/50 1,536,890**	
1943	67,510	**Mileage at 31/12/60 2,010,236**	
1944	60,597	**Withdrawn week ending 8/12/62**	
1945	72,016	**Scrapped Crewe Works 5/63**	

Looking sleeker than ever, 46133 with its smoke deflectors, in the early 1950s at Corkerhill. The peculiar framework on the right, by the tender, is the water sprinkler apparatus, for slaking coal, ash wagons and so on. At this early time, the loco has the 'strengthened' plain cross section coupling rods, ordered to be fitted to the new engines; by 1961 (see next picture) it had reverted to the 'unsuitable' fluted rods! Photograph John Pattison, B.P. Hoper Collection.

46128 THE LOVAT SCOUTS

Built North British, cost £7,744
LM 'date built' 11/9/27
Taper boiler fitted 4/6/46
First named METEOR (by 4/28), renamed 11/36
Original smoke deflectors – not listed
BR smoke deflectors fitted period ending 28/6/51
Renumbered 6128 to 46128 week ending 26/2/49

TENDERS

No.	Fitted
3924	11/9/27
9042	10/3/36
9053	9/11/38

REPAIRS

1/6/29-28/6/29**HG**	29/3/40-19/4/40**HG**
25/9/30-12/11/30**HG**	19/11/40-5/12/40**LS**
5/10/31-27/10/31**HS**	25/8/41-15/9/41**HS**
3/2/32-3/3/32**LO**	10/3/42-4/4/42**LS**
13/4/32-11/5/32**HG**	16/12/42-9/1/43**LS**
10/12/32-28/12/32**LS**	24/6/43-17/7/43**HG**
22/5/33-14/6/33**HS**	26/11/43-10/12/43**LO**
28/10/33-21/11/33**HS**	21/4/44-6/5/44**LO**
13/4/34-17/5/34**HG**	1/6/44-15/7/44**HS**
27/10/34-15/11/34**LS**	16/4/45-1/5/45**LS**
26/3/35-15/4/35**LS**	15/4/46-4/6/46**HG**
16/5/35-24/5/35**LO**	5/6/47-16/8/47**LS**
18/9/35-4/10/35**HS**	5/8/47-23/8/47**TRO(Rect)**
14/4/36-15/4/36**LO**	22/11/47-8/1/48**LO**
10/2/36-10/3/36**HG**	30/1/48-25/2/48**LO**
19/5/36-22/5/36**LO**	12/1/49-21/2/49**HG**
6/9/36-22/9/36**LS**	27/4/50-18/5/50**LI**
14/4/36-15/4/36**LO**	27/5/51-28/6/51**HG**
19/5/36-22/5/36**LO**	24/7/52-30/8/52**HI**
6/9/36-22/9/36**LS**	3/9/53-8/10/53**HG**
24/1/37-22/2/37**HS**	2/8/54-28/8/54**LC(EO)**
31/5/37-25/6/37**LO**	27/3/55-22/4/55**HI**
1/10/37-18/10/37**LS**	15/5/56-28/6/56**HG**
14/3/38-31/3/38**LO**	1/10/57-8/11/57**HI**
21/7/38-17/8/38**HG**	8/1/59-14/2/59**HG**
10/3/39-24/3/39**LS**	24/3/60-6/5/60**LI**
8/8/39-24/8/39**LO**	4/5/61-9/6/61**LI**

SHEDS

Polmadie 18/8/27
'Northern Division' 12/11/30
Camden 25/2/31
Willesden 29/5/37
Crewe North (loan) 27/8/38
Longsight 15/10/38
Crewe North 28/10/39
Holyhead 27/12/41
Crewe North 4/12/43
Carlisle 6/10/45
Camden 28/9/45
Leeds (loan) 17/8/46
Leeds 21/9/46
Crewe North (loan) 21/12/46
Crewe North 25/1/47
Carlisle Upperby 17/5/47
Crewe North 2/10/48
Holyhead (loan) 18/6/49
Leeds (loan) 19/11/49
Crewe North 7/1/50
Holyhead 5/4/52
Crewe North 11/10/52
Camden 13/6/53
Crewe North 19/9/53
Camden 12/6/54
Crewe North 18/9/54
Longsight 30/11/54
Crewe North 26/3/55
Holyhead 4/5/57
Crewe North 11/5/57
Carlisle Upperby 8/8/62
Crewe North 26/5/62
Springs Branch 15/9/62
Carlisle Upperby 3/11/62

MILEAGES

Year	Miles	Year	Miles
1927	18,211	1948	52,326
1928	62,271	1949	64,625
1929	65,717	1950	61,625
1930	60,870	1951	50,299
1931	73,139	1952	54,666
1932	60,391	1953	64,299
1933	81,064	1954	53,049
1934	72,332	1955	59,334
1935	83,823	1956	55,110
1936	79,996	1957	51,464
1937	68,931	1958	59,287
1938	78,255	1959	56,239
1939	58,966	1960	42,683
1940	58,256	1961	43,955
1941	61,992	1962	36,868
1942	61,722	1963	23,508
1943	59,245		
1944	58,315		
1945	63,917		
1946	59,021		
1947	40,995		

Mileage at 31/12/50 1,506,005
Mileage at 31/12/63 2,156,766
Withdrawn week ending 1/5/65
Scrapped Motherwell Machinery & Scrap Co. Ltd, 7/65

BOILERS

Fitted	No.	From			
12/6/29	-	6124	15/9/41	8121	6148
22/10/30	-	6133	17/7/43	7214	6140
18/4/32	-	6169	15/7/44	8136	6150
26/5/33	-	6112	*Taper 102A*		
3/5/34	-	6142	4/6/46	12525	new
21/2/36	-	6166	21/2/49	12090	6149
15/2/37	5576	6127	28/6/51	12091	46121
17/8/38	7219	6104	8/10/53	12526	-
19/4/40	7254	6115	28/6/56	12030	-
			14/2/60	12542	-

After years at Holbeck, 46133 was one of the Royal Scots which came to the London end of the Midland, arriving at Kentish Town in November 1958, leaving for Newton Heath and oblivion two years later. Here it is, in splendid form at Leicester shed on 18 April 1961, some five months before transfer to Manchester. On this occasion it was on the Leicester-St Pancras semi-fasts; unsuspected by the photographer at the time, the picture became famous at Leicester shed for the unfamiliar light it cast upon one Norman, who always wore cycle clips... Photograph Alec Swain, B.P. Hoper Collection.

46129 THE SCOTTISH HORSE

Built North British, cost £7,744
LM 'date built' 11/9/27
Taper boiler fitted 31/12/44
First named COMET (by 4/28), renamed 12/35
Original smoke deflectors – not listed
BR smoke deflectors fitted period ending 17/6/50
Renumbered 6129 to 46129 week ending 26/6/48

BOILERS

Fitted From	No.	
6/10/31	-	6103
18/5/33	-	6107
31/12/34	-	6144
3/12/34	-	6144
26/10/37	7242	6148
3/11/39	9883	6100
3/10/42	11037	6168
Taper 102A		
21/11/44	12036	new
26/6/48	12035	6120
13/6/50	12089	6149
11/8/51	11733	
46133		
30/7/55	12656	-
8/8/59	12534	-

TENDERS

No.	Fitted
9043	10/6/36
9142	18/3/54
2716	?

SHEDS

Polmadie 18/10/27
'Northern Division' 5/12/30
Camden 25/2/31
Carlisle Kingmoor 15/8/36
Crewe North 17/4/37
Bangor 3/7/37
Carlisle Upperby 25/9/37
Crewe North 27/11/37
Camden (loan) 18/12/37
Crewe North 1/1/38
Longsight (loan) 19/4/38
Perth (loan) 30/4/38
Perth 14/5/38
Carlisle Kingmoor 30/3/40
Preston (loan) 19/10/40
Preston 16/11/40
Edge Hill 15/2/41
Longsight 19/4/47
Holyhead 21/2/53
Crewe North 7/8/54
Camden 22/6/57
Crewe North 21/9/57
Camden 21/9/57
Carlisle Upperby 19/10/57
Crewe North 23/11/57
Carlisle Kingmoor 1/7/61
Carlisle Upperby 30/9/61
Crewe North 10/3/62

MILEAGES

1927	11,109	1948	60,912
1928	63,442	1949	56,712
1929	64,925	1950	65,897
1930	44,932	1951	52,932
1931	52,218	1952	61,816
1932	78,644	1953	57,376
1933	61,669	1954	39,427
1934	69,454	1955	44,316
1935	64,748	1956	52,318
1936	58,492	1957	53,039
1937	45,610	1958	54,566
1938	55,864	1959	51,469
1939	69,877	1960	52,214
1940	51,439	1961	47,290
1941	62,307	1962	41,503
1942	49,993	1963	18,067
1943	65,351	**Mileage at 31/12/50 1,374,993**	
1944	49,370	**Mileage at 1963 2,001,326**	
1945	43,567	**Withdrawn week ending 6/6/64**	
1946	84,220	**Scrapped Central Wagon Co., Ince,**	
1947	64,235	**Wigan, 11/64**	

REPAIRS

15/4/29-15/5/29**HG**	2/10/44-29/11/44**HG**
7/5/30-12/7/30**HG**	21/12/45-28/1/46**LO**
22/10/30-5/12/30**HS**	20/3/46-16/4/46**LS**
22/9/31-5/11/31**HG**	19/8/46-21/9/46**HO**
22/10/32-8/11/32**LS**	3/4/47-1/5/47**HS**
10/5/33-7/6/33**HG**	4/12/47-2/2/48**LO**
8/5/34-24/5/34**LS**	29/5/48-26/6/48**LS**
24/11/34-14/12/34**HG**	11/4/49-10/5/49**LI**
14/3/35-17/3/35**LO**	5/10/49-11/11/49**HC**
4/11/35-19/11/35**LS**	11/5/50-13/6/50**HG**
22/5/36-10/6/36**LO**	18/6/51-11/8/51**HG**
19/10/36-11/12/36**HS**	5/9/52-30/9/52**LI**
18/10/37-9/11/37**HG**	25/6/53-11/8/53**LI**
26/11/38-20/12/38**LS**	23/4/54-29/5/54**LC(EO)**
3/11/39-16/12/39**HG**	21/8/54-7/9/54**LC(EO)**
9/2/40-23/2/40**LO**	2/6/55-30/7/55**HG**
23/4/40-1/5/40**LO**	20/8/56-22/9/56**HI**
16/9/40-4/10/40**LS**	22/7/57-7/9/57**LC(EO)**
14/4/41-29/4/41**LS**	13/4/58-10/5/58**LI**
13/3/42-15/4/42**LS**	21/6/59-8/8/59**HG**
15/10/42-31/10/42**HG**	14/9/60-22/10/60**LI**
14/5/43-29/5/43**LS**	18/8/61-28/9/61**HI**
18/2/44-6/3/44**LO**	

46130 THE WEST YORKSHIRE REGIMENT

Built North British, cost £7,744
LM 'date built' 6/11/27
Taper boiler fitted 6/12/49
First named LIVERPOOL (by 4/28), renamed 6/35
Original smoke deflectors – not listed
BR smoke deflectors fitted period ending 31/12/49
Renumbered 6130 to 46130 week ending 22/5/48

TENDERS

No.	Fitted
3926	6/11/27
9124	23/12/36

SHEDS

Polmadie 13/10/27
Camden 25/2/31
Carlisle Upperby 30/3/35
Camden 28/9/35
Edge Hill 29/4/39
Speke Junction 16/9/29
Crewe North 30/9/39
Camden 2/12/39
Bushbury (loan) 8/3/41
Edge Hill (loan) 17/10/42
Camden 3/4/43
Crewe North 2/10/48
Holyhead (loan) 17/6/50
Crewe North 29/7/50
Holyhead (loan) 28/10/50
Crewe North 16/12/50
Longsight 13/6/53
Carlisle 18/6/55
Edge Hill 22/6/57
Holyhead 27/7/57
Edge Hill 5/10/57
Kentish Town 7/2/59
Edge Hill 18/4/59
Kentish Town 19/9/59
'NER' (presumably Leeds
Holbeck) 12/59

BOILERS

Fitted	No.	From
6/3/31	-	6106
3/2/33	-	6155
11/12/34	-	6108
2/3/36	-	6168
8/12/36	-	6117
18/2/38	7251	6123
13/10/39	9884	6103
27/6/42	7261	6142
22/7/44	11040	6127
1/8/46	8128	6155
Taper 102A		
6/12/49	13240	new
8/5/53	13240	-
22/3/55	11731	-
29/5/58	12531	-

MILEAGES

1927	10,946	1945	58,873
1928	57,430	1946	63,818
1929	42,942	1947	60,684
1930	54,569	1948	57,670
1931	58,430	1949	38,096
1932	66,843	1950	55,020
1933	71,709	1951	48,945
1934	46,278	1952	46,755
1935	86,974	1953	50,283
1936	67,919	1954	58,785
1937	70,504	1955	44,433
1938	74,327	1956	53,464
1939	63,902	1957	65,407
1940	72,729	1958	58,704
1941	65,952	**Mileage at 31/12/50 1,442,944**	
1942	59,115	**Mileage at 31/12/58 2,068,916**	
1943	76,359	**Withdrawn week ending 22/12/62**	
1944	62,455	**Scrapped Crewe Works 10/63**	

REPAIRS

18/12/28-23/2/29**LS**	21/6/44-22/7/44**HG**
24/6/29-3/8/29**HG**	16/2/45-23/3/45**LO**
9/9/29-27/9/29**LS**	4/10/45-3/11/45**LS**
22/10/30-6/11/30**LO**	7/6/46-1/8/46**HG**
21/2/31-27/9/31**HG**	3/12/46-3/1/47**LO**
4/2/32-19/2/32**LS**	23/6/47-1/8/47**LS**
24/9/32-13/10/32**LO**	2/10/47-7/11/47**LO**
30/1/33-8/3/33**HG**	12/4/48-18/5/48**LS**
23/10/33-10/11/33**LS**	7/2/49-7/3/49**HI**
10/3/34-12/4/34**HS**	27/4/49-2/5/49**NC**
29/11/34-20/12/34**HG**	8/12/49-16/12/49**NC(Rect)**
8/8/35-26/8/35**LS**	19/12/49-10/1/50**NC**
20/2/36-16/3/36**HG**	16/2/50-25/3/50**NC**
3/11/36-23/12/36**HS**	3/6/51-28/6/51**LI**
21/6/37-12/7/37**LS**	28/3/52-24/4/52**LC(EO)**
16/11/37-22/11/37**LO**	6/4/53-8/5/53**HG**
14/2/38-7/3/38**HG**	9/4/54-1/5/54**HI**
19/5/38-20/6/38**LO**	14/1/55-22/3/55**HG**
10/12/38-9/1/39**LS**	24/8/55-15/9/55**LC(EO)**
13/10/39-25/11/39**HG**	26/2/56-15/3/56**LC(EO)**
19/9/40-5/10/40**LS**	29/6/56-13/7/56**LC(EO)**
13/2/41-1/3/41**LO**	5/9/56-10/10/56**HG**
22/3/41-4/4/41**LO**	6/5/57-29/5/57**HI**
17/7/41-1/8/41**LS**	9/4/58-29/5/58**HG**
11/6/42-27/6/42**HG**	9/4/59-16/5/59**HI**
6/4/43-22/4/43**LS**	23/5/60-29/6/60**LI**
8/11/43-25/11/43**HS**	4/4/61-8/5/61**LI**

Late in the 1950s, and 46134 THE CHESHIRE REGIMENT leads a trio of light engines – probably running back to Crewe after unbalanced workings to Shrewsbury. Photograph B.P. Hoper Collection.

46131 THE ROYAL WARWICKSHIRE REGIMENT

Built North British, cost £7,744
LM 'date built' 11/9/27
Taper boiler fitted 14/10/44
First named PLANET (by 4/28), renamed 3/36
Original smoke deflectors 12/1/32
BR smoke deflectors fitted period ending 15/7/50
Renumbered 6131 to 46131 week ending 7/8/48

SHEDS
Polmadie 3/9/27
Crewe North 3/2/32
Longsight 7/9/32
Crewe North 31/1/32
Holyhead 23/7/35
Longsight 26/2/38
Crewe North 5/11/38
Preston 21/6/41
Crewe North 15/11/41
Holyhead 27/12/41
Crewe North 30/4/43
Holyhead (loan) 3/2/45
Crewe North 3/3/45
Longsight 5/4/47
Camden (loan) 18/10/47
Longsight 29/11/47
Kentish Town 19/10/57
Trafford Park 5/7/58
Crewe North 19/7/58
Camden 2/8/58
Crewe North 20/9/58
Longsight 18/10/58
Llandudno Junction 3/3/62

REPAIRS
25/3/29-10/5/29**HS**	27/7/44-14/10/44**HG**
7/8/29-18/9/29**LS**	30/6/45-2/8/45**LO**
7/1/30-1/5/30**HG**	13/5/46-5/6/46**LS**
1/6/31-19/6/31**HS**	2/6/47-26/7/47**HG**
5/12/31-12/1/32**HG**	10/7/48-3/8/48**LS**
22/8/32-9/9/32**LS**	11/6/49-30/6/49**HI**
26/5/33-12/7/33**HG**	31/8/49-28/9/49**LC**
10/5/34-27/6/34**HS**	23/11/49-20/12/49**LC**
1/1/35-29/1/35**LS**	2/6/50-3/7/50**HG**
8/7/35-23/7/35**HS**	15/7/50-27/7/50 'Painting Only'
11/3/36-26/3/36**LS**	1/5/51-21/5/51**HI**
16/10/36-13/11/36**HG**	11/2/52-20/3/52**HG**
21/6/37-14/7/37**HS**	16/4/52-26/4/52**NC(Rect)**
31/12/37-17/1/38**HS**	30/12/52-27/1/53**HI**
5/3/38-23/3/38**LO**	5/9/53-2/10/53**LI**
5/10/38-26/10/38**LS**	28/1/54-19/2/54**LC**
12/1/39-13/2/39**HG**	10/6/54-27/7/54**LC(EO)**
28/7/39-14/8/39**LO**	13/2/55-14/3/55**HG**
16/12/39-2/1/40**LS**	23/4/56-2/6/56**HI**
9/8/40-24/8/40**LS**	9/11/56-18/12/56**HI**
28/4/41-24/5/41**HG**	31/7/57-17/9/57**HG**
14/8/41-29/8/41**LO**	20/10/57-23/11/57**LC(EO)**
3/3/42-25/3/42**LS**	17/6/58-1/8/58**LC(EO)**
8/10/42-24/10/42**LO**	13/4/59-14/5/59**HI**
1/3/43-13/3/43**HS**	10/9/60-19/10/60**HI**
7/12/43-23/12/43**LS**	20/6/61-10/8/61**HC(EO)**

MILEAGES
1927	16,015	1946	61,818
1928	62,148	1947	61,528
1929	42,832	1948	66,442
1930	46,208	1949	51,163
1931	59,522	1950	64,533
1932	60,175	1951	68,033
1933	59,101	1952	55,342
1934	72,427	1953	60,071
1935	58,665	1954	47,508
1936	62,541	1955	55,493
1937	75,790	1956	56,334
1938	67,921	1957	58,916
1939	61,961	1958	50,859
1940	65,677	1959	59,155
1941	52,579	1960	2,395
1942	57,740	**Mileage at 31/12/50 1,393,763**	
1943	56,946	**Mileage at 31/12/60 1,907,849**	
1944	54,653	**Withdrawn week ending 3/11/62**	
1945	55,378	**Scrapped Crewe Works 11/62**	

TENDERS
No.	Fitted
3927	11/9/27
3918	1933
9004	13/11/36

BOILERS
Fitted	No.	From
8/4/30	–	6140
8/12/31	–	6102
2/6/33	–	6159
19/6/34	–	6115
26/10/36	–	6133
10/1/38	7217	6147
13/2/39	8132	6169
24/5/41	7243	6109
Taper 102A		
14/10/44	12034	new
26/7/47	12527	new
3/7/50	11731	6169
20/3/52	12032	–
13/4/55	12090	–
17/9/57	13891	–

46132 THE KING'S REGIMENT LIVERPOOL

Built North British, cost £7,744
LM 'date built' 11/9/27
Taper boiler fitted 5/11/43
First named PHOENIX (by 4/28), renamed 4/36
Original smoke deflectors – not listed
BR smoke deflectors fitted period ending 6/10/51
Renumbered 6132 to 46132 week ending 24/4/48

BOILERS

Fitted	No.	From
19/3/31	-	6104
6/4/32	-	6151
1/5/33	-	6116
20/4/34	-	6145
7/4/36	-	6105
5/11/37	9882	new
10/1/40	5820	6139
Taper 102A		
5/11/43	11731	new
2/7/47	12533	new
4/10/51	11725	-
1/8/53	12534	-
26/5/56	12033	-
19/4/62	12089	-

SHEDS

Polmadie 3/9/27	Crewe North 24/5/52
Camden 25/2/31	Camden (loan) 24/5/52
Preston 12/1/35	Crewe North 31/5/52
Carlisle (loan) 13/5/39	Holyhead 5/7/52
Preston 8/7/39	Edge Hill 2/10/54
Crewe North 28/2/42	Longsight 13/11/54
Holyhead (loan) 16/6/45	Edge Hill 15/1/55
Crewe North 30/6/45	Kentish Town (loan) 19/9/59
Leeds 8/9/45	Kentish Town 7/11/59
Crewe North 20/10/45	Saltley 14/10/61
Holyhead 21/9/46	Carlisle Upperby (loan) 30/6/62
Edge Hill 24/5/47	Carlisle Upperby 21/7/62
Holyhead 21/6/47	Carlisle Kingmoor 23/9/63

REPAIRS

19/2/29-20/4/29**HS**	1/12/43-11/12/43**LO**
4/3/30-4/4/30**LO**	24/1/45-22/2/45**HS**
4/10/29-14/11/29**HG**	23/7/45-14/8/45**LO**
3/3/31-31/3/31**HG**	20/10/45-3/11/45**LO**
2/4/32-4/5/32**HG**	24/7/46-8/8/46**LS**
1/12/32-16/12/32**HS**	5/5/47-2/7/47**HG**
22/4/33-17/5/33**HS**	6/3/48-19/4/48**LO**
9/10/33-26/10/33**HS**	1/11/48-25/11/48**HS**
22/3/34-10/5/34**HG**	10/6/49-19/7/49**LC**
6/10/34-24/10/34**HS**	17/10/49-8/11/49**LI**
1/4/35-17/4/35**LS**	14/6/50-21/7/50**LI**
15/8/35-22/8/35**LO**	6/11/50-2/12/50**LC**
25/10/35-13/11/35**LS**	17/7/51-4/10/51**HG**
31/3/36-27/4/36**HG**	1/9/52-20/9/52**LI**
15/9/36-29/9/36**LO**	10/12/52-24/12/52**NC(EO)**
25/1/37-8/2/37**LS**	24/6/53-1/8/53**HG**
27/10/37-24/11/37**HG**	10/4/54-13/5/54**LI**
18/5/38-10/6/38**LO**	4/2/55-14/3/55**HI**
10/11/38-15/12/38**LS**	28/7/55-25/8/55**HC(EO)**
14/12/39-10/1/40**HG**	19/4/56-26/5/56**HG**
18/10/40-1/11/40**LS**	28/12/56-19/1/57**LI**
5/8/41-18/8/41**LO**	23/5/57-19/6/57**LC(EO)**
12/2/42-28/2/42**HS**	17/2/58-3/4/58**LI**
1/8/42-15/8/42**LO**	7/3/59-7/4/59**HI**
8/9/43-5/11/43**HG**	3/12/59-20/1/60**HC(EO)**
	24/8/60-6/10/60**LI**

TENDERS

No.	Fitted
3928	11/9/27
1913	26/12/31
2863	28/6/34
3913	11/8/34
9013	27/4/36
9782	12/7/52
9013	5/11/52

MILEAGES

1927	12,129
1928	60,822
1929	47,664
1930	58,956
1931	63,688
1932	63,497
1933	77,445
1934	71,563
1935	66,714
1936	67,657
1937	61,309
1938	59,221
1939	56,768
1940	43,474
1941	58,926
1942	57,309
1943	45,146
1944	54,803
1945	54,144
1946	53,156
1947	59,973
1948	61,046
1949	56,133
1950	54,981
1951	53,244
1952	61,666
1953	65,114
1954	60,760
1955	57,751
1956	55,408
1957	56,254
1958	52,157
1959	50,033
1960	54,317

Mileage at 31/12/50 1,366,524
Mileage at 31/12/60 1,933,228
Withdrawn week ending 1/2/64
Scrapped West of Scotland
Shipbreaking Co.,Troon, 4/65

6135 SAMSON (later named THE EAST LANCASHIRE REGIMENT, in May 1936) around 1928. The train, at a guess, is the Down Royal Scot, between Stafford and Crewe. Photograph B.P. Hoper Collection.

46137, with the later curving style of smoke deflectors, at Crewe North on 8 August 1953. For an express engine, 46137 (with the very greatest respect to the regiment concerned of course) had one of those less than resonant names – THE PRINCE OF WALES'S VOLUNTEERS SOUTH LANCASHIRE and VESTA, despite a later association with freeze-dried food, had the better of it. 46137 was the last Royal Scot to be transformed, appearing in its new guise in March 1955. Note the 'Lanky Claughton' behind. Photograph A.G. Ellis, B.P. Hoper Collection.

46133 THE GREEN HOWARDS

Built North British, cost £7,744
LM 'date built' 9/10/27
Taper boiler fitted 1/7/44
First named VULCAN (by 4/28), renamed 5/36
Original smoke deflectors 7/1/32
BR smoke deflectors fitted period ending 16/6/51
Renumbered 6133 to 46133 week ending 29/1/49

BOILERS

Fitted	No.	From
2/6/30	-	6107
25/8/30	-	6115
5/5/31	-	6119
30/3/33	-	6145
27/4/34	-	6140
6/2/35	-	6136
20/8/36	-	6159
12/10/38	7246	6163
3/6/41	7218	6143
Taper 102A		
1/7/44	12030	new
24/12/47	11733	6145
26/5/51	12534	46168
21/3/53	12029	-
20/10/56	12527	-
4/3/59	12031	-

TENDERS

No.	Fitted
3929	9/10/27
3938	26/12/31
9357	3/9/36
9047	6/10/56
9035	11/2/57

MILEAGES

Year	Mileage
1927	5,211
1928	51,775
1929	55,516
1930	60,602
1931	55,944
1932	65,637
1933	57,841
1934	70,553
1935	71,011
1936	78,199
1937	75,630
1938	85,219
1939	71,166
1940	51,538
1941	70,243
1942	48,255
1943	59,459
1944	43,750
1945	61,101
1946	51,597
1947	62,289
1948	68,323
1949	65,671
1950	60,612
1951	74,898
1952	68,617
1953	55,562
1954	73,161
1955	61,929
1956	75,114
1957	65,076
1958	57,430
1959	44,220
1960	45,810
1961	33,146
1962	36,544
1963	399

Mileage at 31/12/50 1,447,142
Mileage at 2/63 2,548,329
Withdrawn week ending 23/2/63
Scrapped Crewe Works 5/63

REPAIRS

4/11/27-19/12/27**L**	7/3/42-21/3/42**HS**
19/10/28-18/12/28**LS**	20/8/42-5/9/42**LO**
10/4/29-11/5/29**HG**	4/3/43-19/3/43**LS**
16/12/29-23/1/30**LS**	29/12/43-24/1/44**HS**
26/5/30-17/6/30**HG**	28/4/44-1/7/44**HG**
21/8/30-28/8/30**HO**	24/2/45-10/3/45**LO**
2/5/31-23/5/31**HG**	22/8/45-25/9/45**HS**
5/8/31-26/8/31**LG**	25/10/46-23/11/46**HS**
8/12/31-7/1/32**HS**	24/11/47-24/12/47**HG**
31/3/32-1/4/32**LO**	20/11/48-25/1/49**HI**
5/9/32-20/9/32**LS**	19/11/49-16/12/49**LI**
21/3/33-25/4/33**HG**	11/4/50-10/5/50**LC**
16/9/33-6/10/33**LS**	13/10/50-18/11/50**HI**
9/4/34-7/5/34**HS**	31/3/51-26/5/51**HG**
15/10/34-2/11/34**LS**	21/3/52-24/4/52**HI**
28/1/35-26/2/35**HG**	14/2/53-21/3/53**HG**
16/9/35-5/10/35**LO**	28/3/53-1/4/53**LC(EO)**
14/2/36-28/2/36**LS**	8/7/53-13/8/53**HC(EO)**
18/7/36-3/9/36**HG**	25/2/54-27/3/54**LI**
13/6/37-30/6/37**LS**	8/1/55-8/2/55**HI**
19/11/37-8/12/37**LS**	1/11/55-1/12/55**HI**
3/10/38-22/10/38**HG**	14/9/56-20/10/56**HG**
28/8/39-15/9/39**LS**	13/5/57-6/6/57**HI**
28/2/40-20/3/40**LO**	5/3/58-25/3/58**HI**
10/6/40-24/6/40**HS**	27/1/59-14/3/59**HG**
12/5/41-3/6/41**HG**	5/4/59-4/5/59**NC(Rect)(EO)**
9/8/41-23/8/41**LO**	29/3/60-7/5/60**LI**
	11/1/61-7/3/61**LI**

SHEDS

Crewe North 17/9/27
Camden 22/4/31
Crewe North 24/6/31
Edge Hill 10/8/40
Holyhead 9/11/40
Crewe North 9/8/41
Carlisle Upperby 20/9/41
Leeds (loan) 15/7/44
Carlisle 12/8/44
Crewe North 31/8/46
Leeds (loan) 21/12/46
Leeds 25/1/47
Kentish Town 18/10/58
Trafford Park (loan) 1/11/58
Trafford Park 8/11/58
Kentish Town 29/11/58
Newton Heath 16/9/61

46134 THE CHESHIRE REGIMENT

Built North British, cost £7,744
LM 'date built' 9/10/27
Taper boiler fitted 31/12/53
First named ATLAS (3/28), renamed 5/36
Original smoke deflectors 27/1/32
BR smoke deflectors fitted period ending 2/1/54
Renumbered 6134 to 46134 week ending 13/11/48

TENDERS

No.	Fitted
3930	9/10/27
3945	26/12/31
3928	31/12/32
9041	16/3/36
9358	25/8/36
9356	30/12/37

SHEDS

Crewe North 17/9/27
Carlisle 30/6/28
Crewe North 26/9/28
Preston (loan) 26/11/38
Crewe North 10/12/38
Edge Hill 10/8/40
Carlisle Upperby 19/7/41
Edge Hill 25/10/41
Holyhead (loan) 19/4/47
Edge Hill 17/5/47
Carlisle Upperby 5/6/48
Edge Hill 5/6/48
Bushbury 27/1/51
Crewe North 7/7/51
Camden 23/10/54
Holyhead 20/11/54
Crewe North 26/2/55
Holyhead 20/9/58
Crewe North 27/9/58
Edge Hill 28/10/61
Carlisle Upperby 28/5/62

BOILERS

Fitted	No.	From
5/9/30	-	6110
18/6/31	-	6105
10/5/33	-	6143
23/2/34	-	6133
24/9/35	-	6154
21/7/37	8119	61261
21/7/38	7237	6116
13/3/39	7225	6154
13/1/41	9220	6106
8/4/43	9882	6158
20/10/45	8125	6147
12/11/48	11037	6100
Taper 102A		
31/12/53	11037	-
2/5/58	12662	-

REPAIRS

7/10/27-20/10/27**L**	29/9/41-10/10/41**LO**
21/3/29-19/4/29**HG**	2/1/42-17/1/42**HS**
12/2/30-6/3/30**LS**	9/6/42-30/6/42**LO**
3/9/30-27/9/30**HG**	15/3/43-8/4/43**HG**
20/10/30-4/11/30**L**	25/6/43-7/7/43**LO**
13/6/31-16/7/31**HG**	26/10/43-6/11/43**LO**
7/1/32-27/1/32**LS**	18/7/44-3/8/44**LS**
4/6/32-29/6/32**LS**	24/5/45-9/6/45**LO**
12/12/32-30/12/32**LS**	2/10/45-20/10/45**HG**
1/5/33-29/5/33**HG**	25/7/46-15/8/46**LS**
17/10/33-10/11/33**HS**	21/2/47-24/3/47**HS**
7/2/34-5/3/34**HO**	17/11/47-12/12/47**LO**
26/5/34-11/6/34**LS**	5/8/48-12/11/48**HG**
26/10/34-16/11/34**LS**	7/3/49-1/4/49**LC**
6/3/35-28/3/35**LS**	26/11/49-16/12/49**LI**
18/4/35-3/5/35**LO**	4/7/50-8/8/50**LC**
6/9/35-7/10/35**HG**	9/1/51-30/1/51**LI**
27/2/36-16/3/36**HS**	13/6/51-20/6/51**LC**
23/7/36-25/8/36**LS**	22/7/51-14/8/51**LC(EO)**
2/11/36-24/11/36**LO**	22/8/51-7/9/51**NC(Rect)(EO)**
24/12/36-8/1/37**LO**	10/5/52-1/7/52**HI**
1/7/37-4/8/37**HG**	6/1/53-14/2/53**LC**
31/12/37-14/1/38**LO**	10/10/53-31/12/53**HG**
14/7/38-1/8/38**HS**	4/1/54-12/1/54**NC(Rect)(EO)**
8/2/39-13/3/39**HG**	21/7/55-10/9/55**HI**
29/3/40-16/4/40**HS**	22/11/56-24/12/56**LI**
9/10/40-22/10/40**LO**	20/8/59-10/10/59**LI**
30/11/40-13/1/41**HG**	25/2/61-1/4/61**HI**
23/6/41-14/7/41**LO**	21/4/61-22/4/61**NC(Rect)(EO)**
3/9/41-24/9/41**LO**	

MILEAGES

1927	8,919	1947	56,843
1928	69,302	1948	52,963
1929	59,230	1949	44,147
1930	53,626	1950	55,796
1931	70,457	1951	46,814
1932	58,012	1952	44,428
1933	64,316	1953	36,278
1934	77,284	1954	63,849
1935	68,834	1955	51,179
1936	72,941	1956	59,347
1937	79,533	1957	59,394
1938	76,920	1958	53,462
1939	63,114	1959	52,941
1940	48,050	1960	58,386
1941	50,241	1961	41,139
1942	57,256	1962	26,915
1943	53,122	Mileage at 31/12/50 1,412,779
1944	60,241	Mileage at 1962 2,007,911
1945	51,129	Withdrawn week ending 1/12/62
1946	60,503	Scrapped Crewe Works 4/63

Transformation. 46137 at Dalry Road shed, Edinburgh, 17 August 1955, carrying little of its predecessor except the nameplate (it has been suggested that the splashers were re-used too) and the cab. A beautiful swan from well, not exactly an ugly duckling – but you get the idea. Photograph J. Robertson, B.P. Hoper Collection.

46135 THE EAST LANCASHIRE REGIMENT

Built North British, cost £7,744
LM 'date built' 9/10/27
Taper boiler fitted 1/1/47
Original smoke deflectors 7/12/31
BR smoke deflectors fitted period ending – not listed but post-7/48
Renumbered 6135 to 46135 week ending – not listed but after 7/48

SHEDS
Crewe North 24/9/27
Edge Hill 15/10/27
Carlisle 13/3/29
Crewe North 22/8/29
Carlisle 21/12/29
Crewe North 12/11/30
Bangor 13/10/34
Carlisle 30/3/35
Edge Hill (loan) 21/1/39
Longsight (loan) 15/4/39
Carlisle 29/4/39
Edge Hill 31/7/43
Holyhead 3/4/54
Carlisle 31/7/54
Crewe North 15/9/56
Longsight 29/9/56
Crewe 16/2/57
Camden 20/6/59
Crewe North 12/9/59
Longsight 11/6/60
Crewe North 10/9/60

BOILERS
Fitted	No.	From
2/2/29	-	6147
27/3/30	-	6108
17/3/31	-	6100
13/3/33	-	6115
28/1/35	-	6162
9/10/36	-	6139
7/10/37	8130	6141
25/7/39	9878	6113
11/12/41	8132	6131
9/11/44	7261	6130
Taper 102A		
1/1/47	12531	new
10/11/50	12029	6159
15/1/52	13893	-
12/11/55	12539	-
9/7/58	12667	-

REPAIRS
25/1/29-11/3/29HG
8/8/29-22/8/29LO
10/12/29-21/12/29LO
21/3/30-15/4/30HG
14/3/31-7/4/31HG
16/6/31-29/6/31LO
8/12/31-13/1/32HS
31/3/32-20/4/32LO
23/8/32-9/9/32LS
7/3/33-4/4/33HG
21/8/33-7/9/33LS
15/1/34-13/2/34HS
28/5/34-16/6/34LS
17/1/35-13/2/35HG
30/3/35-15/4/35HO
30/8/35-18/9/35LO
18/1/36-29/1/36LO
24/4/36-12/5/36HS
2/10/36-27/10/36HG
16/7/37-2/8/37LS
1/10/37-14/10/37HO
31/1/38-22/2/38LS
25/7/38-8/8/38LO
31/12/38-16/1/39LS
19/6/39-25/7/39LS
27/6/40-11/7/40LS
24/2/41-15/3/41LS
25/7/41-9/8/41LO
20/11/41-11/12/41HG
23/4/42-13/5/42LO
6/11/42-21/11/42LS
29/6/43-24/7/43LS
28/12/43-14/1/44LO
23/10/44-9/11/44HG
15/9/45-20/10/45LS
1/12/45-5/1/46LO
10/10/46-1/1/47HG
9/9/47-30/9/47LO
9/9/48-28/9/48LS
27/10/48-23/11/48LO
19/9/49-14/10/49LI
25/9/50-10/11/50HG
8/4/51-10/5/51HI
12/1/52-14/2/52HI
11/10/52-15/11/52HG
11/5/53-30/5/53LC(EO)
9/1/54-9/2/54HI
1/11/54-27/11/54LI
5/10/55-12/11/55HG
11/2/57-12/3/57LI
14/5/58-9/7/58HG
28/11/59-15/1/60LI
20/1/60-1/2/60NC(Rect)(EO)
13/7/61-18/8/61HI

MILEAGES
1927	15,851	1946	42,265
1928	74,052	1947	54,575
1929	52,206	1948	63,661
1930	63,099	1949	72,059
1931	52,105	1950	58,733
1932	58,668	1951	62,890
1933	78,851	1952	56,838
1934	74,635	1953	69,279
1935	67,476	1954	60,866
1936	70,752	1955	58,205
1937	75,602	1956	74,588
1938	69,680	1957	56,890
1939	73,069	1958	52,713
1940	61,365	1959	51,177
1941	59,976	1960	50,929
1942	55,265		
1943	60,571	**Mileage at 31/12/50 1,453,114**	
1944	51,161	**Mileage at 31/12/60 2,047,489**	
1945	47,437	**Withdrawn week ending 29/12/62**	
		Scrapped Crewe Works 4/63	

TENDERS
No.	Fitted
3931	9/10/27
3932	20/12/31
4254	1933
9049	12/5/36
9033	27/10/36
9132	14/4/51

THE LONDON IRISH RIFLEMAN, in super shape, reborn and at Polmadie shed in immediately post-Nationalisation condition – plain coupling rods. The awkward M on the smokebox plate is a bolted on addition; on the cab it's different, resulting in the curious effect of *two* numbers – M6138 and 6138M!. Photograph W. Hermiston, B.P. Hoper Collection.

46140 THE KING'S ROYAL RIFLE CORPS, in
perfect nick, at Crewe North in the early 1950s.
Photograph B.P. Hoper Collection.

46136 THE BORDER REGIMENT

Built North British, cost £7,744
LM 'date built' 9/10/27
Taper boiler fitted 22/3/50
First named GOLIATH (by 4/28), renamed 4/36
Original smoke deflectors 7/12/31
BR smoke deflectors fitted period ending 25/3/50
Renumbered 6136 to 46136 week ending 31/7/48

SHEDS
Crewe North 24/9/27
Carlisle 17/12/27
Crewe North 12/11/30
'Carlisle' 20/2/31
'Carlisle' 28/9/35
Camden 20/1/40
Edge Hill (loan) 19/9/43
Edge Hill 22/5/43
Carlisle Upperby 5/6/48
Edge Hill 1/10/49
Carlisle Upperby 15/10/49
Longsight 2/3/57
Carlisle Upperby 30/3/57
Preston 7/11/59
Carlisle Upperby 17/9/60
Crewe North 29/10/60
'loan to NER' 12/8/62
'return to LM(W)' 9/9/62
Carlisle Upperby 15/9/62

MILEAGES

Year	Mileage
1927	20,202
1928	64,304
1929	51,461
1930	68,797
1931	42,207
1932	73,225
1933	72,022
1934	67,689
1935	73,837
1936	79,939
1937	78,807
1938	76,359
1939	62,661
1940	79,337
1941	69,699
1942	70,062
1943	52,093
1944	53,387
1945	59,959
1946	71,795
1947	58,759
1948	46,153
1949	44,021
1950	46,886
1951	55,756
1952	53,054
1953	56,887
1954	51,450
1955	60,027
1956	59,169
1957	53,296
1958	61,113
1959	66,102
1960	49,545
1961	50,250
1962	13,294
1963	23,125

Mileage at 31/12/50 1,483,661
Mileage at 16/10/63 2,136,729
Withdrawn week ending 28/3/64
Scrapped Crewe Works 4/64

REPAIRS

14/12/28-5/2/29**HG**	26/6/44-18/7/44**LS**
11/6/29-28/6/29**LO**	27/10/44-11/11/44**LO**
4/12/29-31/12/29**HS**	23/4/45-11/5/45**HS**
27/1/31-20/2/31**HG**	19/11/45-8/12/45**LO**
6/11/31-7/12/31**HS**	3/5/46-25/5/46**HG**
26/4/32-20/5/32**HG**	31/3/47-29/4/47**LS**
13/3/33-31/3/33**HS**	12/1/48-5/2/48**LO**
16/8/33-14/9/33**HS**	14/6/48-30/7/48**LS**
16/2/34-19/4/34**HG**	16/1/50-22/3/50**HG**
6/10/34-26/10/34**HS**	26/9/50-30/10/50**LC**
18/3/35-5/4/35**LS**	24/2/51-2/4/51**LC**
7/10/35-31/10/35**HG**	4/8/51-28/8/51**LI**
4/4/36-28/4/36**LO**	3/10/52-28/10/52**HI**
30/12/36-22/1/37**HG**	2/2/54-23/2/54**HG**
26/10/37-10/11/37**LS**	19/11/54-5/1/55**LI**
13/8/38-15/9/38**HG**	9/11/55-3/12/55**LI**
12/9/39-26/9/39**LS**	1/10/56-11/11/56**HG**
13/5/40-28/5/40**LS**	14/9/57-26/10/57**HI**
7/9/40-27/9/40**HG**	31/10/57-5/11/57**NC(Rect)(EO)**
17/4/41-3/5/41**LS**	31/10/58-5/12/58**HI**
11/12/41-1/1/42**HS**	23/9/59-6/10/59**NC(EO)**
3/8/42-22/8/42**LS**	17/11/59-9/1/60**HG**
3/7/43-27/8/43**HG**	4/11/60-14/1/61**HI**
	21/8/61-18/9/61**LC(EO)**

BOILERS

Fitted	No.	From
12/28	-	6114
12/12/29	-	6126
29/1/31	-	6124
29/4/32	-	6166
20/3/33	-	6122
27/3/34	-	6150
18/10/34	-	6156
16/10/35	-	6165
6/1/37	-	6112
15/9/38	5821	6112
27/9/40	7223	6138
27/8/43	7222	6147
25/5/46	10182	6111
Taper 102A		
22/3/50	13241	new
23/2/54	12665	-
17/11/56	13894	-
9/1/60	13287	-

TENDERS

No.	Fitted
3932	9/10/27
3940	26/12/31
9337	28/4/36
9331	3/12/55
9343	26/10/57

46137 THE PRINCE OF WALES'S VOLUNTEERS SOUTH LANCASHIRE

Built North British, cost £7,744
LM 'date built' 9/10/27
Taper boiler fitted 26/3/55
First named VESTA (by 4/28), renamed 5/36
Original smoke deflectors 1/12/31
BR smoke deflectors fitted period ending – not listed
Renumbered 6137 to 46137 week ending 8/5/48

BOILERS

Fitted	No.	From
12/28	-	6120
19/11/29	-	6120
5/2/31	-	new
11/4/32	-	6111
23/1/34	-	6165
3/10/34	-	6149
2/9/36	-	6167
28/10/37	7212	6154
25/10/38	5573	6117
18/6/42	7226	6101
12/8/44	10185	6124
4/5/48	11039	6155
25/4/52	8125	-
Taper 102A		
16/3/55	13593	-
20/6/58	14001	-

TENDERS

No.	Fitted
3933	9/10/27
3922	26/12/31
9012	27/2/36

SHEDS
Crewe North 1/10/27
Carlisle 17/12/27
Crewe North 13/11/37
Carlisle (loan) 18/12/37
Crewe North 1/1/38
Carnforth (loan) 15/1/38
Carlisle Upperby 26/2/38
Crewe North 5/11/38
Edge Hill (loan) 19/11/38
Crewe North 10/12/38
Carlisle 17/12/38
Camden 20/1/40
Edge Hill (loan) 21/3/42
Camden 4/4/42
Crewe North 10/7/43
Carlisle Upperby 24/3/45
Edge Hill (loan) 13/11/48
Carlisle Upperby 27/11/48
Edge Hill 12/3/49
Crewe North 24/1/53
Longsight 17/11/56
Crewe North 23/2/57
Holyhead 4/5/57
Carlisle Upperby 17/8/57
Longsight 5/10/57
Edge Hill 24/10/57
Longsight 7/12/57
Newton Heath 30/4/60
Crewe North 17/9/60
Newton Heath 17/9/60
Crewe North 14/1/61
Trafford Park (loan) 14/1/61
Trafford Park 4/2/61
Derby 17/6/61
Trafford Park 2/9/61*
Saltley 2/9/61*
Carlisle Upperby 30/6/62
'Carlisle' 21/7/68
*same date – no explanation

REPAIRS

28/2/28-21/3/28**L**	20/7/44-12/8/44**HG**
27/11/28-22/12/28**HG**	25/10/44-11/11/44**LO**
4/5/29-3/6/29**LO**	5/6/45-18/7/45**LS**
19/10/29-6/12/29**HG**	24/4/46-24/5/46**LO**
3/2/31-3/3/31**HG**	1/10/46-26/10/46**HS**
13/7/31-29/7/31**HS**	14/7/47-15/8/47**LO**
7/4/32-3/5/32**HG**	21/10/47-11/11/47**LO**
6/3/33-22/3/33**LS**	3/4/48-4/5/48**HG**
15/1/34-12/2/34**HG**	24/11/48-22/12/48**LO**
26/9/34-11/10/34**HS**	11/3/49-12/4/49**LC**
4/3/35-22/3/35**LS**	30/8/49-30/9/49**HI**
2/9/35-26/9/35**LS**	8/5/50-9/6/50**HG**
5/2/36-27/2/36**LS**	24/7/50-18/8/50**LC**
26/8/36-21/9/36**HG**	17/2/51-16/3/51**HI**
31/5/37-15/6/37**LS**	14/8/51-22/9/51**LC(EO)**
11/10/37-5/11/37**HS(Rect)**	15/3/52-25/4/52**HG**
3/10/38-25/10/38**HG**	13/8/52-20/9/52**LC**
1/7/39-31/7/39**LS**	2/9/53-30/9/53**LI**
27/5/40-12/6/40**LS**	4/3/54-13/4/54**LC(EO)**
7/1/41-24/1/41**LS**	24/12/54-16/3/55**HG**
29/7/41-14/8/41**LS**	28/4/55-24/5/55**NC(Rect)(EO)**
12/12/41-27/12/41**LO**	5/11/55-1/12/55**LC(EO)**
30/5/42-18/6/42**HG**	19/2/57-23/3/57**LI**
17/12/42-5/1/43**LS**	17/4/58-20/6/58**HG**
13/3/43-30/3/43**LO**	1/7/58-10/7/58**NC(Rect)(EO)**
23/9/43-9/10/43**HS**	20/8/59-19/9/59**HI**
22/4/44-13/5/44**LO**	23/11/60-11/1/61**HI**
	16/1/61-10/2/61**NC(Rect)(EO)**

MILEAGES

Year	Mileage	Year	Mileage
1927	18,946	1946	56,843
1928	50,494	1947	50,446
1929	52,865	1948	42,333
1930	58,813	1949	49,121
1931	62,770	1950	52,154
1932	72,578	1951	52,483
1933	46,507	1952	49,711
1934	85,835	1953	46,709
1935	67,269	1954	47,095
1936	75,455	1955	47,338
1937	69,867	1956	59,583
1938	71,356	1957	63,442
1939	76,570	1958	53,764
1940	73,150	1959	69,770
1941	67,399	1960	58,536
1942	79,352		
1943	74,024		
1944	50,728		
1945	51,363		

Mileage at 31/12/50 1,456,238
Mileage at 31/12/60 2,004,341
Withdrawn week ending 3/11/62
Scrapped 5/63

46138 THE LONDON IRISH RIFLEMAN

Built North British, cost £7,744
LM 'date built' 9/10/27
Taper boiler fitted 9/6/44
First named FURY (by 4/28), renamed 10/29
Original smoke deflectors 20/1/32
BR smoke deflectors fitted period ending 9/9/50
Renumbered 6138 to 46138 week ending 15/1/49

BOILERS

Fitted	No.	From
23/4/30	-	6135
16/7/31	-	6112
25/4/33	-	6169
5/10/34	-	6152
19/10/36	-	6128
21/6/38	7223	6144
13/7/40	9881	6144
18/7/42	5824	6100
Taper 102A		
9/6/44	12029	new
28/2/48	11730	6146
23/8/50	12028	6146
11/2/54	12089	-
4/1/57	12526	-
23/12/60	12029	-

SHEDS

Crewe North 1/10/27
Edge Hill 15/10/27
Carlisle 17/12/27
Aberdeen 12/11/34
Edge Hill 5/10/35
Crewe North 22/6/36
Bangor 3/7/37
Carlisle Upperby 25/9/37
Crewe North 20/1/40
Preston 9/3/40
Edge Hill 31/8/40
Holyhead 15/9/51
Camden 12/4/52
Crewe North 3/5/52
Camden 25/4/53
Crewe North 6/6/53
Camden 13/6/53
Crewe 19/9/53
Longsight 27/11/54
Crewe North 1/1/55
Carlisle 4/8/56
Crewe North 3/11/56
Llandudno Junction 7/11/59
Holyhead 18/6/60
Llandudno Junction 17/9/60
Holyhead 11/3/61
Carlisle Upperby 10/11/62

MILEAGES

Year	Miles
1927	9,138
1928	65,495
1929	65,350
1930	73,876
1931	54,023
1932	63,930
1933	96,004
1934	64,660
1935	64,980
1936	81,052
1937	82,043
1938	81,953
1939	78,090
1940	50,891
1941	62,843
1942	52,670
1943	62,838
1944	44,764
1945	69,651
1946	52,748
1947	60,570
1948	55,111
1949	60,804
1950	65,891
1951	69,315
1952	57,220
1953	58,863
1954	59,862
1955	47,120
1956	49,298
1957	54,748
1958	50,782
1959	54,825
1960	44,918

Mileage at 31/12/50 1,519,375
Mileage at 31/12/60 2,046,326
Withdrawn week ending 9/2/63
Scrapped Crewe Works 5/63

REPAIRS

19/3/29-25/4/29**HG**
22/11/29-7/12/29**LO**
14/4/30-9/5/30**HG**
22/9/30-7/10/30**LS**
9/4/31-30/4/31**LO**
15/7/31-7/8/31**HG**
16/4/32-6/5/32**HS**
13/9/32-30/9/32**LS**
18/4/33-16/5/33**HG**
8/1/34-8/2/34**HS**
27/9/34-24/10/34**HG**
2/1/36-20/1/36**LS**
5/6/36-22/6/36**LS**
12/10/36-30/10/36**HG**
8/9/37-27/9/37**LS**
1/6/38-15/7/38**HG**
10/5/39-24/5/39**LS**
27/11/39-13/12/39**LS**
24/6/40-13/7/40**HG**
19/8/40-28/8/40**LO**
29/9/41-11/10/41**LS**
23/6/42-18/7/42**HG**
15/9/42-26/9/42**LO**
8/5/43-22/5/43**LS**
14/3/44-9/6/44**HG**
10/3/45-7/4/45**LO**
15/9/45-19/10/45**LS**
25/11/46-27/12/46**HS**
2/5/47-3/6/47**LO**
4/7/47-12/8/47**HS**
5/1/48-28/2/48**HG**
19/3/48-31/3/48**NC**
30/10/48-14/1/49**HI**
17/6/49-26/7/49**LC**
17/1/50-9/2/50**LI**
21/7/50-23/8/50**HG**
24/8/51-22/9/51**LI**
29/10/52-22/11/52**HI**
6/1/54-11/2/54**HG**
22/6/55-30/7/55**LI**
15/4/56-24/5/56**HC(EO)**
5/11/56-4/1/57**HG**
26/2/57-8/3/57**NC(Rect)(EO)**
7/4/58-1/5/58**HI**
25/11/58-2/1/59**LC**
20/4/59-2/5/59**NC(EO)**
21/7/59-28/8/59**HI**
28/11/60-22/12/60**HG**

TENDERS

No.	Fitted
3914	20/12/31
9017	20/1/36

46141 THE NORTH STAFFORD-SHIRE REGIMENT , late in the day (note electrification warning label and speedo off left-hand trailing crank pin); a bit scruffy but still exuding power and grace. A few gallons have gone up the chimney but the water was well treated, for the streaks down the smokebox have not dried white. The date is not given, though the year would be, at a guess, about 1962 (the speedo was fitted at the very end of 1960) and the location, astonishingly is – Eastleigh shed, a number of exotic locomotives finding their way to Southampton in those strange times. Reed, it turns out, in his *Loco Profile* actually mentions 46141's visit, giving the date as February 1963 – so the guess was only a year out. Photograph Les Elsey.

46139 THE WELCH REGIMENT

Built North British, cost £7,744
LM 'date built' 9/10/27
Taper boiler fitted 12/11/46
First named AJAX (3/28), renamed 3/36
Original smoke deflectors 21/12/31
BR smoke deflectors fitted period ending 29/5/50
Renumbered 6139 to 46139 week ending 22/5/48

BOILERS

Fitted	No.	From
6/3/29	-	6146
19/2/30	-	6147
30/12/30	-	6123
6/10/32	-	6161
6/6/34	-	6107
6/3/36	-	6111
11/10/37	5820	6153
31/5/39	8135	6167
2/8/41	7229	6116
5/11/43	11031	6169
Taper 102A		
12/11/46	12538	new
29/5/50	12204	6157
31/7/53	12535	-
23/6/55	12208	-
26/4/58	13239	-

REPAIRS

25/2/29-25/3/29HG	28/9/43-5/11/43HG
17/7/29-27/7/29LO	6/3/44-18/3/44LO
27/1/30-7/3/30HG	19/9/44-6/10/44LS
20/12/30-17/1/31HG	21/8/45-15/9/45HS
15/8/31-1/9/31HS	9/8/46-12/11/46HG
9/3/32-31/3/32LS	11/12/47-22/1/48HS
4/10/32-3/11/32HG	16/4/48-21/5/48HO
19/5/33-13/6/33LS	12/7/48-12/8/48LO
20/11/33-7/12/33LS	4/10/48-5/11/48LO
4/5/34-20/6/34HG	21/7/49-5/8/49LI
7/12/34-27/12/34HS	12/4/50-29/5/50HG
20/5/35-5/6/35LS	24/8/50-31/8/50LC
11/10/35-25/10/35LO	20/11/50-3/1/51HI
26/2/36-20/3/36HG	29/11/51-5/1/52HI
4/2/37-22/2/37HS	27/8/52-23/9/52HI
2/10/37-21/10/37HG	21/6/53-31/7/53GEN
7/6/38-20/6/38LO	22/3/54-20/4/54LI
8/11/38-12/12/38LS	22/10/54-11/11/54LC(EO)
6/5/39-31/5/39HG	5/5/55-23/6/55HG
15/4/40-26/4/40LS	10/2/56-10/3/56LC(EO)
23/10/40-7/11/40LS	17/1/57-16/2/57HI
16/1/41-31/1/41LO	15/3/58-26/4/58HG
24/3/41-23/4/41LO	1/7/58-12/7/58NC(Rect)(EO)
9/7/41-2/8/41HG	7/3/59-13/4/59HI
23/1/42-14/2/42LO	4/4/60-17/5/60HI
14/8/42-29/8/42LS	11/10/60-4/11/60LC(EO)
27/1/43-15/2/43LS	31/1/61-13/3/61HI
	31/7/61-25/8/61NC(EO)

TENDERS

No.	Fitted
3935	9/10/27
3921	26/12/31
9014	20/3/36

SHEDS
Crewe North 8/10/27
Camden 5/11/27
Carlisle 17/12/27
Crewe North 17/6/33
Preston 23/9/33
Holyhead 26/2/38
Carlisle 24/9/38
Holyhead 14/1/39
Carlisle 27/4/40
Camden 17/1/42
Crewe South 29/9/45
Camden 29/12/45
Crewe North 12/10/46
Holyhead 24/5/47
Camden 21/6/47
Kentish Town 7/11/59
Newton Heath 16/9/61

MILEAGES

1927	10,904
1928	61,059
1929	72,447
1930	70,905
1931	65,003
1932	50,374
1933	78,683
1934	65,408
1935	76,954
1936	73,448
1937	67,351
1938	60,994
1939	67,235
1940	58,195
1941	53,214
1942	74,104
1943	72,928
1944	65,732
1945	79,955
1946	50,501
1947	64,588
1948	51,316
1949	75,749
1950	49,831
1951	60,904
1952	61,705
1953	67,066
1954	59,765
1955	59,282
1956	63,989
1957	62,769
1958	52,125
1959	62,569
1960	51,536

Mileage at 31/12/50 1,517,778
Mileage at 31/12/60 2,120,088
Withdrawn week ending 13/10/62
Scrapped Crewe Works 5/63

46140 THE KING'S ROYAL RIFLE CORPS

Built North British, cost £7,744
LM 'date built' 9/10/27
Taper boiler fitted 30/5/52
First named HECTOR (by 4/28), renamed 5/36
Original smoke deflectors 23/6/31
BR smoke deflectors fitted period ending 14/6/52
Renumbered 6140 to 46140 week ending 8/1/49

TENDERS

No.	Fitted
3936	9/10/27
9341	27/5/36

REPAIRS

8/11/28-28/12/28LO	25/11/43-24/12/43HS
22/4/29-22/5/29HG	24/8/44-13/9/44HS
5/3/30-1/4/30HG	3/2/45-3/3/45LO
21/5/31-23/6/31HG	15/6/45-4/8/45HS
5/4/32-25/4/32HS	26/11/45-22/12/45LO
2/1/33-27/1/33HG	28/6/46-15/8/46HG
28/2/33-4/3/33LO	26/2/47-3/4/47LO
22/8/33-19/9/33HS	16/1/48-6/2/48HS
28/3/34-24/5/34HG	30/10/48-7/1/49HG
8/10/34-25/10/34LS	31/3/49-26/4/49LC
4/3/35-19/3/35LO	10/11/49-9/12/49LI
2/9/35-26/9/35HG	27/3/50-27/4/50LC
11/5/36-27/5/36LS	18/11/50-22/11/50LC
12/4/37-29/4/37HG	15/1/51-26/2/51LI
30/8/37-15/9/37LO	26/1/52-30/5/52HG
16/10/37-5/11/37LO	5/10/53-29/10/53LI
9/4/38-9/5/38HS	9/11/53-19/11/53LC(EO)
28/11/38-12/12/38LS	2/12/53-2/1/54HC(EO)
18/8/39-1/9/39LS	27/4/54-22/5/54LC(EO)
18/10/39-2/12/39LS	8/11/54-8/12/54HI
19/4/40-15/5/40HG	3/1/56-18/2/56LC(EO)
25/10/40-11/11/40LO	21/4/56-17/5/56LC
15/5/41-2/6/41LS	6/4/57-1/5/57HI
9/9/41-27/9/41LO	27/2/58-29/3/58HG
31/1/42-17/2/42LS	16/3/59-15/4/59LI
25/3/42-7/5/42LO	16/4/60-3/6/60HI
14/9/42-26/9/42LS	16/1/61-4/3/61HG
26/4/43-13/5/43HG	
12/8/43-11/9/43LO	

SHEDS
Crewe North 8/10/27
Camden 5/11/27
Edge Hill 17/12/27
Carlisle 30/6/28
Edge Hill 26/9/28
Carlisle 20/4/30
Edge Hill 23/6/31
Preston 2/7/38
Carlisle Upperby 4/9/38
Holyhead (loan) 15/10/38
Carlisle Upperby 19/11/38
Holyhead (loan) 7/1/39
Camden 28/1/39
Carlisle 3/2/45
Camden 10/2/45
Bushbury 30/9/50
Crewe North 7/7/51
Longsight 12/6/54
Kentish Town 26/9/59
Nottingham 7/11/59
Kentish Town 19/12/59
Newton Heath 16/9/61
Longsight 22/6/63

BOILERS

Fitted	No.	From
13/3/30	-	6125
27/5/31	-	6146
8/4/32	-	6132
9/1/33	-	6139
6/9/33	-	6166
17/5/34	-	6147
13/9/35	-	6103
19/4/37	-	6155
29/4/38	8120	6110
15/5/40	7214	6116
13/5/43	8120	6163
15/8/46	7259	6164
7/1/49	10183	6156
Taper 102A		
30/5/52	13592	-
18/2/56	12658	-
29/3/58	14002	-
4/3/61	13591	-

MILEAGES

1927	8,161
1928	43,548
1929	47,188
1930	58,322
1931	61,598
1932	57,849
1933	77,170
1934	58,888
1935	79,999
1936	93,741
1937	72,653
1938	70,307
1939	68,153
1940	70,358
1941	69,243
1942	68,108
1943	63,715
1944	75,178
1945	54,060
1946	73,676
1947	56,536
1948	60,454
1949	60,706
1950	64,761
1951	47,220
1952	38,151
1953	48,070
1954	56,024
1955	69,553
1956	59,797
1957	70,943
1958	69,112
1959	63,266
1960	64,365

Mileage at 31/12/50 1,514,372
Mileage at 31/12/60 2,100,873
Withdrawn week ending 30/10/65
Scrapped J.McWilliam, Shettleston, 3/66

6142 LION on the turntable at Camden shed in the early 1930s – another parallel boiler Scot lurks in the background. Both have the first 'straight up' pattern of smoke deflectors. Photograph B.P. Hoper Collection.

THE YORK & LANCASTER REGIMENT, at this time an Edge Hill engine, passing Earlestown No.2 box in the late 1950s – probably on a Liverpool-Newcastle train. The abandoned board leaning against the wall is headed NOTICES – observe also the Signalman's external loo and, in the distance, the (doubtless long gone) *Curzon* cinema. Photograph Les Elsey.

46141 THE NORTH STAFFORDSHIRE REGIMENT

Built North British, cost £7,744
LM 'date built' 6/11/27
Taper boiler fitted 28/10/50
First named CALEDONIAN (by 4/28), renamed 4/36
Original smoke deflectors 7/1/32
BR smoke deflectors fitted period ending 4/11/50
Renumbered 6141 to 46141 week ending 3/7/48

MILEAGES

Year	Mileage
1927	10,742
1928	44,347
1929	48,874
1930	55,599
1931	52,914
1932	69,729
1933	74,042
1934	59,908
1935	56,931
1936	74,294
1937	74,294
1938	72,616
1939	68,176
1940	75,018
1941	73,709
1942	70,472
1943	78,303
1944	65,494
1945	68,874
1946	75,328
1947	58,064
1948	50,085
1949	44,700
1950	44,562
1951	62,146
1952	64,986
1953	64,477
1954	53,836
1955	48,001
1956	44,088
1957	54,873
1958	63,177
1959	60,781
1960	54,101

Mileage at 31/12/50 1,467,078
Mileage at 31/12/63 2,037,544
Withdrawn week ending 18/4/64
Scrapped Crewe Works 7/64

SHEDS

Crewe North 15/10/27
Camden 5/11/27
Edge Hill 17/12/27
Carlisle 23/6/28
Edge Hill 30/6/28*
Carlisle 30/6/28*
Edge Hill 24/4/29
Carlisle 23/3/30
Edge Hill 18/4/36
Longsight 30/9/39
Carlisle 7/10/39
Camden 20/1/40
Crewe North 12/10/46
Camden 8/11/47
Longsight 10/2/51
Camden 24/3/51
Carlisle 25/9/54
Leeds 7/1/56
Carlisle Upperby 18/1/56
Bushbury 7/11/59
Willesden 3/12/60
Trafford Park 31/12/60
Saltley 17/6/61
Carlisle Upperby 7/7/62
'Carlisle' 21/7/62
*same dates – reason unknown

REPAIRS

4/3/29-20/4/29**HG**	10/8/43-28/8/43**LO**
18/2/30-19/3/30**HG**	20/1/44-4/2/44**LS**
25/9/31-27/10/31**HG**	18/8/44-2/9/44**LS**
5/9/32-21/9/32**LS**	19/12/44-20/1/45**LO**
9/2/33-16/3/33**HG**	7/5/45-9/6/45**LS**
4/1/34-25/1/34**HS**	19/12/45-10/1/46**HG**
20/11/34-10/12/34**LS**	7/5/47-5/6/47**HS**
21/6/35-26/7/35**HG**	5/10/47-3/11/47**LO**
4/9/35-6/9/35**LO**	22/5/48-3/7/48**HG**
2/10/35-16/10/35**LO**	20/8/48-14/9/48**LO**
28/3/36-20/4/36**HS**	25/8/49-28/9/49**LI**
28/11/36-19/12/36**HG**	1/9/50-28/10/50**HG**
4/8/37-19/8/37**LS**	13/5/52-14/6/52**HI**
19/11/37-7/12/37**HO**	25/1/53-17/3/53**HG**
2/3/38-17/3/38**HS**	9/2/54-8/3/54**LI**
12/10/38-1/12/38**HG**	14/3/55-30/4/55**HI**
23/8/39-12/9/39**LS**	17/10/55-11/11/55**HI**
22/4/40-7/5/40**LS**	5/6/56-29/6/56**LC(EO)**
9/12/40-8/1/41**HG**	10/11/56-13/12/56**HG**
24/5/41-7/6/41**HS**	23/11/57-20/12/57**HI**
24/10/41-13/11/41**LS**	5/7/58-21/8/58**LC**
11/4/42-29/4/42**LS**	20/5/59-27/6/59**HG**
16/10/42-14/11/42**LS**	24/9/60-25/10/60**LI**
22/4/43-8/5/43**HG**	

BOILERS

Fitted	No.	From
28/2/30	-	6100
5/10/31	-	6117
15/2/33	-	6158
12/1/34	-	6104
15/7/35	-	6120
4/12/36	-	6131
30/11/37	8138	6162
1/12/38	7253	6137
8/1/41	10183	6149
8/5/43	11032	6126
10/1/46	11034	6167
3/7/48	9879	6111
Taper 102A		
28/10/50	12538	6139
17/3/53	12660	-
13/12/56	12672	-
27/6/59	13893	-

TENDERS

No.	Fitted
3937	6/11/27
3934	26/12/31
9045	20/4/36

46142 THE YORK & LANCASTER REGIMENT

Built North British, cost £7,744
LM 'date built' 6/11/27
Taper boiler fitted 14/2/51
First named LION (by 4/28), renamed 5/36
Original smoke deflectors 4/1/32
BR smoke deflectors fitted period ending 24/2/51
Renumbered 6142 to 46142 week ending 3/7/48

BOILERS

Fitted	No.	From
21/3/29	-	6148
22/1/30	-	6122
8/5/31	-	6114
29/11/32	-	6114
4/12/33	-	6161
20/8/34	-	6118
12/12/35	-	6136
3/6/37	-	new
2/3/39	7261	6107
21/4/42	7258	6114
6/10/44	11036	6146
24/6/47	9878	6109
Taper 102A		
14/2/51	13590	new
5/12/53	12674	-
24/7/56	12536	-
25/8/59	12530	-

MILEAGES

Year	Mileage
1927	11,096
1928	40,170
1929	46,202
1930	48,488
1931	59,810
1932	49,207
1933	58,734
1934	74,615
1935	73,171
1936	84,399
1937	78,231
1938	68,735
1939	58,289
1940	59,725
1941	51,922
1942	66,970
1943	73,373
1944	60,762
1945	42,216
1946	68,851
1947	55,846
1948	64,170
1949	62,921
1950	54,132
1951	59,846
1952	54,590
1953	62,932
1954	70,430
1955	62,137
1956	62,648
1957	48,771
1958	59,562
1959	57,200
1960	47,270
1961	49,358
1962	19,971
1963	31,586

Mileage at 31/12/50 1,412,035
Mileage at 31/12/63 2,008,336
Withdrawn week ending 11/1/64
Scrapped Crewe Works 1/64

REPAIRS

4/3/29-17/4/29**HG**	20/1/45-17/2/45**LO**
3/1/30-7/2/30**HG**	19/6/45-28/7/45**LO**
7/5/31-5/6/31**HG**	8/3/46-4/4/46**HS**
7/12/31-4/1/32**HO**	1/1/47-22/1/47**LO**
23/11/32-2/1/33**HG**	17/5/47-24/6/47**HG**
5/7/33-31/7/33**LO**	28/5/48-1/7/48**LS**
25/11/33-20/12/33**HS**	27/11/48-23/12/48**TRO**
10/8/34-4/9/34**HG**	4/5/49-23/5/49**LI**
1/5/35-24/5/35**HS**	24/2/50-22/3/50**LI**
27/11/35-24/12/35**HG**	23/3/50-24/3/50**TRO**
24/9/36-14/10/36**LS**	6/12/50-14/2/51**HG**
25/5/37-22/6/37**HG**	31/3/51-19/4/51**NC**
8/1/38-29/1/38**LS**	16/4/52-21/5/52**LI**
22/7/38-16/8/38**LS**	7/8/52-4/9/52**LC(EO)**
28/1/39-2/3/39**HG**	7/11/53-5/12/53**HG**
27/12/39-11/1/40**LS**	17/11/54-16/12/54**LC(EO)**
11/9/40-24/9/40**LS**	21/5/55-15/6/55**LI**
6/3/41-26/3/41**LO**	12/6/56-24/7/56**HG**
21/6/41-12/7/41**HS**	11/5/57-20/6/57**HI**
28/11/41-13/12/41**LO**	22/10/57-23/11/57**LC**
30/3/42-21/4/42**HG**	14/8/58-12/9/58**LI**
13/6/42-27/6/42**LO**	22/6/59-25/8/59**HG**
21/11/42-12/12/42**LS**	20/7/60-23/8/60**HI**
22/3/43-17/4/43**LO**	31/10/60-2/12/60**LC(EO)**
21/9/43-6/10/43**LS**	9/6/61-4/8/61**HI**
7/9/44-6/10/44**HG**	

SHEDS

Crewe North 15/10/27
Edge Hill 5/11/27
Edge Hill 18/4/36
Bushbury 21/10/39
Camden 13/12/41
Carlisle Upperby 17/6/44
Crewe North 31/8/46
Edge Hill 30/11/46
Crewe North 29/3/47
Camden 21/6/47
Edge Hill 24/9/55
Kentish Town (loan) 19/9/59
Kentish Town 7/11/59
Newton Heath 16/9/61
Longsight 22/6/63

TENDERS

No.	Fitted
3938	6/11/27
2898	26/12/31
3929	31/12/32
9040	14/10/36
9133	18/6/45
9765	23/11/57
9779	22/6/59

46143 THE SOUTH STAFFORDSHIRE REGIMENT

Built North British, cost £7,744
LM 'date built' 6/11/27
Taper boiler fitted 7/6/49
First named MAIL (by 4/28), renamed7/34
Original smoke deflectors – not listed
BR smoke deflectors fitted period ending 18/4/53
Renumbered 6143 to 46143 week ending 4/9/48

BOILERS

Fitted	No.	From
19/5/30	-	6117
2/12/30	-	6117
5/11/31	-	6121
6/4/33	-	6130
7/2/34	-	6162
15/11/34	-	6100
4/2/36	-	6110
16/6/37	7236	6159
15/2/39	7241	6131
14/4/41	11039	new
24/2/45	11033	6120
Taper 102A		
7/6/49	12659	new
2/4/53	12668	-
14/10/55	12203	-
30/4/60	12197	-

TENDERS

No.	Fitted
3939	6/11/27
3903	26/12/31
9036	19/2/36

SHEDS

Crewe North 22/10/27
Edge Hill 5/11/27
Carlisle 3/7/37
Edge Hill 26/2/38
Preston (loan) 21/5/38
Edge Hill 18/6/38
Bushbury 21/10/39
Crewe 3/1/42
Polmadie (loan) 14/9/43
Polmadie 2/10/43
Crewe North (loan) 13/5/44
Crewe North 17/6/44
Polmadie (loan) 16/9/44
Polmadie 23/12/44
Longsight (loan) 18/6/49
Longsight 23/7/49
Crewe North 3/2/51
Camden 24/3/51
Holyhead 20/9/52
Crewe North 11/10/52
Longsight 6/12/52
Leeds 29/10/55
Longsight 19/11/55
Bushbury 7/11/59
Trafford Park 17/12/60
Trafford Park 4/2/61
Annesley 29/2/62

MILEAGES

Year	Mileage
1927	3,271
1928	33,220
1929	39,211
1930	51,926
1931	63,655
1932	62,784
1933	70,896
1934	66,626
1935	54,189
1936	70,085
1937	68,152
1938	73,813
1939	55,978
1940	51,147
1941	63,040
1942	60,517
1943	56,591
1944	51,291
1945	56,619
1946	62,696
1947	40,699
1948	32,757
1949	50,120
1950	68,464
1951	67,545
1952	64,394
1953	60,451
1954	55,733
1955	50,332
1956	58,753
1957	53,920
1958	68,089
1959	60,715
1960	44,665

Mileage at 31/12/50 1,307,747
Mileage at 31/12/60 1,892,344
Withdrawn week ending 21/12/63
Scrapped Crewe Works 1/64

REPAIRS

26/11/27-10/3/28LO
8/5/29-8/6/29HG
9/5/30-3/6/30HG
1/12/30-12/12/30HO
11/6/31-30/6/31LS
2/11/31-1/12/31HG
10/10/32-25/10/32LS
1/4/33-26/4/33HS
29/1/34-28/2/34HG
25/6/34-27/7/34HS
5/11/34-24/11/34HS
15/12/34-21/12/34LO
4/5/35-27/5/35HO
29/7/35-13/8/35LS
17/1/36-19/2/36HG
29/5/37-21/6/37HS
19/11/37-6/12/37LS
8/8/38-26/8/38LS
7/1/39-15/2/39HG
7/7/39-31/7/39LO
28/3/40-13/4/40LS
7/3/41-4/4/41HG
25/9/42-13/10/42LS
29/3/43-20/4/43LS
14/6/44-30/6/44LS
25/1/45-24/2/45HG
16/11/45-17/12/45LS
29/8/46-25/9/46HS
21/11/47-27/12/47LS
6/8/48-31/8/48LO
3/2/49-7/6/49HG
14/8/50-7/9/50LI
24/2/52-22/3/52LI
3/7/52-8/8/52LC
4/2/53-2/4/53HG
18/8/54-22/9/54LI
9/8/55-14/10/55HG
8/6/56-2/7/56HI
19/12/56-25/1/57LC(EO)
5/10/57-8/11/57HI
28/7/58-20/8/58LI
3/3/59-4/4/59LI
26/3/60-30/4/60HG
18/9/61-18/10/61HI

The Up Blackpool (North) express to Euston, with the 6.35am Workington and Barrow portion attached, south of Tring at 2.55 in the afternoon on 3 October 1953, with Longsight's 46143 THE SOUTH STAFFORDSHIRE REGIMENT in charge, and running at about 60mph. Photograph E.D. Bruton.

46144 HONOURABLE ARTILLERY COMPANY

Built North British, cost £7,744
LM 'date built' 6/11/27
Taper boiler fitted 9/6/45
First named OSTRICH (by 4/28), renamed 1/33
Original smoke deflectors 30/1/32
BR smoke deflectors fitted period ending 17/5/52
Renumbered 6144 to 46144 week ending 5/6/48

MILEAGES

1927	9,360	1948	62,535
1928	40,810	1949	70,644
1929	39,150	1950	67,632
1930	41,564	1951	68,779
1931	50,387	1952	52,205
1932	55,103	1953	59,375
1933	68,411	1954	55,464
1934	68,065	1955	68,072
1935	70,273	1956	59,193
1936	86,274	1957	52,358
1937	74,697	1958	53,379
1938	74,970	1959	65,596
1939	62,934	1960	53,412
1940	55,261	1961	36,976
1941	47,378	1962	40,514
1942	58,840	1963	23,103
1943	53,143	**Mileage at 31/12/50 1,404,713**	
1944	59,123	**Mileage at 31/12/63 2,093,139**	
1945	56,092	**Withdrawn week ending 11/1/64**	
1946	66,327	**Scrapped Crewe Works 1/64**	
1947	65,740		

REPAIRS

18/10/28-8/12/28**HG**	26/11/41-20/12/41**LO**
17/6/29-27/6/29**LO**	1/6/42-20/6/42**HG**
11/12/29-8/1/30**HG**	8/1/43-27/1/43**LO**
10/10/31-16/11/31**HS**	12/3/43-10/4/43**LS**
4/3/31-8/4/31**HG**	8/9/43-23/9/43**LO**
1/4/32-20/4/32**LS**	6/5/44-24/5/44**LS**
9/11/32-12/12/32**HG**	5/4/45-9/6/45**HG**
25/1/33-30/1/33**LO**	26/2/46-2/4/46**HS**
13/3/33-3/4/33**LO**	31/5/46-19/6/46**LO**
3/5/33-5/5/33**LO**	12/2/47-6/3/47**HS**
26/9/33-19/10/33**HS**	2/12/47-30/12/47**LS**
2/3/34-23/3/34**LS**	5/5/48-2/6/48**LO**
21/8/34-19/9/34**HG**	8/11/48-4/1/49**HG**
20/10/34-22/10/34**LO**	12/10/49-12/11/49**LC**
15/3/35-3/4/35**LS**	5/5/50-25/5/50**LI**
29/5/35-17/6/35**HO**	15/3/51-8/6/51**HI**
30/8/35-19/9/35**LS**	22/3/52-13/5/52**HG**
20/1/36-4/2/36**LS**	21/9/53-22/10/53**HI**
3/6/36-19/6/36**HS**	24/11/53-8/12/53**NC(Rect)(EO)**
16/2/37-11/3/37**HG**	22/9/54-27/10/54**HG**
22/4/37-1/5/37**LO**	24/11/54-23/12/54**LC(EO)**
1/11/37-29/11/37**HS**	2/2/56-12/3/56**LI**
10/10/38-8/11/38**LS**	13/4/57-1/6/57**HG**
15/2/39-1/3/39**LO**	29/6/58-2/8/58**HI**
5/6/39-19/6/39**LS**	4/3/59-25/3/59**LC(EO)**
25/3/40-16/4/40**HG**	21/5/59-16/6/59**HI**
18/10/40-31/10/40**LS**	13/6/60-5/8/60**HG**
4/10/41-24/10/41**HS**	9/8/60-19/8/60**NC(Rect)(EO)**
	30/1/61-16/3/61**LC(EO)**

BOILERS

Fitted	No.	From
11/28	-	6103
17/12/29	-	6106
10/3/31	-	new
15/11/32	-	6147
4/10/33	-	6126
28/8/34	-	6121
6/6/35	-	6159
23/2/37	-	6136
22/11/37	9881	new
16/4/40	7238	6102
20/6/42	7235	6110
Taper 102A		
9/6/45	12197	new
4/1/49	12201	6159
13/5/52	12525	-
27/10/54	12533	-
1/6/57	12540	-
5/8/60	13999	-

TENDERS

No.	Fitted
3940	6/11/27
3929	26/12/30
3898	31/12/32
9347	19/6/36

SHEDS

Crewe North 22/10/27
Edge Hill 5/11/27
Camden 2/7/38
Edge Hill 29/4/39
Preston 15/6/40
Edge Hill 7/12/40
Crewe North 3/2/51
Edge Hill 24/3/51
Camden 20/12/52
Willesden 10/6/61
Llandudno Junction 23/9/61
Crewe North 22/6/63

6144 OSTRICH exits Shugborough tunnel with an Up train; the LNW distant signal with sighting board is worth a look, and the fogman's hut too. Photograph Collection B.P. Hoper.

46145 THE DUKE OF WELLINGTON'S REGT. (WEST RIDING)

Built North British, cost £7,744
LM 'date built' 31/12/27
Taper boiler fitted 29/1/44
First named CONDOR (2/28), renamed 1/33
Original smoke deflectors 12/1/32
BR smoke deflectors fitted period ending 27/1/51
Renumbered 6145 to 46145 week ending 2/10/48

The sophisticated LMS 1946 lined black suited the Scots, the rather art deco lettering sitting perfectly with the livery. 6147 THE NORTHAMPTONSHIRE REGIMENT basks in its own glory a year or so before Nationalisation. Photograph J. Pattison B.P. Hoper Collection.

BOILERS

Fitted	No.	From
11/4/30	-	6113
13/8/31	-	6109
26/1/33	-	6144
14/2/34	-	6122
12/10/34	-	6139
10/9/36	-	6130
21/4/38	10185	new
5/7/40	11036	new
Taper 102A		
29/1/44	11733	new
26/9/47	12034	6131
5/1/51	12526	6116
6/7/53	12527	-
24/5/56	12667	-
22/3/58	12205	-

TENDERS

No.	Fitted
3941	31/12/27
8907	26/12/31
9026	1936

SHEDS

Crewe North 5/11/27
Rugby 5/11/27
Edge Hill 17/12/27
Crewe North 17/12/30
Edge Hill 7/9/32
Camden 8/4/33
Preston 23/9/33
Camden 11/7/36
Crewe North 2/1/37
Camden (loan) 23/1/37
Camden 10/4/37
Preston 21/6/41
Crewe North 29/11/44
Holyhead 28/11/42
Crewe North 30/4/43
Holyhead (loan) 26/2/44
Crewe North 8/4/44
Holyhead 12/8/44
Crewe North 10/8/46
Longsight 5/4/47
Camden (loan) 19/11/49
Longsight 17/12/49
Holyhead (loan) 21/7/51
Longsight 22/9/51
Holyhead (loan) 20/10/51
Longsight 24/11/51
Leeds 24/1/53

REPAIRS

29/10/28-18/12/28**LS**
2/5/29-4/6/29**HG**
7/4/30-1/5/30**HG**
14/2/31-2/3/31**LS**
10/8/31-1/9/31**HG**
2/10/31-9/10/31**LO**
14/6/32-30/6/32**LS**
19/1/33-1/3/33**HG**
2/7/33-4/7/33**LO**
14/8/33-31/8/33**HS**
5/2/34-28/2/34**HS**
5/10/34-29/10/34**GH**
29/4/35-27/5/35**HS**
12/12/35-30/12/35**LO**
5/5/36-25/5/36**LS**
1/9/36-29/9/36**HG**
9/10/36-17/10/36**LO**
7/6/37-28/6/37**LS**
12/4/38-16/5/38**HG**
13/1/39-30/1/39**LS**
8/1/40-23/1/40**HS**
15/6/40-5/7/40**HG**
3/3/41-21/3/41**LS**
21/9/42-10/10/42**HS**
16/4/43-1/5/43**LS**
18/11/43-29/1/44**HG**
15/3/45-14/4/45**LS**
14/6/45-21/7/45**LO**
12/6/46-22/7/46**HS**
11/8/47-26/9/47**HG**
6/9/48-28/9/48**LS**
12/12/48-8/2/49**HC**
7/10/49-29/10/49**LI**
9/2/50-8/3/50**LC**
29/4/50-23/5/50**LG**
27/11/50-5/1/51**HG**
24/11/51-22/12/51**HI**
11/6/52-2/7/52**LI**
12/6/53-6/7/53**HG**
27/8/54-22/9/54**LI**
20/5/55-15/6/55**HG**
14/4/56-24/5/56**HG**
11/12/56-11/1/57**HI**
9/2/58-22/3/58**HG**
21/1/59-6/3/59**LI**
7/1/60-12/2/60**HI**
27/2/61-25/4/61**HI**

MILEAGES

1927	4,119
1928	40,257
1929	56,315
1930	55,426
1931	59,887
1932	67,247
1933	68,068
1934	53,790
1935	63,258
1936	59,025
1937	70,190
1938	87,419
1939	79,263
1940	70,604
1941	64,629
1942	64,759
1943	69,004
1944	62,374
1945	57,708
1946	66,227
1947	54,219
1948	64,680
1949	48,639
1950	53,749
1951	66,248
1952	73,685
1953	72,629
1954	67,765
1955	67,867
1956	63,690
1957	71,608

Mileage at 31/12/50 1,440,856
Mileage at 31/12/57 1,924,348
Withdrawn week ending 8/12/62
Scrapped Crewe Works 10/63

46146 THE RIFLE BRIGADE

Built North British, cost £7,744
LM 'date built' 6/11/27
Taper boiler fitted 8/10/43
First named JENNY LIND (by 4/28), renamed 5/36
Original smoke deflectors 21/12/31
BR smoke deflectors fitted period ending 8/10/49
Renumbered 6146 to 46146 week ending 12/6/48

SHEDS

Crewe North 5/11/27
Rugby 5/11/27
Edge Hill 17/12/27
Bangor 22/10/30
Crewe North 12/10/35
Holyhead (loan) 5/3/38
Crewe North 14/5/38
Camden 27/4/40
Preston (loan) 26/10/40
Camden 16/11/40
Bushbury 18/1/41
Preston 10/5/41
Crewe North 28/2/42
Leeds (loan) 13/11/43
Crewe North 4/12/43
Holyhead 5/8/44
Holyhead 7/4/45
Crewe North 5/5/45
Leeds 2/3/46
Crewe North 27/4/46
Edge Hill 10/4/47
Crewe North 7/6/47
Holyhead 10/4/48
Crewe North 15/5/48
Holyhead (loan) 25/12/48
Crewe North 1/1/49
Holyhead (loan) 28/5/49
Crewe North 9/7/49
Carlisle Upperby 7/7/51
Camden 12/4/52
Carlisle Upperby 23/1/54
Camden 6/3/54
Willesden 21/1/61

BOILERS

Fitted	No.	From
18/2/29	-	6105
24/10/29	-	6102
6/3/31	-	6114
12/7/33	-	6129
10/1/35	-	6169
12/2/37	-	6156
20/2/39	7230	6148
30/1/42	8122	6156
Taper 102A		
8/10/43	11730	new
9/9/47	12028	6116
5/10/49	12209	6121
1/11/52	11727	-
16/8/55	12542	-
16/8/58	12671	-

TENDERS

No.	Fitted
3942	6/11/27
3943	26/12/31
9018	5/5/36

MILEAGES

1927	7,575
1928	52,840
1929	46,199
1930	49,918
1931	45,746
1932	64,643
1933	66,748
1934	76,589
1935	54,277
1936	90,900
1937	77,207
1938	69,185
1939	67,406
1940	63,320
1941	30,540
1942	56,206
1943	58,066
1944	60,530
1945	53,447
1946	55,600
1947	51,320
1948	71,160
1949	51,002
1950	59,612
1951	51,297
1952	57,379
1953	67,703
1954	73,620
1955	51,239
1956	67,782
1957	55,320
1958	47,118
1959	57,732
1960	57,816

Mileage at 31/12/50 1,400,036
Mileage at 31/12/60 1,987,042
Withdrawn week ending 1/12/62
Scrapped Crewe Works 3/63

REPAIRS

12/2/29-9/3/29**HG**
16/3/29-23/3/29**LO**
15/10/29-15/11/29**HG**
4/3/31-27/3/31**HG**
25/11/31-21/12/31**H**
25/5/32-13/6/32**LS**
6/12/32-5/1/33**HS**
27/6/33-3/8/33**HG**
30/12/33-19/1/34**HS**
22/10/34-5/11/34**LO**
31/12/34-30/1/35**HS**
3/12/35-20/12/35**LS**
20/4/36-5/5/36**LO**
11/9/36-2/10/36**LS**
25/1/37-25/2/37**HG**
26/7/37-6/8/37**LO**
31/12/37-14/1/38**LS**
15/8/38-7/9/38**LS**
16/1/39-20/2/39**HG**
26/2/40-9/3/40**HS**
30/9/40-19/10/40**LS**
21/2/41-12/3/41**LO**
9/1/42-30/1/42**HG**
3/8/42-19/8/42**LO**
13/7/43-8/10/43**HG**
30/1/45-14/2/45**LS**
19/9/45-3/11/45**HS**
10/10/46-13/11/46**LS**
5/7/47-9/9/47**HG**
29/4/48-7/6/48**LO**
17/1/49-15/2/49**LI**
25/8/49-5/10/49**HG**
27/10/50-15/11/50**LI**
24/8/51-15/9/51**LC**
1/10/52-1/11/52**HG**
11/3/53-26/3/53**LC**
15/10/53-11/11/53**HI**
4/8/54-21/8/54**HI**
24/6/55-16/8/55**HG**
4/4/56-4/5/56**LC(EO)**
28/4/57-22/5/57**LI**
11/6/58-16/8/58**HG**
30/9/59-11/11/59**LI**
24/9/60-4/11/60**LI**
27/4/61-5/6/61**LC(EO)**

46147 THE NORTHAMPTONSHIRE REGIMENT

Built North British, cost £7,744
LM 'date built' 6/11/27
Taper boiler fitted 26/9/46
First named COURIER (by 4/28), renamed 7/35
Original smoke deflectors 18/1/32
BR smoke deflectors fitted period ending 9/2/51
Renumbered 6147 to 46147 week ending 15/1/49

SHEDS

Crewe North 5/11/27
Edge Hill 17/12/27
Crewe North 3/7/29
Edge Hill 20/10/29
Crewe North 22/10/30
Holyhead 5/1/35
Crewe North -
Carlisle (loan) 29/5/37
Camden 3/7/37
Edge Hill 29/4/39
Bushbury 21/10/39
Camden 13/12/41
Crewe North 29/9/45
Carlisle Upperby (loan) 2/8/47
Crewe North 30/8/47
Edge Hill 12/6/48
Carlisle (Upperby) 12/3/49
Camden 12/4/52
Holyhead 24/9/55
Edge Hill 9/6/56
Longsight 23/6/56*
Holyhead 23/6/56*
Longsight 1/9/56
Holyhead 15/9/56
Edge Hill 22/6/57*
Holyhead 22/6/57*
followed by
Holyhead 21/9/57
Carlisle Upperby 19/10/57
Holyhead 23/11/57
Edge Hill 14/6/58
Crewe North 12/9/59
Willesden 3/3/62
*same dates – reason unknown

BOILERS

Fitted	No.	From
29/1/29	-	6126
14/2/30	-	6142
9/12/30	-	6107
11/5/32	-	6156
29/3/34	-	6116
1/2/35	-	6130
20/1/36	7217	6119
21/9/37	9880	new
15/4/39	7213	6156
3/7/40	7222	6111
16/4/43	8125	6118
27/10/44	7214	6128
Taper 102A		
26/9/46	12528	new
9/2/51	12535	5530
21/5/53	12538	-
23/3/55	11729	-
18/5/57	12091	-

MILEAGES

1927	9,764
1928	55,087
1929	44,331
1930	49,233
1931	59,448
1932	50,835
1933	76,765
1934	70,900
1935	78,854
1936	77,396
1937	71,774
1938	73,161
1939	54,809
1940	53,458
1941	45,759
1942	79,029
1943	73,013
1944	70,381
1945	74,067
1946	46,799
1947	59,979
1948	58,829
1949	50,001
1950	49,537
1951	59,054
1952	62,305
1953	50,190
1954	71,079
1955	55,431
1956	59,167
1957	55,229
1958	53,763
1959	51,646
1960	4,057

Mileage at 31/12/50 1,433,209
Mileage at 1960 1,955,130
Withdrawn week ending 1/12/62
Scrapped Crewe Works 3/63

REPAIRS

14/1/29-8/3/29**HG**
4/6/29-17/6/29**LO**
17/1/30-1/3/30**HG**
5/12/30-7/1/31**HG**
14/10/31-6/11/31**HS**
18/12/31-18/1/32**LO**
6/2/32-29/2/32**LO**
11/5/32-2/6/32**HG**
11/11/32-28/11/32**LS**
8/4/33-3/5/33**HS**
25/9/33-9/10/33**LS**
27/2/34-20/4/34**HG**
25/1/35-12/2/35**HS**
8/7/35-25/7/35**LS**
3/1/36-4/2/36**HG**
23/11/36-12/12/36**HS**
28/4/37-13/5/37**LO**
15/9/37-7/10/37**HG**
13/7/38-29/7/38**LS**
18/8/38-6/9/38**LO**
17/3/39-15/4/39**HG**
15/6/40-3/7/40**HS**
10/7/41-6/8/41**HS**
23/10/41-7/11/41**LO**
19/5/42-6/6/42**LS**
26/3/43-16/4/43**HG**
16/11/43-1/12/43**LS**
11/10/44-27/10/44**HG**
24/9/45-19/10/45**HS**
19/6/46-26/9/46**HG**
11/2/48-3/3/48**LS**
8/3/48-23/3/48**LO**
19/12/48-13/1/49**LC**
7/9/49-13/10/49**HI**
19/12/50-9/2/51**HG**
26/5/51-15/6/51**LC**
12/5/52-10/6/52**LI**
21/4/53-21/5/53**HG**
26/5/53-26/6/53**HC**
17/10/53-10/11/53**LC(EO)**
7/12/53-12/1/54**LC(EO)**
9/6/54-3/7/54**HI**
1/2/55-23/3/55**HG**
23/4/56-26/5/56**HI**
29/3/57-18/5/57**HG**
10/1/58-31/1/58**LC(EO)**
26/9/58-24/10/58**LI**
28/7/59-27/8/59**LI**
6/6/61-3/7/61**LI**

TENDERS

No.	Fitted
3943	6/11/27
3916	26/12/31
9011	4/2/36

46148 THE MANCHESTER REGIMENT

Built North British, cost £7,744
LM 'date built' 4/12/27
Taper boiler fitted 9/7/54
First named VELOCIPEDE (by 4/28), renamed 1935
Original smoke deflectors 18/1/32
BR smoke deflectors fitted period ending 17/7/54
Renumbered 6148 to 46148 week ending 26/6/48

BOILERS

Fitted	No.	From
28/2/29	-	6125
8/1/30	-	6136
17/8/31	-	6133
22/5/33	-	6152
7/5/35	-	6135
26/4/37	-	6110
14/1/39	8121	6121
2/4/41	5821	6136
31/5/44	5820	6132
27/9/46	7238	6168
28/10/47	11038	6154
4/11/50	11032	6110
Taper 102A		
9/7/54	14002	-
1/2/58	13591	-
1/10/60	11729	-

TENDERS

No.	Fitted
3944	4/11/27
3942	26/12/31
9033	30/3/36
9049	17/10/36
9352	16/10/39
9034	14/12/45
9348	20/12/57
9034	1/2/58

SHEDS

Crewe North 12/11/27
Edge Hill 17/12/27
Crewe North 3/7/29
Edge Hill 20/10/29
Crewe North 22/10/30
Longsight 5/10/35
Camden 2/7/38
Longsight 29/4/39
Bushbury 21/10/39
Camden 13/12/41
Edge Hill (loan) 4/4/42
Camden 16/5/42
Crewe North 27/11/48
Camden 10/6/50
Crewe North 30/9/50
Bushbury 14/10/50
Crewe North 7/7/51
Camden 22/6/57
Crewe North 21/9/57
Camden 21/9/57
Carlisle Upperby (loan) 19/10/57
Carlisle Upperby 9/11/57
Longsight 10/1/59
Kentish Town 14/2/59
Carlisle Upperby 11/4/59
Willesden 3/3/62
Crewe North 21/4/62
Llandudno Junction 22/9/62
Holyhead 7/12/63

REPAIRS

23/2/29-23/3/29**HG**
30/12/30-25/1/30**HG**
6/2/31-19/2/31**LS**
15/9/31-13/10/31**HO**
12/8/31-9/9/31**HG**
2/5/32-23/5/32**LS**
16/11/32-2/12/32**LS**
10/5/33-12/6/33**HG**
1/11/33-20/11/33**LS**
24/4/34-14/5/34**LS**
7/11/34-28/11/34**LS**
9/9/35-23/9/35**LO**
22/4/35-24/5/35**HG**
12/3/36-30/3/36**HS**
3/10/36-17/10/36**LS**
15/4/37-8/5/37**HG**
28/7/37-12/8/37**LO**
18/2/38-3/3/38**LS**
10/11/38-14/1/39**HG**
11/8/39-25/8/39**LS**
12/7/40-26/7/40**LS**
7/10/40-19/10/40**LO**
10/3/41-2/4/41**HG**
6/1/42-24/1/42**LS**
23/7/42-8/8/42**HO**
27/10/42-11/11/42**LO**
18/1/43-16/2/43**LS**
21/10/43-5/11/43**LS**
13/5/44-31/5/44**HG**
20/4/45-19/5/45**HS**
10/12/45-12/1/46**LS**
2/9/46-27/9/46**HG**
24/9/47-28/10/47**HS**
28/5/48-25/6/48**LO**
22/10/48-27/10/48**TRO**
1/12/48-21/12/48**LS**
7/12/49-10/1/50**HI**
22/8/50-4/11/50**HG**
10/7/51-6/8/51**LI**
20/2/52-20/3/52**LC**
5/6/52-26/7/52**LC**
30/10/52-4/12/52**LI**
19/2/54-9/7/54**HG**
22/5/56-19/6/56**HI**
25/6/56-3/7/56**NC(Rect)(EO)**
21/12/57-1/2/58**HG**
2/4/59-8/5/59**HI**
10/8/60-1/10/60**HG**

MILEAGES

1927	6,502
1928	55,657
1929	55,451
1930	42,227
1931	50,978
1932	65,981
1933	75,067
1934	65,417
1935	79,291
1936	68,050
1937	76,184
1938	72,185
1939	77,818
1940	46,472
1941	57,125
1942	64,841
1943	72,293
1944	70,365
1945	72,006
1946	65,853
1947	56,139
1948	63,363
1949	46,831
1950	55,415
1951	45,016
1952	33,711
1953	48,583
1954	33,735
1955	61,913
1956	62,981
1957	55,966
1958	67,630
1959	53,944
1960	5,025
1961	62,001*
1962	36,173
1963	21,062

probably includes mileage from 1960
Mileage at 31/12/50 1,461,511
Mileage at 31/12/63 2,076,369
Withdrawn week ending 14/11/64
Scrapped Bird Group, Morriston, 1/65

46148 THE MANCHESTER REGIMENT at Camden shed on 21 August 1955, with Driver's oil bottle on the deck. Two other Scots stand beyond – 46167 and another, unidentified. Photograph R.C. Riley.

46149 THE MIDDLESEX REGIMENT

Built North British, cost £7,744
LM 'date built' 4/12/27
Taper boiler fitted 17/4/45
First named LADY OF THE LAKE (by 4/28), renamed 5/36
Original smoke deflectors 7/1/32
BR smoke deflectors fitted period ending 3/12/49
Renumbered 6149 to 46149 week ending 24/4/48

MILEAGES

1927	3,834	1946	72,430
1928	49,773	1947	61,017
1929	51,722	1948	55,193
1930	55,955	1949	65,731
1931	52,547	1950	70,177
1932	67,878	1951	62,588
1933	67,228	1952	63,460
1934	59,555	1953	65,256
1935	75,877	1954	57,488
1936	74,787	1955	51,382
1937	81,051	1956	62,712
1938	75,079	1957	42,783
1939	75,226	1958	56,522
1940	51,883	1959	63,213
1941	66,353	1960	45,259
1942	50,224	**Mileage at 31/12/50 1,469,729**	
1943	70,937	**Mileage at 31/12/60 2,040,390**	
1944	65,907	**Withdrawn week ending 31/8/63**	
1945	49,365	**Scrapped Crewe Works 11/63**	

TENDERS

No.	Fitted
3945	4/12/27
3912	26/12/31
9008	10/6/36

REPAIRS

17/4/28-8/6/28**LS**	9/3/42-31/3/42**LO**
10/4/29-14/5/29**HG**	18/9/42-15/10/42**HG**
??/5/30-7/6/30**HG**	19/4/43-8/5/43**LS**
5/3/31-23/3/31**LS**	26/1/44-10/2/44**LS**
31/8/31-24/9/31**HG**	22/9/44-10/10/44**LO**
7/3/32-6/4/32**LS**	24/1/45-17/4/45**HG**
15/9/32-3/10/32**LS**	4/9/45-18/10/45**LO**
13/3/33-19/4/33**HG**	26/8/46-27/9/46**HS**
1/6/33-15/6/33**LO**	9/10/47-31/10/47**LS**
9/10/33-23/10/33**LS**	30/3/48-21/4/48**LO**
16/1/34-14/2/34**LO**	5/11/48-9/12/48**HG**
1/5/34-18/6/34**HS**	29/10/49-30/11/49**HG**
10/11/34-3/12/34**LS**	30/10/50-22/11/50**LI**
17/5/35-15/6/35**HG**	18/9/51-15/11/51**HG**
16/11/35-10/12/35**LS**	30/8/52-6/10/52**LI**
21/5/36-10/6/36**LS**	5/9/53-9/10/53**HI**
10/11/36-1/12/36**HG**	22/7/54-3/9/54**HG**
10/4/37-3/5/37**LO**	13/4/55-12/5/55**LC**
20/9/37-4/10/37**LS**	17/9/55-14/10/55**LI**
2/3/38-28/3/38**HG**	23/7/56-1/9/56**HG**
19/11/38-5/12/38**LS**	21/6/57-23/8/57**LI**
18/5/39-15/6/39**LO**	10/6/58-5/7/58**LI**
15/3/40-9/4/40**HG**	2/3/59-8/4/59**HG**
3/12/40-19/12/40**LO**	28/4/60-14/6/60**LI**
7/7/41-2/8/41**LS**	4/8/60-21/9/60**LC(EO)**
2/1/42-17/1/42**LO**	

BOILERS

Fitted	No.	From
22/5/30	-	6138
3/9/31	-	6116
20/3/33	-	6101
10/6/34	-	6166
31/5/35	-	6146
16/11/36	-	6163
9/3/38	10183	new
9/4/40	8130	6135
15/10/42	7591	6152
Taper 102A		
17/4/45	12090	new
9/12/48	12089	6160
30/11/49	12032	6119
15/11/51	12206	-
3/9/54	10753	-
1/9/56	12534	-
8/4/59	12529	-

SHEDS

Crewe North 19/11/27
Edge Hill 17/12/27
Crewe North 3/7/29
Edge Hill 20/10/29
Crewe North 22/10/30
Leeds (loan) 25/8/45
Crewe North 8/9/45
Camden 28/9/45
Longsight 12/10/46
Holyhead (loan) 18/12/48
Longsight 15/1/49
Edge Hill 24/1/53
Longsight 23/6/56
Holyhead 15/9/56
Crewe North 30/4/60
Longsight 24/6/61

6149 curiously unadorned, at Crewe about 1932, before getting coal rails on the tender. Its LADY OF THE LAKE plate has gone, though the little plaque with a diagram and historical note of the original engine of that name is still there. The perfect name for a minor mystery! Photograph B.P. Hoper Collection.

46150 THE LIFE GUARDSMAN

Built LMS Derby, cost £6,467
LM 'date built' 2/6/30
Named 10/31
Taper boiler fitted 19/12/45
Original smoke deflectors 15/1/32
BR smoke deflectors fitted period ending 24/2/51
Renumbered 6150 to 46150 week ending 22/1/49

BOILERS

Fitted	No.	From
24/2/32	-	6129
16/2/34	-	6144
12/11/35	-	6126
15/9/37	9879	new
26/6/39	5823	6112
12/4/41	8136	6166
17/12/43	7248	6117
Taper 102A		
19/12/45	12203	new
19/1/49	12198	6126
3/2/51	11732	6117
28/3/53	11726	-
8/10/55	11733	-
1/3/58	12199	-
24/1/62	12206	-

MILEAGES

1930	39,044
1931	57,401
1932	70,796
1933	63,825
1934	78,952
1935	79,236
1936	82,242
1937	74,800
1938	84,920
1939	63,492
1940	68,735
1941	71,057
1942	74,038
1943	68,363
1944	73,696
1945	64,902
1946	80,991
1947	60,524
1948	66,010
1949	64,622
1950	63,680
1951	59,652
1952	71,112
1953	62,111
1954	58,388
1955	47,203
1956	58,037
1957	54,591
1958	47,371
1959	59,549
1960	54,556

Mileage at 31/12/50 1,451,326
Mileage at 31/12/60 2,023,896
Withdrawn week ending 23/11/63
Scrapped Crewe Works 12/63

REPAIRS

6/1/31-9/2/31**LO**	29/4/46-11/5/46**LO**
14/5/31-27/5/31**LS**	21/10/46-15/11/46**LS**
22/2/32-24/3/32**HG**	23/12/46-24/1/47**HO**
18/1/33-10/2/33**LS**	3/11/47-2/12/47**LS**
28/8/33-11/9/33**HS**	30/11/48-19/1/49**HG**
6/2/34-12/3/34**HG**	20/12/49-12/1/50**HI**
31/12/34-15/1/35**HS**	5/6/50-3/7/50**LC**
3/6/35-18/6/35**LS**	2/1/51-3/2/51**HG**
8/11/35-28/11/35**HG**	26/5/51-21/6/51**LC**
- 11/5/36**L**	12/2/52-13/3/52**HI**
17/7/36-20/7/36**LO**	7/2/53-28/3/53**HG**
26/9/36-21/10/36**LS**	13/5/54-8/6/54**HI**
15/3/37-8/4/37**LO**	21/9/54-30/10/54**LC(EO)**
6/9/37-29/9/37**HG**	21/8/55-8/10/55**HG**
24/2/38-10/3/38**LO**	5/11/55-2/12/55**LC(EO)**
23/7/38-18/8/38**LS**	15/10/56-24/11/56**HI**
30/5/39-26/6/39**HG**	26/4/57-25/5/57**LC(EO)**
25/6/40-10/7/40**LS**	30/1/58-1/3/58**HG**
19/3/41-12/4/41**HG**	17/10/58-15/11/58**LC(EO)**
31/10/41-15/11/41**LS**	20/11/58-2/12/58**NC(Rect)(EO)**
20/5/42-6/6/42**HS**	16/4/59-14/5/59**LI**
22/9/42-8/10/42**LO**	17/5/59-26/5/59**NC(Rect)(EO)**
15/3/43-30/3/43**HS**	30/1/60-11/3/60**LI**
25/11/43-17/12/43**HG**	1/5/61-25/5/61**LI**
12/10/44-28/10/44**LS**	3/7/61-13/7/61**LC(EO)**
27/10/45-19/12/45**HG**	28/7/61-22/8/61**NC(Rect)(EO)**

SHEDS

Crewe North -
Camden 27/4/40
Bushbury (loan) 27/7/40
Camden 17/8/40
Bushbury (loan) 8/3/41
Longsight 5/4/47
Holyhead (loan) 21/7/51
Holyhead 29/9/51
Carlisle 7/8/54
Crewe North 29/1/55
Edge Hill 28/4/56
Holyhead 11/8/56
Crewe North 1/9/56
Carlisle Upperby 22/9/56
Crewe North 27/10/56
Camden 22/6/57
Crewe North 21/9/57
Llandudno Jct 7/11/59
Holyhead 18/6/60
Crewe North 9/3/63
Holyhead 20/4/63
Willesden 22/6/63

TENDERS

No.	Fitted
4235	2/6/30
9051	11/5/36

We've had a Scot on the Southern, at Eastleigh, so here is one on the Western. Only just, however; this is 46150 THE LIFE GUARDSMAN in 1961, on the ash road at Bristol Barrow Road, a Midland Railway shed incorporated into the Western Region. 46150 has just taken coal (note the screen to stop lumps falling on the main line, which was unusually close at this shed) and is now dropping ash. It's also a long way from home – Holyhead. Photograph B.P. Hoper Collection.

46151 THE ROYAL HORSE GUARDSMAN

Built LMS Derby, cost £6,467
LM 'date built' 11/6/30
Named 10/31
Taper boiler fitted 16/4/53
Original smoke deflectors 17/12/31
BR smoke deflectors fitted period ending 18/4/53
Renumbered 6151 to 46151 week ending 23/10/48

TENDERS

No.	Fitted
4236	11/6/30
9238	26/12/31
9133	7/8/36
9040	18/6/45

SHEDS

Crewe North -
Carlisle Upperby 24/3/45
Crewe North 2/2/46
Camden 4/5/46
Bushbury 28/10/50
Edge Hill 7/7/51
Crewe North 15/9/51
Holyhead 2/7/55
Camden 9/6/56
Crewe North 15/9/56
Longsight 31/5/58
Crewe North 7/6/58
Longsight 18/7/59

MILEAGES

1930	40,057	1948	65,701
1931	68,701	1949	52,412
1932	48,182	1950	46,836
1933	66,331	1951	47,221
1934	78,469	1952	49,859
1935	82,813	1953	38,265
1936	71,015	1954	47,547
1937	83,049	1955	60,405
1938	79,711	1956	60,205
1939	59,951	1957	52,281
1940	55,867	1958	52,384
1941	63,028	1959	63,013
1942	60,085	1960	4,764
1943	61,733	**Mileage at 31/12/50 1,328,991**	
1944	61,834	**Mileage at 1960 1,804,935**	
1945	53,022	**Withdrawn week ending 29/12/62**	
1946	63,133	**Scrapped Crewe Works 8/63**	
1947	66,991		

REPAIRS

9/3/31-25/3/31**LS**	18/9/42-21/10/42**HG**
18/9/31-12/10/31**LS**	27/9/43-9/10/43**HS**
5/2/32-4/3/32**HG**	22/12/43-20/1/44**LO**
19/5/32-17/6/32**LO**	19/7/44-4/8/44**LO**
22/10/32-7/11/32**LS**	16/2/45-3/3/45**HG**
19/4/33-10/5/33**LS**	2/1/46-6/2/46**LS**
2/10/33-6/11/33**HG**	13/11/46-12/12/46**LS**
1/5/34-16/5/34**HS**	30/12/47-30/1/48**HG**
22/5/34-1/6/34**LO**	24/9/48-22/10/48**LO**
16/10/34-31/10/34**HS**	26/5/49-21/6/49**HI**
6/3/35-25/3/35**LS**	24/6/49-29/6/49**NC(Rect)**
4/6/35-20/6/35**LO**	22/9/49-7/10/49**LC**
27/8/35-12/9/35**LS**	6/5/50-30/6/50**HG**
14/2/36-3/3/36**HS**	7/9/50-13/10/50**LG**
16/7/36-7/8/36**HG**	28/6/51-5/7/51**LC**
25/11/36-9/12/36**LO**	22/8/51-21/9/51**LI**
12/4/37-27/4/37**LS**	20/4/52-17/5/52**LC**
9/9/37-23/9/37**HS**	13/1/53-16/4/53**HG**
2/3/38-16/3/38**LO**	3/9/54-2/10/54**HI**
15/8/38-20/9/38**HG**	13/5/55-8/6/55**LC(EO)**
15/2/39-1/3/39**LO**	1/3/56-28/3/56**HI**
16/8/39-11/9/39**HS**	26/8/57-5/10/57**HG**
6/3/40-2/4/40**HO**	29/5/58-27/6/58**LC**
19/7/40-2/8/40**LS**	6/5/59-2/6/59**HI**
3/9/41-23/9/41**LS**	8/6/59-19/6/59**NC(Rect)(EO)**
16/2/42-5/3/42**LO**	18/5/60-29/7/60**HG**

BOILERS

Fitted	No.	From			
9/2/32	-	6107	21/10/42	8127	6111
19/10/33	-	6100	3/3/45	5574	6166
23/10/34	-	6164	30/1/48	7238	6148
24/7/36	-	6150	30/6/50	10187	6165
20/9/38	7216	6167	*Taper 102A*		
11/9/39	9899	6142	16/4/53	13998	-
2/4/40	8133	6127	5/10/57	13241	-
			29/7/60	13895	-

46154 THE HUSSAR, in one of those glorious Carlisle Citadel moments, 8 June 1957, waiting on the middle road to take over an Up W545 – the Fireman is trimming the coal to render it safer on the journey ahead. 46154 was well into a ten year spell as a Camden engine and Carlisle must have been one of the few places where a London Scot could be found alongside one from Holbeck – in this case 46117 WELSH GUARDSMAN. Photograph J.L. Stevenson

46152 THE KING'S DRAGOON GUARDSMAN

Built LMS Derby, cost £6,467
LM 'date built' 19/6/30
Named 10/31
Taper boiler fitted 11/8/45
Original smoke deflectors – not listed
BR smoke deflectors fitted period ending 31/12/49
Renumbered 6152 to 46152 week ending 19/6/48

BOILERS

Fitted	No.	From
5/11/31	-	6145
13/7/33	-	6119
21/6/34	-	6114
24/6/35	-	6163
6/5/37	-	6128
6/4/38	7285	6101
15/6/39	8134	6155
1/11/41	7591	6124
6/6/42	8126	6121
Taper 102A		
11/8/45	12199	new
21/12/49	12207	6125
14/12/51	11734	-
25/9/54	12034	-
18/4/57	12089	-

SHEDS

Crewe North -
Longsight (loan) 19/2/38
Crewe North 12/3/38
Camden 29/9/45
Longsight 10/2/51
Edge Hill 24/1/53
Kentish Town 19/10/57
Trafford Park 5/7/58
Camden 19/7/58
Crewe North 20/9/58
Holyhead 16/7/60
Crewe North 13/8/60
Willesden 10/6/61
Llandudno Junction 23/9/61
Holyhead 10/3/62

REPAIRS

7/4/31-28/4/31LS
3/11/31-2/12/31HG
20/6/32-18/7/32LS
10/1/33-2/2/33LS
8/7/33-9/8/33HG
10/5/34-28/6/34HS
29/12/34-15/1/35LS
14/6/35-11/7/35HG
2/12/35-17/12/35LS
15/5/36-28/5/36LS
1/10/36-27/10/36LS
28/4/37-26/5/37HG
14/3/38-13/4/38HS
7/5/38-20/5/38LO
19/11/38-5/12/38LS
19/5/39-15/6/39HG
8/6/40-22/6/40LS
16/10/41-1/11/41HS
11/5/42-6/6/42HS
6/3/43-22/3/43LS
17/1/44-31/1/44LS
29/9/44-14/10/44LS
16/6/45-11/8/45HG
26/7/46-23/8/46LS
13/9/47-11/10/47LS
28/11/47-10/1/48LO
31/3/48-17/6/48HO
16/12/48-14/1/49LI
24/10/49-21/12/49HG
15/2/51-15/3/51LI
12/11/51-14/12/51HG
30/9/52-22/10/52HI
22/3/53-23/4/53LC(EO)
22/5/53-20/6/53LC(EO)
16/10/53-9/11/53HI
27/8/54-25/9/54HG
25/5/55-25/6/55LC
6/10/55-2/11/55LI
16/7/56-22/8/56LI
23/2/57-18/4/57HG
4/3/58-29/3/58LI
1/8/59-4/9/59HI
1/1/60-3/2/60LC(EO)
15/8/60-24/9/60HI

MILEAGES

1930	39,012
1931	59,177
1932	58,136
1933	68,523
1934	71,864
1935	72,775
1936	91,040
1937	82,898
1938	72,069
1939	69,066
1940	66,350
1941	64,223
1942	58,506
1943	61,494
1944	61,496
1945	71,220
1946	64,385
1947	51,391
1948	59,035
1949	62,780
1950	81,926
1951	55,652
1952	67,220
1953	57,101
1954	69,500
1955	63,781
1956	56,768
1957	56,580
1958	52,174
1959	41,715
1960	46,991

Mileage at 31/12/50 1,387,366
Mileage at 31/12/60 1,954,848
Withdrawn week ending 17/4/65
Scrapped Motherwell
Machinery & Scrap
Co. Ltd, 7/65

TENDERS

No.	Fitted
4239	19/6/30
3931	1933
9126	28/5/36

46154 THE HUSSAR, clean and tidy at Birmingham New Street, 22 August 1958. It had been one of the two Royal Scots in the 1948 Interchange, hauling a WD eight wheel tender, on the Southern. The emblem is interesting for its forward facing lion; this apparently transgressed some basic tenet of heraldry but BR was stuck with its expensive stock of transfers. They were thus used on the right-hand side from 1957 to about 1959, until the spares ran out. After that, the right-hand, left facing lion was used. Photograph Michael Mensing.

46153 THE ROYAL DRAGOON

Built LMS Derby, cost £6,467
LM 'date built' 30/6/30
Named 10/31
Taper boiler fitted 19/8/49
Original smoke deflectors 21/12/31
BR smoke deflectors fitted period ending 10/9/49
Renumbered 6153 to 46153 week ending 20/8/49

TENDERS

No.	Fitted
4238	30/6/30
4236	26/12/31
9340	21/5/36

SHEDS

Crewe North 21/5/36
Camden 21/6/47
Crewe North 22/5/48
Carlisle Upperby 12/6/48
Edge Hill 15/10/49
Crewe North 3/2/50
Edge Hill 24/3/51
Longsight 9/7/55
Bushbury 7/11/59
Trafford Park (loan) 7/1/61
Trafford Park 4/2/61
Annesley 29/2/62

BOILERS

Fitted	No.	From
26/11/31	-	6134
20/7/33	-	6148
27/11/34	-	6167
6/11/35	-	6155
18/6/37	-	6120
12/5/38	7233	6100
9/11/40	11035	new
24/8/43	10184	6161
24/12/46	8120	6140
Taper 102A		
19/8/49	13237	new
15/11/52	12537	-
26/2/55	12525	-
25/1/57	13590	-

MILEAGES

1930	35,729
1931	64,304
1932	64,944
1933	60,128
1934	75,468
1935	78,292
1936	89,695
1937	76,042
1938	79,589
1939	66,996
1940	60,684
1941	63,812
1942	55,287
1943	62,055
1944	58,215
1945	52,332
1946	56,522
1947	64,165
1948	53,830
1949	33,848
1950	66,345
1951	70,329
1952	59,734
1953	63,717
1954	61,315
1955	53,333
1956	64,380
1957	64,759
1958	57,157
1959	59,756
1960	48,448

Mileage at 31/12/50 1,319,282
Mileage at 31/12/60 1,922,210
Withdrawn week
ending 22/12/62
Scrapped Crewe Works 5/63

REPAIRS

8/5/31-22/5/31**LS**
23/11/31-21/12/31**HG**
4/10/32-24/10/32**LS**
12/7/33-27/9/33**HG**
28/2/34-16/3/34**LS**
17/11/34-13/12/34**HG**
7/5/35-27/5/35**LS**
29/10/35-15/11/35**HS**
10/12/35-16/12/35**LO**
24/4/36-21/5/36**HS**
14/9/36-13/10/36**LS**
22/2/37-9/3/37**LO**
6/6/37-3/7/37**HG**
25/4/38-20/5/38**HS**
16/9/38-6/10/38**LS**
30/5/39-17/6/39**LS**
19/4/40-3/5/40**HS**
19/10/40-9/11/40**HG**
7/2/41-21/2/42**LS**
16/11/42-10/12/42**HS**
30/6/43-24/8/43**HG**
3/2/44-3/3/44**LO**
14/11/44-1/12/44**LS**
26/11/45-2/1/46**LS**
26/11/46-24/12/46**HG**
17/7/47-22/8/47**LO**
21/2/48-16/3/48**LS**
11/5/49-19/8/49**HG**
31/8/49-12/9/49**NC(Rect)**
14/10/50-18/11/50**HI**
13/5/51-16/6/51**HC**
9/1/52-4/2/52**LI**
11/10/52-15/11/52**HG**
12/8/53-18/9/53**LI**
20/6/54-30/7/54**HI**
28/12/54-26/2/55**HG**
1/4/56-28/4/56**HI**
18/12/56-25/1/57**HG**
24/12/57-24/1/58**LI**
7/2/58-20/2/58**LC**
10/2/59-7/3/59**LI**
27/2/60-2/4/60**HI**
3/3/61-14/4/61**LI**

The days of the Birmingham expresses now far off, THE HUSSAR trundles under the wires with an Up container train, on Queensville Curve, Stafford, 6 October 1962. Photograph Michael Mensing.

46154 THE HUSSAR

Built LMS Derby, cost £6,467
LM 'date built' 7/7/30
Named 10/31
Taper boiler fitted 16/3/48
Original smoke deflectors 18/1/32
BR smoke deflectors fitted period ending 25/10/51
Renumbered 6154 to 46154 week ending 17/4/48

BOILERS

Fitted	No.	From
31/5/32	-	6136
18/6/34	-	6131
8/7/35	-	6148
16/3/36	-	6101
30/6/37	7225	6113
7/1/39	7259	6133
2/11/40	10186	6119
11/12/43	10183	6141
14/10/44	11038	6119
16/6/45	8137	6105
Taper 102A		
16/3/48	12665	new
8/11/49	12536	6161
25/10/51	12667	-
20/6/53	12530	-
18/2/56	12671	-
10/4/58	12200	-

SHEDS

Crewe North 22/10/30
'Northern Division' 17/12/30
Camden 13/11/32
Crewe North 30/12/33
Longsight (loan) 4/12/37
Crewe North 1/1/38
Holyhead 17/7/43
Crewe North 8/4/44
Camden 24/4/48
Kentish Town 9/5/59
Camden 13/6/59
Preston 12/9/59
Edge Hill 17/9/60
Willesden 8/7/61
Llandudno Junction 23/9/61
Holyhead 10/3/62
Willesden 23/6/62

TENDERS

No.	Fitted
4239	7/7/30
3896	9/5/33
4239	28/6/33
9019	30/3/36
-	7/6/48
9019	21/6/48

REPAIRS

28/12/31-18/1/32**LS**	14/5/45-16/6/45**HS**
28/5/32-21/6/32**HG**	26/11/45-2/1/46**LO**
17/7/33-4/8/33**LS**	5/11/46-21/11/46**LS**
10/1/34-14/2/34**HS**	9/12/47-16/3/48**HG**
1/6/34-28/6/34**HG**	13/4/48-16/4/48**NC**
23/11/34-13/12/34**LS**	21/6/48-26/6/48**NC**
15/3/35-1/4/35**HO**	27/8/48-15/10/48**HO**
21/6/35-15/7/35**HS**	3/8/49-31/8/49**HI**
3/3/36-30/3/36**HG**	10/10/49-8/11/49**HC**
27/4/36-11/5/36**LO**	4/10/50-9/11/50**HI**
31/8/36-30/9/36**LS**	21/9/51-25/10/51**HG**
18/1/37-2/2/37**HS**	29/4/52-28/5/52**LC(EO)**
14/6/37-22/7/37**HG**	21/10/52-26/11/52**LC**
28/4/38-25/5/38**LS**	22/5/53-20/6/53**HG**
17/6/38-18/7/38**LO**	18/10/54-20/11/54**HI**
29/11/38-7/1/39**HG**	9/1/56-18/2/56**HG**
5/11/39-25/11/39**LS**	12/6/56-26/7/56**LC(EO)**
14/10/40-2/11/40**HG**	29/3/57-27/4/57**HI**
6/7/41-31/7/41**HS**	4/3/58-10/4/58**HG**
18/3/42-3/4/42**LS**	24/2/59-2/4/59**LI**
17/12/42-8/1/43**HS**	3/4/59-9/4/59**NC(EO)**
13/3/43-9/4/43**LO**	17/4/59-28/4/59**NC(Rect)(EO)**
3/11/43-4/12/43**HG**	28/5/60-1/7/60**LI**
30/9/44-14/10/44**HS**	29/11/60-14/12/60**LC(EO)**
	10/8/61-22/9/61**LI**

MILEAGES

1930	34,684	1948	52,552
1931	61,004	1949	70,322
1932	57,821	1950	70,891
1933	71,392	1951	55,959
1934	70,348	1952	65,109
1935	73,225	1953	73,086
1936	69,790	1954	65,059
1937	79,371	1955	64,964
1938	70,395	1956	57,125
1939	77,590	1957	60,709
1940	60,772	1958	61,941
1941	64,626	1959	58,867
1942	52,641	1960	48,347
1943	58,192	**Mileage at 31/12/50 1,317,426**	
1944	63,763	**Mileage at 31/12/60 1,928,589**	
1945	55,598	**Withdrawn week ending 1/12/62**	
1946	53,148	**Scrapped Crewe Works 3/63**	
1947	49,281		

46155 THE LANCER, with *left* facing lion, outside Camden shed on 31 March 1963. Presumably the engine is ready to back down to Euston; there is some steam from the top and the tender is full, but as yet there is no tail lamp at the front. Photograph Peter Groom.

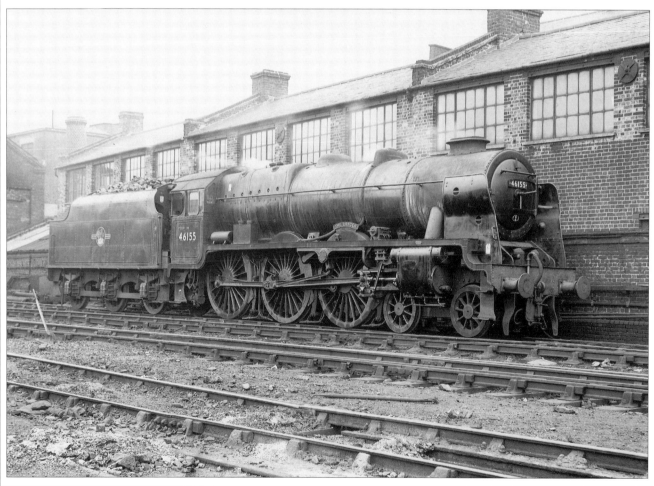

46155 THE LANCER

Built LMS Derby, cost £6,467
LM 'date built' 14/7/30
Named 10/31
Taper boiler fitted 18/8/50
Original smoke deflectors 16/12/31
BR smoke deflectors fitted period ending 28/1/50
Renumbered 6155 to 46155 week ending 3/7/48

BOILERS

Fitted	No.	From
2/6/32	-	6100
30/4/34	-	6155
2/8/35	-	6127
11/1/37	-	6124
9/9/38	7257	6168
20/6/40	7244	6165
2/2/43	8128	6108
28/11/45	11039	6143
14/5/47	10184	6153
Taper 102A		
18/8/50	12530	6118
2/4/53	12669	-
25/5/55	13591	-
23/11/57	12661	-

MILEAGES

1930	30,926
1931	63,253
1932	83,091
1933	77,504
1934	70,506
1935	68,040
1936	74,620
1937	78,652
1938	74,968
1939	82,719
1940	67,863
1941	73,591
1942	76,141
1943	73,791
1944	60,756
1945	65,131
1946	58,085
1947	55,526
1948	59,986
1949	50,038
1950	30,921
1951	60,326
1952	52,020
1953	54,607
1954	49,484
1955	60,210
1956	53,522
1957	51,503
1958	56,952
1959	56,926
1960	41,801

Mileage at 31/12/50 1,376,108
Mileage at 31/12/60 1,913,459
Withdrawn week ending 12/12/64
Scrapped West of Scotland
Shipbreaking Co., Troon, 2/65

TENDERS

No.	Fitted
4240	14/7/30
9339	13/5/36

SHEDS

Carlisle 19/7/30
Holyhead 19/5/34
Bangor 11/5/35
Camden 15/4/36
Willesden 29/5/37
Camden 8/4/39
Crewe North 12/10/46
Willesden (loan) 12/7/47
Crewe North 20/9/47
Holyhead 7/7/67
Crewe North (loan) 18/8/51
Crewe North 15/9/51
Camden 5/7/52
Crewe North 20/9/52
Carlisle Upperby 16/2/57
Crewe North 23/2/57
Edge Hill 14/6/58
Crewe North 12/9/59
Camden 24/12/60
Crewe North 31/12/60
Llandudno Junction 15/9/62
Crewe North 22/6/63
Holyhead 24/8/63

REPAIRS

3/12/31-16/12/31**LS**	3/2/45-9/3/45**LO**
31/5/32-30/6/52**HG**	31/10/45-28/11/45**HG**
27/3/33-15/4/33**HS**	28/7/46-16/8/46**LO**
24/10/33-1/12/33**LS**	4/2/47-12/3/47**HS**
16/2/34-30/4/34**HG**	12/4/47-14/5/47**HO**
28/2/35-19/3/35**LS**	3/6/48-2/7/48**LS**
25/7/35-8/8/35**HS**	31/3/49-21/4/49**HI**
3/9/35-13/9/35**LO**	29/4/50-18/8/50**HG**
28/1/36-12/2/36**LS**	12/9/50-28/9/50**LC**
18/4/36-13/5/36**LO**	20/10/50-9/11/50**NC**
1/1/37-28/1/37**HG**	11/4/52-13/5/52**LI**
30/9/37-19/10/37**HS**	26/2/53-2/4/53**HG**
28/2/38-22/3/38**LO**	24/3/54-21/4/54**HI**
3/8/38-9/9/38**HG**	13/4/55-25/5/55**HG**
1/12/38-23/12/38**LO**	10/8/56-20/9/56**LI**
22/5/39-7/6/39**LS**	10/10/57-23/11/57**HG**
3/6/40-20/6/40**HG**	3/9/58-2/10/58**HI**
16/8/40-27/8/40**LO**	29/5/59-2/7/59**LC(EO)**
24/2/41-11/3/41**LS**	31/12/59-6/2/60**LI**
13/10/41-1/11/41**LS**	16/3/60-20/4/60**LC(EO)**
18/4/42-8/5/42**HS**	26/9/60-29/10/60**LC(EO)**
26/12/42-2/2/43**HG**	8/6/61-8/8/61**LI**
15/9/43-30/9/43**LS**	14/8/61-25/8/61**NC(Rect)(EO)**
11/9/44-27/9/44**LS**	

46156 THE SOUTH WALES BORDERER

Built Derby, cost £6,467
LM 'date built' 27/10/30
Named 10/31
Taper boiler fitted 28/5/54
Original smoke deflectors 30/1/32
BR smoke deflectors fitted period ending 19/6/54
Renumbered 6156 to 46156 week ending 5/2/49

TENDERS

No.	Fitted
4241	21/7/30
9053	9/9/36
9042	9/11/38
9039	26/7/52
9129	10/4/53
9049	20/3/59

REPAIRS

17/9/31-30/9/31**LS**	14/8/45-12/9/45**HG**
11/4/32-9/5/32**HG**	30/11/45-9/1/46**LO**
26/4/33-11/5/33**LS**	22/8/46-11/9/46**LS**
18/8/34-21/9/34**HG**	7/4/47-29/4/47**LO**
13/9/35-11/10/35**LS**	29/12/47-26/1/48**HS**
19/8/36-9/9/36**HO**	17/12/48-1/2/49**HG**
14/10/36-23/11/36**HG**	23/2/49-15/3/49**LC**
12/8/37-30/8/37**LS**	11/8/49-3/9/49**LC**
22/1/38-4/2/38**HS**	17/2/50-8/3/50**LI**
11/7/38-29/7/38**LS**	29/3/50-24/4/50**NC(Rect)**
17/9/38-4/10/38**LO**	29/1/51-22/2/51**LC**
27/1/39-15/3/39**HG**	2/7/51-22/8/51**HG**
10/7/39-9/8/39**HS**	11/9/51-4/10/51**LC(EO)**
29/3/40-13/4/40**HS**	15/11/52-24/12/52**HI**
19/11/40-6/12/40**LS**	17/3/53-10/4/53**NC(EO)**
18/4/41-4/6/41**HG**	9/2/54-28/5/54**HG**
6/10/41-25/10/41**LO**	26/3/56-2/5/56**LI**
7/2/42-21/2/42**LS**	30/6/56-20/7/56**LC(EO)**
19/10/42-10/11/42**HS**	16/6/57-6/7/57**HI**
12/6/43-1/7/43**HG**	27/7/58-26/8/58**HG**
28/7/44-12/8/44**LS**	3/10/59-14/4/59**HI**
12/3/45-29/3/45**LO**	28/1/61-4/3/61**HI**
	1/4/61-18/4/61**NC**

MILEAGES

1930	33,618	1948	52,490
1931	87,358	1949	55,966
1932	68,496	1950	55,466
1933	63,828	1951	47,497
1934	71,616	1952	41,220
1935	57,077	1953	44,041
1936	26,424	1954	42,816
1937	75,187	1955	61,830
1938	65,998	1956	50,842
1939	61,056	1957	53,684
1940	54,478	1958	56,254
1941	55,181	1959	65,280
1942	59,683	1960	68,829
1943	63,174	**Mileage at 31/12/50 1,234,088**	
1944	60,128	**Mileage at 31/12/60 1,177,381**	
1945	50,379	**Withdrawn week ending 10/10/64**	
1946	62,508	**Scrapped A. Draper, Hull, 2/65**	
1947	53,977		

SHEDS

Carlisle 26/7/30
Camden 15/8/36
Crewe North 24/10/36
Longsight 30/1/37
Holyhead 26/2/38
Camden (loan)13/8/38
Holyhead 27/8/38
Longsight 24/9/38
Crewe North (loan) 26/11/38
Longsight 31/12/38
Crewe North 8/4/39
Holyhead 29/4/39
Crewe North 21/10/39
Holyhead 31/1/42
Crewe North 28/2/42
Holyhead (loan) 14/3/42
Crewe North 16/5/42
Edge Hill 30/11/46
Crewe North 24/1/53
Carlisle Upperby 25/8/56
Crewe North 1/9/56
Edge Hill 14/6/58
Llandudno Junction 7/11/59
Longsight 27/2/60
Llandudno Junction 26/3/60
Holyhead 18/6/60
Camden 9/3/63
Holyhead 20/4/63
Willesden 22/6/63
Annesley 12/10/63

BOILERS

Fitted	No.	From
15/4/32	-	6120
21/8/34	-	6119
2/11/36	-	6160
15/3/39	8122	6158
14/6/41	8129	6164
1/7/43	7249	6103
12/9/45	10187	6107
1/2/49	8125	6134
22/8/51	11038	-
Taper 102A		
28/5/54	14000	-
26/8/58	12208	-
19/4/62	13244	-

46157 THE ROYAL ARTILLERYMAN

Built LMS Derby, cost £6,467
LM 'date built' 28/7/30
Named 10/31
Taper boiler fitted 19/1/46
Original smoke deflectors 5/2/32
BR smoke deflectors fitted period ending 22/4/50
Renumbered 6157 to 46157 week ending 18/12/48

BOILERS

Fitted	No.	From
14/1/32	-	6152
12/9/33	-	6103
25/4/35	-	6147
17/9/36	-	6132
13/5/39	8138	6141
23/8/41	6028	6158
25/8/42	9879	6162
3/2/45	7258	6142
Taper 102A		
19/1/46	12204	new
5/4/50	12033	6124
7/2/53	12209	-
4/1/56	12035	-
10/7/57	12198	-
24/5/61	10753	-

TENDERS

No.	Fitted
4242	21/7/30
9131	1936

SHEDS

Carlisle Kingmoor 12/10/30
Camden 21/2/32
'Western Division'
Camden 26/9/34
Carlisle 29/9/34
Crewe North 7/11/36
Camden (loan) 13/2/37
Crewe North 27/2/37
Camden 14/8/37
Crewe North 21/8/37
Holyhead (loan) 2/2/46
Crewe North 4/5/46
Holyhead 13/12/47
Crewe North 10/1/47
Holyhead 5/6/48
Crewe North 2/10/48
Holyhead (loan) 1/1/49
Crewe North 5/2/49
Longsight (loan) 12/2/49
Edge Hill (loan) 12/3/49
Crewe North 9/7/49
Holyhead 24/3/51
Camden 14/8/54
Longsight 18/9/54
Edge Hill 2/10/54
Kentish Town 19/10/57
Camden (loan) 14/6/58
Camden 21/6/58
Crewe North 20/9/58
Camden 20/6/59
Nottingham (loan) 7/11/59
Nottingham 2/1/60
Saltley 17/6/61
Carlisle Upperby 30/6/62
Carlisle Kingmoor 22/6/63

MILEAGES

1930	26,946
1931	70,412
1932	61,296
1933	69,114
1934	71,636
1935	82,870
1936	68,866
1937	74,554
1938	82,200
1939	68,610
1940	64,427
1941	57,159
1942	58,242
1943	62,807
1944	56,342
1945	40,517
1946	60,284
1947	59,373
1948	43,427
1949	64,704
1950	47,183
1951	55,341
1952	62,794
1953	62,086
1954	62,119
1955	51,558
1956	63,548
1957	65,980
1958	57,942
1959	53,752
1960	55,455

Mileage at 31/12/50 1,291,969
Mileage at 31/12/60 1,882,544
Withdrawn week ending 4/1/64
Scrapped Crewe Works 2/64

REPAIRS

8/1/32-5/2/32**HG**
29/8/32-19/9/32**LS**
27/2/33-22/3/33**HS**
30/8/33-28/9/33**HG**
19/4/34-8/5/34**LS**
8/9/34-26/9/34**LS**
4/1/35-22/1/35**LS**
5/4/35-13/5/35**HG**
7/3/36-24/3/36**HS**
7/9/36-3/10/36**HG**
3/12/36-4/1/37**LO**
22/8/37-14/9/37**LS**
26/1/38-10/2/38**LS**
7/10/38-25/10/38**HS**
21/4/39-13/5/39**HG**
13/5/40-28/5/40**LS**
7/8/41-23/8/41**HG**
16/12/41-10/1/42**HS**
8/8/42-25/8/42**HS**
10/6/43-26/6/43**LS**
17/2/44-8/3/44**HS**
17/1/45-3/2/45**HS**
29/7/45-30/8/45**LS**
30/9/45-19/1/46**HG**
30/7/47-6/9/47**HS**
30/12/47-24/1/48**LO**
18/11/48-15/12/48**LS**
15/12/48-1/1/49**NC(Rect)**
25/6/49-28/7/49**LC**
1/12/49-6/12/49**TRO**
14/2/50-5/4/50**HG**
16/11/50-19/12/50**HI**
14/2/52-8/3/52**LI**
28/7/52-2/8/52**LC(EO)**
31/12/52-7/2/53**HG**
2/9/53-25/9/53**LC(EO)**
26/6/54-6/8/54**LI**
19/3/55-22/4/55**LC**
21/11/55-4/1/56**HG**
2/9/56-5/10/56**HI**
11/6/57-10/7/57**HG**
9/1/58-25/1/58**LC(EO)**
12/5/58-9/6/58**LI**
30/6/59-15/8/59**LI**
5/7/60-26/8/60**HI**
14/4/61-24/5/61**HG**

A dirty 46156 THE SOUTH WALES BORDERER at Manchester Victoria – possibly on a Newcastle job and in BR 'mixed traffic' lined black livery (which a few Scots got). The date is not recorded, though with full BRITISH RAILWAYS legend (the lion and wheel emblem appeared in 1949) the period would be about 1948-49. Photograph B.P. Hoper Collection.

46158 THE LOYAL REGIMENT

Built LMS Derby, cost £6,467
LM 'date built' 4/8/30
Named 7/31
Taper boiler fitted 24/9/52
Original smoke deflectors 19/2/32
BR smoke deflectors fitted period ending 4/10/52
Renumbered 6158 to 46158 week ending 9/10/48

BOILERS

Fitted	No.	From
16/6/32	-	6104
27/8/34	-	6109
18/3/36	-	6107
8/3/37	8122	6115
20/6/38	6028	6106
24/7/40	9882	6132
28/1/43	8124	6125
30/5/47	11040	6130
13/2/50	9884	6167
Taper 102A		
24/9/52	11731	-
12/11/54	13243	-
6/9/57	12028	-
1/7/60	13894	-

SHEDS
Camden 26/11/30
Preston 23/9/33
Camden 12/1/35
Preston 11/7/36
Carlisle 16/9/39
Camden 15/1/49
Carlisle Upperby 12/2/49
Crewe North 12/3/49
Holyhead 20/5/50
Crewe North 28/10/50
Bushbury 25/11/50
Edge Hill 7/7/51
Longsight 9/7/55
Kentish Town 25/4/59
Longsight 13/6/59
Bushbury 7/11/59
Willesden 3/12/60
Trafford Pk 31/12/60
Annesley 29/2/62

MILEAGES

1930	21,461
1931	70,040
1932	38,041
1933	60,182
1934	57,321
1935	69,100
1936	83,705
1937	63,096
1938	54,934
1939	72,011
1940	58,406
1941	62,218
1942	52,753
1943	58,494
1944	59,068
1945	59,796
1946	53,735
1947	53,728
1948	50,070
1949	52,420
1950	39,254
1951	45,644
1952	39,163
1953	71,945
1954	56,538
1955	54,049
1956	63,630
1957	61,476
1958	57,743
1959	66,413
1960	57,036

Mileage at 31/12/50 1,189,813
Mileage at 31/12/60 1,763,450
Withdrawn week ending 19/10/63
Scrapped Crewe Works 11/63

TENDERS

No.	Fitted
4243	4/8/30
9331	6/4/36
9337	30/11/55

REPAIRS
16/5/31-19/5/31**LO**
31/8/31-15/9/31**LS**
2/2/32-19/2/32**HS**
15/6/32-20/7/32**HG**
11/1/33-8/2/33**LO**
25/7/33-11/8/33**LS**
10/1/34-2/2/34**LS**
16/3/34-20/4/34**LO**
20/8/34-14/9/34**HS**
7/6/35-25/6/35**HS**
10/10/35-7/11/35**LO**
9/3/36-6/4/36**HG**
1/3/37-17/3/37**HS**
31/8/37-17/9/37**LS**
24/1/38-7/2/38**LO**
13/5/38-15/7/38**HG**
4/8/39-19/8/39**LS**
8/7/40-24/7/40**HG**
29/12/40-22/1/41**LO**
25/1/41-6/2/41**LO**
14/4/41-16/5/41**LO**
7/10/41-25/10/41**HS**
30/3/42-18/4/42**LO**
9/1/43-28/1/43**HG**
27/1/44-12/2/44**LS**
23/10/44-11/11/44**HS**
22/5/45-8/6/45**LO**
27/12/45-16/1/46**HS**
17/6/46-19/7/46**LO**
10/4/47-30/5/47**HG**
28/12/47-31/1/48**LO**
9/9/48-9/10/48**LS**
16/2/49-2/3/49**LC**
28/12/49-15/2/50**HG**
24/10/50-18/11/50**LC**
4/12/50-18/12/50**LC**
25/4/51-5/5/51**LC**
30/11/51-12/1/52**HI**
23/5/52-24/9/52**NG**
3/10/52-8/10/52**NC(Rect)(EO)**
23/10/53-12/11/53**HI**
2/10/54-12/11/54**HG**
4/11/55-30/11/55**LI**
27/8/56-24/9/56**LI**
29/7/57-6/9/57**HG**
24/11/58-3/1/59**HI**
28/5/59-25/7/59**LC(EO)**
29/5/60-1/7/60**HG**

Below. 46157 THE ROYAL ARTILLERYMAN, a Carlisle engine, at Holbeck on a Sunday, 8 September 1963. The fierce winter earlier in the year had had the result of prolonging the life of many steam locomotives such as this, though the next great barrier, the end of the summer timetable, saw another surge in withdrawals. Steam had proved far less susceptible than the new diesels in the Great Freeze of early 1963 but the steam heating problems which had been the diesels' undoing remained more or less unchanged even as the *next* winter drew on. Photograph B.P. Hoper Collection.

Above. 46158 THE LOYAL REGIMENT at Polmadie, 2 April 1950. That huge smokebox could never really look right, especially given the ridiculous little chimney. Yet though it spoilt the appearance, the empirically derived chimney-blastpipe proportions were more or less perfect, as good as any later obtained by more experimental procedures – hence the excellent steaming of the Royal Scots. It is somewhat surprising to learn (Radford, *Derby Works and Midland Locomotives,* Ian Allan, 1971) that the boiler design, as drawn out at Derby, owed much to that of the 0-10-0 'Big Bertha' banking engine. Photograph J.L. Stevenson.

46159 THE ROYAL AIR FORCE

Built LMS Derby, cost £6,467
LM 'date built' 11/8/30
Named 10/31
Taper boiler fitted 13/10/45
Original smoke deflectors 30/1/32
BR smoke deflectors fitted period ending 15/7/50
Renumbered 6159 to 46159 week ending 18/9/48

REPAIRS
2/10/31-28/10/31**LS**
8/4/32-3/5/32**HG**
1/10/32-19/10/32**LO**
27/4/33-8/6/33**HS**
20/7/33-14/8/33**HO**
9/6/34-30/6/34**HS**
7/12/34-15/1/35**HG**
8/2/35-28/2/35**HO**
4/11/35-3/12/35**LS**
13/3/36-31/3/36**HO**
21/7/36-6/8/36**LS**
26/4/37-27/5/37**HG**
30/3/38-21/4/38**HS**
31/8/38-30/9/38**HG**
1/9/39-28/9/39**HS**
25/5/40-7/6/40**LS**
7/6/41-24/6/41**LS**
14/3/42-1/4/42**HG**
22/12/42-9/1/43**LS**
6/12/43-24/12/43**HG**
9/9/44-26/9/44**LS**
17/8/45-13/10/45**HG**
1/7/46-1/8/46**LS**
22/7/47-5/9/47**LS**
12/7/48-15/9/48**HG**
11/2/49-19/2/49**NC**
26/5/49-7/6/49**LC**
25/7/49-6/9/49**LI**
5/6/50-1/7/50**HG**
9/6/51-27/6/51**LI**
1/8/52-20/9/52**HG**
22/8/53-17/9/53**HI**
30/9/54-6/11/54**HG**
16/12/55-7/1/56**LI**
13/2/57-16/3/57**HG**
5/8/58-29/8/58**LI**
28/1/59-28/2/59**LC**
14/12/59-16/1/60**NI**
17/3/61-25/4/61**HI**
18/9/61-5/10/61**LC(EO)**

MILEAGES

1930	13,117
1931	58,256
1932	68,119
1933	68,471
1934	56,125
1935	62,298
1936	83,612
1937	67,272
1938	75,861
1939	68,791
1940	65,623
1941	60,188
1942	58,250
1943	58,398
1944	63,925
1945	56,519
1946	67,600
1947	70,274
1948	71,354
1949	70,161
1950	62,408
1951	64,009
1952	61,892
1953	67,601
1954	61,014
1955	56,517
1956	58,689
1957	48,060
1958	53,824
1959	58,676
1960	57,121

Mileage at 31/12/50 1,326,622
Mileage at 31/12/60 1,914,025
Withdrawn week ending 1/12/62
Scrapped Crewe Works 3/63

BOILERS

Fitted	No.	From
11/4/32	-	6164
4/5/33	-	6136
31/12/34	-	6129
23/3/36	-	6123
5/5/37	-	6169
30/9/38	7589	6161
28/9/39	5574	6111
1/4/42	7217	6113
24/12/43	7241	6104
Taper 102A		
13/10/45	12201	new
15/9/48	12029	6138
1/7/50	12031	6112
20/9/52	12201	-
6/11/54	12206	-
16/3/57	12201	-

SHEDS
Holyhead 15/10/30
Crewe North 12/10/35
Carlisle Upperby 3/10/36
Longsight 24/10/36
Crewe North 2/1/37
Preston (loan) 16/1/37
Crewe North 3/4/37
Camden 29/9/45
Holyhead 4/7/53
Crewe North 14/11/53
Camden 12/6/54
Crewe North 18/9/54
Camden 25/6/55
Crewe North 24/9/55
Camden 3/11/56
Crewe North 15/12/56
Willesden 14/1/61

TENDERS

No.	Fitted
4244	11/8/30
4250	26/12/31
9046	12/11/35

46159 THE ROYAL AIR FORCE at Crewe North, July 1949. It has the BR 'mixed traffic' lined black, with larger lettering than on 46156, seen earlier. Photograph J. Robertson, B.P. Hoper Collection.

46159 with smoke deflectors and now in BR Brunswick green, at the Dalry Road coal stage – date unrecorded, though the plates were put on in July 1950. The pair of steps over the inside cylinder cover was something the Scots had which the rebuilt Patriots and Jubilees did not – it was thus an 'early recognition' sign that denoted (mystically, to those not in the know) an approaching Royal Scot. Photograph W. Hermiston, B.P. Hoper Collection.

46160 QUEEN VICTORIA'S RIFLEMAN

Built LMS Derby 27/8/30, cost £6,467.
Named 1932
Taper boiler fitted 10/2/45
Original smoke deflectors – not listed
BR smoke deflectors fitted period ending 28/1/50?
Renumbered 6160 to 46160 week ending 25/9/48

BOILERS

Fitted	No.	From
22/3/32	-	6110
26/4/34	-	6136
5/3/35	-	6133
10/6/36	-	6147
1/12/37	8137	6108
11/4/39	7590	6114
20/3/41	7212	6120
21/11/42	9884	6130
Taper 102A		
16/2/45	12089	new
20/9/48	12037	6166
2/11/51	12533	-
24/12/53	12091	-
21/2/54	12665	-
18/10/61	12526	-

TENDERS

No.	Fitted
4245	27/8/30
9010	21/1/36

MILEAGES

1930	18,383
1931	73,738
1932	48,162
1933	57,621
1934	69,997
1935	78,311
1936	87,451
1937	70,442
1938	77,154
1939	64,250
1940	52,767
1941	58,804
1942	57,806
1943	77,510
1944	65,058
1945	67,759
1946	63,821
1947	65,006
1948	51,380
1949	55,781
1950	62,158
1951	60,206
1952	66,464
1953	60,216
1954	65,929
1955	57,503
1956	72,667
1957	60,928
1958	57,790
1959	59,409
1960	55,654

Mileage at 31/12/50 1,323,359
Mileage at 31/12/60 1,940,125
Withdrawn week ending 1/5/65
Scrapped Motherwell
Machinery & Scrap Co. Ltd, 7/65

REPAIRS

5/8/31-19/8/31**LS**	21/12/44-16/2/45**HG**
18/3/32-3/5/32**HG**	11/6/46-1/7/46**HS**
20/9/32-8/11/32**LO**	21/7/47-28/8/47**LS**
29/5/33-19/6/33**LS**	17/7/48-20/9/48**HG**
15/9/33-4/10/33**HS**	15/10/48-5/11/48**LO**
20/3/34-9/5/34**HG**	1/1/49-21/1/49**LC**
26/2/35-13/3/35**HS**	21/3/49-22/4/49**HC**
29/7/35-14/8/35**LS**	4/1/50-23/1/50**LI**
3/1/36-21/1/36**HS**	16/10/50-4/11/50**LI**
2/6/36-26/6/36**HG**	1/10/51-2/11/51**HG**
1/2/37-15/2/37**LS**	15/3/52-3/4/52**HC**
4/6/37-23/6/37**LO**	12/1/53-4/2/53**LI**
12/11/37-20/12/37**HG**	27/11/53-24/12/53**HG**
4/3/38-23/3/38**LO**	5/12/54-6/1/55**HI**
7/9/38-12/10/38**LS**	18/2/55-9/3/55**LC(EO)**
13/3/39-11/4/39**HG**	25/11/55-31/12/55**HI**
24/6/40-10/7/40**LS**	13/1/57-21/2/57**GEN**
6/10/40-8/11/40**LO**	3/3/58-18/4/58**HI**
22/2/41-20/3/41**HG**	23/3/59-23/4/59**LI**
14/1/42-4/2/42**LS**	19/5/59-23/5/59**NC(Rect)(EO)**
31/10/42-21/11/42**HS**	11/2/60-26/3/60**HI**
23/7/43-7/3/43**LS**	16/9/60-27/10/60**LC(EO)**
15/4/44-5/5/44**HS**	8/9/61-18/10/61**HG**

SHEDS

Holyhead	17/9/30
Carlisle	13/7/32
Camden	12/10/32
Crewe North	18/11/33
Holyhead (loan)	21/9/40
Crewe North	17/4/43
Holyhead	14/8/43
Crewe North	4/9/43
Edge Hill	25/11/44
Crewe	17/2/45
Leeds (loan)	16/6/45
Crewe North (loan)	30/6/45
Holyhead	31/8/46
Longsight	17/5/47
Kentish Town	19/9/59
Saltley	17/6/61
Carlisle Upperby	30/6/62
Carlisle Kingmoor	22/6/63

46161 KING'S OWN

Built LMS Derby, cost £6,467
LM 'date built' 8/9/30
Taper boiler fitted 12/10/46
First named THE KING'S OWN (9/30), renamed 6/31
Original smoke deflectors 27/2/32
BR smoke deflectors fitted period ending 10/9/49
Renumbered 6161 to 46161 week ending 31/7/48

TENDERS

No.	Fitted
4246	8/9/30
9338	12/5/36
9356	2/9/36
9358	30/12/37

BOILERS

Fitted	No.	From
18/5/32	-	6128
15/9/33	-	6131
19/12/34	-	6137
18/8/36	-	6154
31/1/38	8127	6160
12/7/39	8123	6108
18/9/41	10184	6104
10/3/43	7242	6106
19/10/44	9877	6116
Taper 102A		
12/10/46	12536	new
20/8/49	12669	new
20/2/53	13237	-
13/1/56	12670	-
28/6/58	11731	-

SHEDS

Holyhead 22/10/30
Crewe North 12/10/35
Camden (loan) 20/11/37
Crewe North 18/12/37
Edge Hill (loan) 8/5/43
Crewe North 7/4/44
Holyhead 29/4/50
Crewe North 20/10/51
Camden 5/7/52
Crewe North 20/9/52
Longsight 13/6/53
Holyhead (loan) 4/7/53
Holyhead 19/9/53
Longsight 3/10/53
Camden 9/6/56
Crewe North 15/9/56
Camden 20/6/59
Preston 12/9/59
Bushbury 4/3/61
Preston 10/6/61
Bidston 9/9/61
Crewe North 14/7/62

MILEAGES

Year	Miles
1930	15,527
1931	55,002
1932	55,988
1933	65,342
1934	71,210
1935	61,051
1936	77,481
1937	82,797
1938	81,356
1939	68,722
1940	63,118
1941	60,490
1942	61,735
1943	56,541
1944	60,134
1945	58,902
1946	44,711
1947	56,661
1948	30,402
1949	50,684
1950	65,699
1951	64,770
1952	56,582
1953	62,187
1954	54,665
1955	51,173
1956	70,486
1957	58,613
1958	45,439
1959	53,547
1960	48,844
1961	32,234
1962	27,784

Mileage at 31/12/50 1,243,553
Mileage at 31/12/62 1,869,907
Withdrawn week ending 1/12/62
Scrapped Crewe Works 12/63

REPAIRS

10/9/31-2/10/31**LS**
17/5/32-6/6/32**HG**
1/3/33-21/3/33**LS**
29/8/33-28/9/33**HS**
27/2/34-13/3/34**LS**
3/12/34-10/1/35**HG**
18/11/35-2/12/35**HS**
23/4/36-12/5/36**LS**
8/8/36-2/9/36**HG**
23/11/36-17/12/36**LO**
3/4/37-23/4/37**HS**
18/9/37-30/9/37**LO**
24/1/38-16/2/38**HG**
10/12/38-2/1/39**LS**
10/6/39-12/7/39**HG**
8/7/40-20/7/40**HS**
16/1/41-1/2/41**LO**
29/8/41-18/9/41**HG**
4/6/42-20/6/42**LS**
15/2/43-10/3/43**HS**
9/8/43-24/8/43**LO**
6/6/44-24/6/44**HS**
14/9/44-19/10/44**HG**
2/9/45-22/9/45**HS**
14/7/46-12/10/46**HG**
23/1/48-26/2/48**LS**
4/3/48-16/3/48**NC**
7/7/48-31/7/48**LO**
8/9/48-21/10/48**LO**
20/11/48-23/12/48**LO**
11/7/49-20/8/49**HG**
18/9/50-6/10/50**LI**
24/10/51-27/11/51**LI**
24/1/53-20/2/53**HG**
27/7/54-20/8/54**HI**
24/8/54-31/8/54**NC(Rect)(EO)**
12/12/55-13/1/56**HG**
30/1/57-8/3/57**LI**
2/5/58-28/6/58**HG**
7/7/58-11/7/58**NC(EO)**
28/11/59-9/1/60**HI**
29/6/60-20/8/60**LC**

6161 KING'S OWN, south of Crewe (it is thought) with a truly exotic mix of stock, running to no less than sixteen vehicles. The year is uncertain, though the ancient writing on the rear of the print says 1946 – shortly before 6161's conversion to taper boiler form. Photograph B.P. Hoper Collection.

KING'S OWN at Euston (note the conductor rails) in the early 1960s. The 'CS' on the tender is the 'empty carriage stock' headcode; 46161 has brought in its train and is now ready to move off with empty stock back to Stonebridge Park or Willesden. It proved beyond my acquisitive instinct, even combined with that of Irwell Press, to come up with a suitable illustration of *every* Royal Scot so one or two have benefited from an extra coverage. Photograph B.P. Hoper Collection.

46162 QUEEN'S WESTMINSTER RIFLEMAN

Built LMS Derby, cost £6,467
LM 'date built' 9/9/30
Taper boiler fitted 7/1/48
Named 1932
Original smoke deflectors – not listed
BR smoke deflectors fitted period ending 4/11/50
Renumbered 6162 to 46162 week ending 17/4/48

MILEAGES

Year	Mileage	Year	Mileage
1930	21,104	1949	59,564
1931	61,363	1950	62,030
1932	61,058	1951	67,485
1933	59,700	1952	59,194
1934	75,671	1953	65,578
1935	80,458	1954	64,781
1936	77,953	1955	54,271
1937	47,101	1956	62,273
1938	62,827	1957	53,421
1939	61,480	1958	53,437
1940	43,719	1959	59,172
1941	59,029	1960	57,792
1942	46,250	**Mileage at 31/12/50 1,229,157**	
1943	67,424	**Mileage at 31/12/60 1,826,561**	
1944	61,880	**Withdrawn week**	
1945	74,240	**ending 30/5/64**	
1946	62,684	**Scrapped J.N. Connell,**	
1947	31,491	**Coatbridge, 9/64**	
1948	52,131		

TENDERS

No.	Fitted
4247	9/9/30
9041	28/8/36
9041	7/6/48
9342	11/3/52
9041	2/7/52
4648	21/3/61

SHEDS

Holyhead 4/10/30
Bangor 5/12/36
Holyhead 17/4/37
Preston 26/2/38
Longsight (loan) 25/2/39
Preston 1/4/39
Carlisle (loan) 6/5/39
Preston 13/5/39
Bushbury (loan) 8/3/41
Preston 18/4/41
Bushbury 29/11/41
Crewe North 3/1/42
Crewe North 8/4/44
Holyhead (loan) 20/3/48
Crewe North 3/4/48
Camden 24/4/48
Longsight (loan) 15/1/49
Camden 23/4/49
Crewe North 20/9/52
Camden (loan) 25/10/52
Camden 27/6/53
Kentish Town (loan) 7/11/59
Kentish Town 2/1/60
Saltley 17/6/61
Carlisle Upperby 30/6/62
Carlisle Kingmoor 21/7/62

REPAIRS

21/9/31-5/10/31**LS**	31/5/44-16/6/44**LS**
25/1/32-15/2/32**HO**	2/1/45-23/1/45**HG**
25/4/32-20/5/32**HG**	20/10/45-15/11/45**LS**
26/10/32-9/11/32**LS**	11/6/46-28/6/46**LS**
25/5/33-15/6/33**HS**	14/10/47-7/1/48**HG**
4/12/33-2/1/34**HG**	7/4/48-14/4/8**NC**
3/11/34-19/11/34**HS**	1/6/48-4/6/48**TRO**
5/4/35-24/4/35**LS**	4/6/48-15/6/48**Nil**
27/8/35-24/9/35**HG**	1/7/48-14/8/48**HO**
7/3/36-20/3/36**LS**	19/4/49-11/5/49**LI**
17/8/36-28/8/36**LO**	13/5/49-20/5/49**Nil**
8/3/37-8/4/37**HS**	31/10/49-29/11/49**LO**
31/8/37-27/9/37**HG**	18/8/50-18/10/50**HG**
28/12/37-12/1/38**LO**	4/2/52-3/3/52**HI**
28/5/38-17/6/38**LO**	27/1/53-19/2/53**HG**
22/11/38-12/12/38**LS**	19/7/54-14/8/54**LI**
20/10/39-6/12/39**HG**	20/8/55-23/9/55**LC**
20/1/40-9/2/40**LO**	29/12/55-26/1/56**HG**
17/10/40-1/11/40**LO**	21/2/57-28/3/57**HI**
27/11/40-11/12/40**LO**	12/1/58-4/2/58**HI**
28/4/41-16/5/41**LS**	24/2/59-4/4/59**HG**
26/3/42-21/4/42**HG**	24/3/60-10/5/60**LI**
7/8/42-29/8/42**LO**	29/9/60-9/11/60**LC**
25/5/43-10/6/43**LS**	31/1/61-1/3/61**LI**

BOILERS

Fitted	No.	From
28/4/32	-	6165
13/12/33	-	6164
8/11/34	-	6138
6/9/35	8138	6152
13/9/37	7232	6152
20/10/39	9849	6150
21/4/42	9880	6103
23/1/45	7226	6137
Taper 102A		
7/1/48	12658	new
18/10/50	12532	6115
19/2/53	12536	-
26/1/56	13893	-
4/4/59	11732	-

46163 CIVIL SERVICE RIFLEMAN

Built LMS Derby, cost £6,467
LM 'date built' 15/9/30
Taper boiler fitted 8/10/53
Named 1932
Original smoke deflectors – not listed
BR smoke deflectors fitted period ending 31/10/53
Renumbered 6163 to 46163 week ending 20/11/48

BOILERS

Fitted	No.	From
12/4/32	-	6131
31/10/33	-	6146
19/2/35	-	6153
6/10/36	-	6161
9/8/37	7235	6125
23/12/38	7218	6151
15/3/41	8120	6140
9/1/43	8133	6151
17/8/45	9880	6162
19/11/48	11034	6141
29/8/52	11039	-
Taper 102A		
8/10/53	13999	-
15/12/56	12674	-
31/10/59	12673	-

REPAIRS

21/11/31-4/12/31**LS**
11/4/32-5/5/32**HG**
2/11/32-21/11/32**LS**
2/5/33-19/5/33**LS**
18/10/33-24/11/33**HG**
11/2/35-28/2/35**HS**
18/11/35-5/12/35**LS**
15/5/36-1/6/36**HS**
29/9/36-23/10/36**GH**
3/8/37-18/8/37**HS**
13/6/38-27/6/38**LS**
10/11/38-23/12/38**HG**
15/6/39-1/7/39**LO**
28/12/39-12/1/40**HS**
14/2/41-15/3/41**HG**
1/10/41-17/10/41**LO**
9/2/42-3/3/42**LS**
11/12/42-9/1/43**HG**
25/10/43-9/11/43**LS**
30/8/44-27/9/44**LS**
16/7/45-17/8/45**HG**
12/10/46-2/11/46**HS**
15/10/47-15/11/47**LS**
29/9/48-19/11/48**HG**
24/2/49-23/3/49**LC**
12/8/49-16/9/49**HC**
27/10/49-28/11/49**LC**
9/12/49-5/1/50**LC**
16/2/50-13/3/50**LC**
31/5/50-26/6/50**LI**
19/7/50-2/8/50**LC**
7/2/51-21/2/51**LC**
30/3/51-5/5/51**LI**
1/8/51-6/9/51**LC(EO)**
25/1/52-14/2/52**LC**
10/7/52-29/8/52**HG**
21/11/52-4/12/52**LC(EO)**
17/7/53-8/10/53**HG**
13/10/53-19/10/53**NC(Rect)(EO)**
29/7/55-20/8/55**LI**
11/11/56-15/12/56**HG**
11/4/58-9/5/58**HI**
26/6/58-15/7/58**NC(Rect)(EO)**
15/9/59-31/10/59**HC**

TENDERS

No.	Fitted
4248	15/9/30
9342	1/6/36
9759	21/1/52
9041	11/3/52
9342	22/7/52

SHEDS

Holyhead 5/10/35
Crewe North 12/10/35
Holyhead 28/1/39
Crewe North 15/7/39
Edge Hill (loan) 25/5/46
Crewe North 22/6/46
Carlisle Upperby 10/6/50
Bushbury 30/9/50
Carlisle Upperby 7/7/51
Crewe North 12/7/52
Camden 12/6/52
Crewe 18/9/54
Camden 20/6/59
Preston 12/9/59
Holyhead 2/4/60
Preston 30/4/60
Crewe North 30/4/60
Holyhead 11/6/60
Llandudno Junction 17/9/60
Holyhead 11/3/61
Willesden 23/6/62
Annesley 12/1/63

MILEAGES

Year	Mileage	Year	Mileage
1930	16,609	1948	53,592
1931	50,725	1949	35,891
1932	70,746	1950	53,728
1933	65,118	1951	38,357
1934	84,370	1952	40,444
1935	62,297	1953	46,770
1936	82,497	1954	63,026
1937	87,117	1955	52,090
1938	78,171	1956	54,315
1939	64,682	1957	65,306
1940	58,463	1958	44,441
1941	58,665	1959	44,177
1942	55,353	1960	60,589
1943	66,085	**Mileage at 31/12/50 1,259,485**	
1944	64,361	**Mileage at 31/12/60 1,769,064**	
1945	55,158	**Withdrawn week ending 29/8/64**	
1946	54,528	**Scrapped Bird Group, Risca, 2/65**	
1947	41,329		

KING'S OWN, a picture of contentment, resting quietly at Manchester London Road, about 1955, after arriving with The Comet. A super study; under *Weatherlux Coats* advert the oiks sit unconcerned and unminded, and happy enough too, no doubt, despite the fact that they had probably seen this local Longsight engine three times that week already. Photograph B.P. Hoper Collection.

46161 KING'S OWN rattles through Prestbury station and its basic goods yard north of Macclesfield, with the 2.25pm Manchester London Road to Birmingham New Street on Good Friday, 27 March 1959. Photograph Michael Mensing.

46162 QUEEN'S WESTMINSTER RIFLEMAN, one of the two Scots in the 1948 Interchange, at Carlisle Upperby in November 1962. The local tool van stands on the siding beyond – lettered MP CARLISLE UPPERBY. Photograph B.P. Hoper Collection.

46164 THE ARTISTS' RIFLEMAN

Built LMS Derby, cost £6,467
LM 'date built' 22/9/30
Taper boiler fitted 23/6/51
Named 1932
Original smoke deflectors 30/1/32
BR smoke deflectors fitted period ending 28/1/50
Renumbered 6164 to 46164 week ending 17/4/48

BOILERS

Fitted	No.	From
9/2/32	-	6101
14/8/33	-	6128
12/6/34	-	6140
20/12/35	-	6140
31/5/38	7226	6118
28/3/39	8129	6105
5/5/41	10183	6168
3/7/43	7259	6154
29/12/45	7591	6149
11/9/48	7251	6122
Taper 102A		
23/6/51	13591	new
13/4/55	12659	-
26/4/57	12537	-
4/3/61	11730	-

MILEAGES

1930	17,692	1948	47,581
1931	73,011	1949	47,386
1932	84,101	1950	56,935
1933	60,986	1951	65,114
1934	80,639	1952	57,618
1935	60,507	1953	62,101
1936	72,073	1954	60,206
1937	70,465	1955	48,152
1938	77,968	1956	54,514
1939	73,621	1957	63,474
1940	60,776	1958	58,191
1941	68,288	1959	55,184
1942	56,079	1960	1,857
1943	46,945	**Mileage at 31/12/50 1,273,492**	
1944	64,709	**Mileage at 31/12/59 1,798,046**	
1945	48,250	**Withdrawn week ending 29/12/62**	
1946	51,877	**Scrapped Crewe Works 3/63**	
1947	53,663		

SHEDS

Longsight 23/10/30
Carlisle 20/4/32
Camden 7/7/34
Carlisle 29/9/34
Longsight 1/12/34
Bangor 11/7/36
Crewe North 3/10/36
Edge Hill 21/2/42
Crewe 12/9/59
Carries a 41C Millhouses
shed plate in a 1961 photo.

REPAIRS

22/6/31-3/7/31**LS**	23/5/45-7/6/45**HS**
8/2/32-7/3/32**HG**	7/12/45-29/12/45**HG**
31/12/32-1/2/33**LS**	8/11/46-30/11/46**HS**
8/8/33-31/8/33**HG**	27/10/47-25/11/47**LS**
2/5/34-19/6/34**HS**	28/2/48-22/3/48**LO**
19/10/34-7/11/34**LS**	31/3/48-17/4/48**NC**
10/4/35-14/5/35**HS**	29/6/48-11/9/48**HG**
18/6/35-17/7/35**HS**	18/1/49-12/2/49**LC**
21/11/35-14/1/36**HG**	28/5/49-16/6/49**LC**
6/8/36-17/8/36**LO**	8/9/49-3/10/49**LC**
6/10/36-30/10/36**LS**	24/2/50-15/3/50**HI**
15/2/37-4/3/37**HG**	3/8/50-24/8/50**LC**
10/4/37-19/4/37**LO**	30/4/51-23/6/51**HG**
11/8/37-30/8/37**HS**	20/1/52-12/2/52**LC**
3/12/37-24/12/37**LO**	27/10/52-22/11/52**LI**
21/5/38-21/6/38**HG**	22/5/53-13/6/53**LI(EO)**
13/3/39-28/3/39**HS**	22/9/53-22/10/53**LC(EO)**
9/11/39-23/11/39**LS**	23/2/54-23/3/54**HI**
22/7/40-6/8/40**LS**	21/2/55-13/4/55**HG**
5/4/41-2/5/41**HG**	9/1/56-2/2/56**HI**
8/1/42-31/1/42**LS**	30/7/56-10/9/56**LC**
1/8/42-15/8/42**LO**	8/3/57-26/4/57**HG**
16/10/42-4/11/42**LO**	20/3/58-18/4/58**LI**
8/6/43-3/7/43**HG**	2/4/59-30/4/59**HI**
3/12/43-23/12/43**LO**	12/5/60**NC**
17/6/44-12/7/44**LS**	9/12/60-4/3/61**HG**

TENDERS

No.	Fitted
4249	22/9/30
9044	12/12/35

46165 THE RANGER (12TH LONDON REGT.)

Built LMS Derby, cost £6,467
LM 'date built' 29/9/30
Named 1932
Taper boiler fitted 12/7/52
Original smoke deflectors 30/1/32
BR smoke deflectors fitted period ending 12/7/52
Renumbered 6165 to 46165 week ending 23/10/48

MILEAGES

1930	14,107
1931	67,312
1932	55,837
1933	68,556
1934	67,682
1935	64,204
1936	64,517
1937	60,999
1938	74,764
1939	65,526
1940	71,409
1941	72,340
1942	67,664
1943	77,694
1944	61,680
1945	53,465
1946	47,622
1947	43,665
1948	43,916
1949	49,308
1950	46,208
1951	43,124
1952	51,402
1953	47,658
1954	57,582
1955	45,954
1956	44,426
1957	55,571
1958	64,267
1959	52,354
1960	43,412
Mileage at 31/12/50 1,238,475	
Mileage at 31/12/60 1,744,225	
Withdrawn week ending 21/11/64	
Scrapped T.W. Ward Ltd, Beighton, 3/65	

SHEDS

Longsight 22/10/30
Camden 2/7/38
Longsight 8/10/38
Camden 25/11/39
Crewe North 11/1/41
Holyhead (loan) 12/12/42
Crewe North 10/4/43
Carlisle Upperby (loan) 15/7/44
Crewe North 12/8/44
Camden (loan) 10/3/45
Crewe North 31/3/45
Holyhead 2/9/50
Bushbury 30/9/50
Crewe North 10/2/51
Bushbury 24/3/51
Edge Hill 7/7/51
Crewe North 15/9/51
Carlisle Upperby 12/7/52
Rugby Test Centre 10/12/55
Carlisle Upperby 14/1/56
Rugby Test Centre 28/1/56
Carlisle Upperby 9/6/56
Crewe South 4/8/56
Carlisle Upperby 3/11/56
Crewe South 16/2/57
Carlisle Upperby 23/2/57
Preston 7/11/59
Heaton Mersey 9/9/61
Crewe North 14/7/62
Llandudno Junction 22/9/62
Crewe North 22/6/63
Annesley 29/2/64

REPAIRS

6/10/31-21/10/31**LS**	22/11/45-8/12/45**LO**
23/3/32-3/5/32**HG**	22/12/45-19/1/46**LO**
14/10/32-3/11/32**LS**	5/10/46-1/11/46**HG**
19/6/33-18/7/33**LS**	19/7/47-27/8/47**LO**
14/11/33-13/12/33**HG**	21/10/47-5/12/47**LS**
16/1/34-20/2/34**HO**	19/9/48-22/10/48**LO**
15/3/34-18/4/34**LO**	5/4/49-13/5/49**HG**
19/11/34-7/12/34**HS**	26/1/50-8/3/50**HG**
22/2/35-15/3/35**HO**	15/5/50-21/6/50**LC**
24/5/35-24/6/35**HG**	25/1/51-16/2/51**HI**
9/1/36-24/1/36**LS**	26/7/51-30/8/51**LC(EO)**
25/9/36-12/10/36**LS**	1/5/52-24/6/52**HG**
8/3/37-22/3/37**LO**	15/2/54-8/3/54**HI**
7/5/37-11/6/37**HG**	11/3/54-20/3/54**NC(Rect)(EO)**
29/9/37-12/10/37**LO**	20/10/55-19/11/55**HG**
10/2/38-24/2/38**LS**	6/1/56-24/1/56**HC(EO)**
7/10/38-2/11/38**HS**	24/6/56-4/7/56**NC(EO)**
24/3/39-12/4/39**LO**	20/7/56-28/7/56**NC(EO)**
14/10/39-15/11/39**HG**	19/10/57-16/11/57**HI**
18/12/39-29/12/39**LO**	9/1/58-9/1/58**NC(EO)**
10/4/40-2/5/40**LO**	22/1/58-14/2/58**LC(EO)**
7/10/40-25/10/40**HS**	19/6/58-15/7/58**LC(EO)**
27/6/41-24/7/41**LO**	30/12/58-16/1/59**LC(EO)**
7/2/42-21/2/42**HG**	15/4/59-29/5/59**HG**
21/4/43-6/5/43**LS**	8/10/59-8/12/59**HC(EO)**
25/1/44-3/2/44**TRO**	1/6/60-22/7/60**LI**
13/5/44-29/5/44**HG**	8/8/60-30/8/60**LC**
3/10/44-28/10/44**LO**	14/8/61-29/9/61**LC(EO)**
9/6/45-18/7/45**LS**	

BOILERS

Fitted	No.	From
31/3/32	-	6118
21/11/33	-	6102
11/6/35	-	6160
24/5/37	-	6130
14/10/39	5822	6157
21/2/42	8123	6161
29/5/44	7246	6114
1/11/46	7258	6157
13/5/49	10187	6156
8/3/50	9883	6123
Taper 102A		
24/6/52	12671	-
19/11/55	12668	-
29/5/59	13592	-

TENDERS

No.	Fitted
4250	29/9/30
4244	26/12/31
9348	25/6/36
9034	20/12/57
9348	9/1/58
10379	30/8/60

THE ARTIST'S RIFLEMAN again, bearing the hurts of the years, at Sheffield Midland on 20 August 1961. It has a Millhouses shed plate, 41C, a late transfer which no one bothered to note in the Record Card. The train indication contains a home-grown painted N, the paper supply having, presumably, run out. Photograph B.P. Hoper Collection.

46165 THE RANGER (12TH LONDON REGT.) in BR mixed traffic black, at Crewe North, July 1949. This engine was the Scot selected for extensive tests at Rugby Test Plant March-May 1956. Photograph J. Robertson, B.P. Hoper Collection.

46166 LONDON RIFLE BRIGADE

Built LMS Derby, cost £6,467
LM 'date built' 6/10/30
Named 1932
Taper boiler fitted 10/1/45
Original smoke deflectors 4/12/31
BR smoke deflectors fitted period ending 17/5/52
Renumbered 6166 to 46166 week ending 31/7/48

SHEDS

Longsight 22/10/30	Holyhead (loan) 10/3/51
Holyhead 11/7/36	Crewe North 17/3/51
Crewe North 26/2/38	Edge Hill (loan) 28/4/51
Holyhead (loan) 5/7/41	Crewe North 30/6/51
Crewe North 9/8/41	Camden 5/7/52
Edge Hill 9/10/43	Crewe North 20/9/52
Camden 27/11/43	Edge Hill 20/6/53
Leeds (loan) 15/1/44	Crewe North 19/9/53
Camden 19/2/44	Camden 12/6/53
Carlisle Upperby 22/4/44	Crewe North 18/9/54
Crewe North 2/9/44	Longsight 27/11/54
Edge Hill (loan) 4/5/46	Crewe North 1/1/55
Crewe North 18/5/46	Holyhead 15/10/55
Holyhead (loan) 21/9/46	Carlisle 5/11/55
Crewe North 5/10/46	Crewe North 3/12/55
Holyhead (loan) 18/12/48	Longsight 14/6/58
Crewe North 25/12/48	Crewe North 10/9/60
Holyhead 28/5/49	Carlisle Kingmoor 24/6/61
Crewe North 1/10/49	Crewe North 1/7/61
Longsight (loan) 14/1/50	Carlisle Upperby 26/5/62
Crewe North 4/2/50	Carlisle Kingmoor 28/9/63
Holyhead 10/6/50	*Picture shoes it with 12B*
Crewe North 3/2/51	*Upperby shed plate 12/9/64*

MILEAGES

1930	16.232
1931	38,836
1932	68,936
1933	76,335
1934	71,947
1935	69,171
1936	79,261
1937	63,665
1938	69,157
1939	69,755
1940	65,899
1941	58,851
1942	52,878
1943	56,999
1944	50,129
1945	55,646
1946	65,228
1947	38,348
1948	51,341
1949	64,235
1950	58,422
1951	50,868
1952	52,759
1953	49,892
1954	54,144
1955	48,235
1956	50,644
1957	60,183
1958	60,918
1959	66,157
1960	43,475

Mileage at 31/12/50 1,241,271
Mileage at 31/12/60 1,778,546
Withdrawn week ending 19/9/64
Scrapped West of Scotland Shipbreaking Co., Troon, 12/64

REPAIRS

20/8/31-16/9/31**HO**	20/6/44-15/7/44**LO**
2/11/31-4/12/31**LO**	16/11/44-10/1/45**HG**
31/3/32-3/5/32**HG**	14/2/45-14/3/45**LO**
2/11/32-25/11/32**LS**	20/5/46-7/6/46**HS**
4/5/33-31/5/33**HG**	22/6/47-4/10/47**HG**
25/4/34-31/5/34**HG**	11/6/48-29/7/48**LO**
2/3/35-27/3/35**HS**	23/3/49-13/4/49**LI**
26/8/35-16/9/35**LS**	17/4/50-15/5/50**LI**
19/3/36-8/4/36**HS**	16/8/50-15/9/50**HC**
4/9/36-9/10/36**LO**	6/6/51-26/6/51**LI**
8/1/37-15/2/37**HG**	4/7/51-25/7/51**LC**
18/9/37-2/10/37**LS**	22/3/52-29/4/52**HG**
3/12/37-23/12/37**LO**	7/10/52-1/11/52**LC**
11/4/38-27/5/38**LS**	29/1/54-20/2/54**LI**
13/10/38-21/11/38**HG**	15/6/55-19/8/55**HG**
31/5/39-17/6/39**LS**	25/2/56-14/4/56**HC(EO)**
31/5/40-12/6/40**LS**	16/10/56-17/11/56**HI**
30/1/41-21/2/41**HG**	3/1/58-30/1/58**LI**
16/8/41-30/8/41**LO**	27/12/58-31/1/59**HG**
20/5/42-12/6/42**HS**	6/4/59-14/4/59**NC(EO)**
14/12/42-15/1/43**LO**	20/2/60-25/3/60**HI**
8/9/43-24/9/43**LS**	12/10/60-3/12/60**HC(EO)**
8/12/43-7/1/44**LO**	

BOILERS

Fitted	No.	From
5/4/32	-	6157
16/5/33	-	6168
22/5/34	-	6160
14/3/35	-	6161
29/1/37	-	6119
21/11/38	8136	6153
21/2/41	7253	6141
12/6/42	5574	6159
Taper 102A		
10/1/45	12037	new
4/10/47	11728	6108
29/4/52	12207	-
19/8/55	12538	-
31/1/59	11728	-

TENDERS

No.	Fitted
4251	6/10/30
9332	8/4/36

46167 THE HERTFORDSHIRE REGIMENT

Built LMS Derby, cost £6,467
LM 'date built' 13/10/30
Named 1932
Taper boiler fitted 13/12/48
Original smoke deflectors 30/1/32
BR smoke deflectors fitted period ending 9/8/52
Renumbered 6167 to 46167 week ending 18/12/48

BOILERS

Fitted	No.	From
23/3/32	-	6113
22/2/33	-	6109
25/10/34	-	6154
21/7/36	-	6106
1/10/37	8135	6134
15/3/39	7248	6166
21/5/41	7233	6153
17/9/42	11034	6109
18/4/45	9884	6160
Taper 102A		
13/12/48	12670	new
9/8/52	11728	-
31/3/55	12662	-
18/1/58	12664	-

TENDERS

No.	Fitted
4252	13/10/30
9050	2/3/36

SHEDS

Crewe North 26/11/30
Longsight 7/9/32
Camden 2/7/38
Crewe North 11/1/41
Longsight 1/10/49
Crewe North 8/12/51
Camden 21/3/53
Crewe North 19/9/53
Camden 12/6/54
Crewe North 18/9/54
Carlisle Upperby 27/10/56
Preston 7/4/59
Carlisle Upperby 17/9/60
Bushbury 4/3/61
Preston 10/6/61
Heaton Mersey 9/9/61
Crewe North 30/6/62
Holyhead 22/9/62
Crewe North 9/3/63
Holyhead 20/4/63
Willesden 22/6/63
Annesley 21/9/63

MILEAGES

1930	14,385	1948	35,701
1931	75,251	1949	62,417
1932	61,978	1950	66,588
1933	51,981	1951	67,419
1934	70,449	1952	50,047
1935	61,928	1953	57,291
1936	73,586	1954	63,335
1937	77,629	1955	53,108
1938	77,417	1956	47,172
1939	73,706	1957	56,913
1940	77,183	1958	58,594
1941	66,123	1959	56,199
1942	61,765	1960	51,204
1943	62,871	Mileage at 31/12/50 1,308,536	
1944	61,976	Mileage at 31/12/60 1,869,818	
1945	60,189	Withdrawn week ending 11/4/64	
1946	62,186	Scrapped Crewe Works 5/64	
1947	53,227		

REPAIRS

15/9/31-29/9/31**LS**
18/3/32-21/4/32**HG**
15/2/33-7/3/33**HS**
3/10/33-23/10/33**HS**
16/4/34-4/5/34**HS**
24/7/34-4/8/34**LO**
15/10/34-13/11/34**HG**
2/1/35-1/2/35**HO**
26/4/35-13/5/35**LO**
27/9/35-10/10/35**LS**
6/1/36-20/1/36**LO**
7/2/36-2/3/26**HO**
14/7/36-5/8/36**HG**
31/3/37-14/4/37**HS**
30/6/37-21/7/37**LO**
24/9/37-11/10/37**HS**
7/7/38-4/8/38**LS**
11/2/39-15/3/39**HG**
15/12/39-14/12/39**LS**
23/5/40-8/6/40**HS**
24/4/41-21/5/41**HG**
28/1/42-14/2/42**LS**
29/8/42-17/9/42**HO**
29/6/43-20/7/43**HS**
25/6/44-22/7/44**LS**
17/3/45-18/4/45**HG**
10/6/46-26/6/46**HS**
23/9/47-17/10/47**LS**
5/1/48-31/1/48**LO**
3/8/48-13/12/48**HG**
17/5/49-24/6/49**LC**
14/1/50-2/2/50**LI**
31/7/50-19/8/50**LC**
26/2/51-15/3/51**LH**
25/6/52-9/8/52**HG**
27/11/53-23/12/53**LI**
2/2/55-31/3/55**HG**
17/7/56-21/8/56**LI**
5/12/57-18/1/58**HG**
27/3/58-30/4/58**NC(Rect)(EO)**
13/5/59-24/6/59**HI**
7/7/60-17/8/60**HI**

Years after, a few yards away at Crewe station on 7 May 1963, 46165 provides an interesting comparison across the years. One interesting contrast is in the leading crank – the ghastly split bush in 1949 and a proper bush in 1963. 46165 was withdrawn in 1964. Photograph B.P. Hoper Collection.

46166 LONDON RIFLE BRIGADE of Longsight, Manchester, waits on the Down Slow (electric) line at Camden on 21 September 1958. She is waiting to cross to Camden shed, probably after banking empty stock out of Euston. The background is Camden goods shed. Photograph R.C. Riley.

46168 THE GIRL GUIDE

Built LMS Derby, cost £6,467
LM 'date built' 10/10/30
Named 12/30
Taper boiler fitted 27/4/46
Original smoke deflectors 14/1/32
BR smoke deflectors fitted period ending 7/4/51
Renumbered 6168 to 46168 week ending 4/9/48

TENDERS

No.	Fitted
4253	20/10/30
9350	16/7/36

BOILERS

Fitted	No.	From
10/5/32	-	6163
19/4/33	-	6167
9/5/34	-	6132
23/1/36	-	6118
31/8/37	7257	6140
24/2/38	10182	new
21/8/40	11037	new
10/10/42	7238	6144
Taper 102A		
27/4/46	12208	new
2/9/48	12534	new
7/4/51	12528	6147
17/2/53	12199	-
7/9/54	12037	-
28/6/57	12034	-

SHEDS

Crewe North 26/11/30
Longsight 7/9/32
Crewe North 5/10/35
Holyhead 9/8/41
Crewe North 30/5/42
Holyhead 31/8/46
Crewe North 21/9/46
Camden 9/11/46
Preston 12/9/59
Heaton Mersey 9/9/61

MILEAGES

Year	Mileage
1930	9,846
1931	72,887
1932	65,458
1933	64,624
1934	53,284
1935	83,045
1936	70,127
1937	78,976
1938	64,209
1939	71,675
1940	57,967
1941	64,463
1942	62,573
1943	65,336
1944	65,502
1945	56,573
1946	52,016
1947	57,792
1948	68,498
1949	58,067
1950	73,827
1951	65,925
1952	70,869
1953	69,132
1954	56,714
1955	67,435
1956	58,420
1957	49,527
1958	52,320
1959	55,932
1960	38,097

Mileage at 31/12/50 1,316,745
Mileage at 31/12/60 1,901,116
Withdrawn week ending 2/5/64
Scrapped Crewe Works 8/64

REPAIRS

31/8/31-16/9/31**LS**
19/2/32-24/3/32**HO**
9/5/32-2/6/32**HG**
7/4/33-5/5/33**HS**
26/10/33-15/11/33**HS**
23/4/34-22/5/34**HG**
2/2/35-22/2/35**LS**
30/7/35-15/8/35**HS**
6/1/36-11/2/36**HG**
27/6/36-16/7/36**LO**
28/10/36-12/11/36**LS**
1/4/37-16/4/37**LO**
9/8/37-16/9/37**HG**
12/2/38-10/3/38**HS**
28/6/38-27/7/38**LO**
26/10/38-21/11/38**HS**
9/10/39-26/10/39**LS**
6/4/40-23/4/40**LO**
29/7/40-21/8/40**HG**
8/5/41-31/5/41**LS**
19/1/42-4/2/42**LS**
17/9/42-10/10/42**HG**
21/5/43-4/6/43**LS**
19/7/43-31/7/43**LO**
13/6/44-29/6/44**HS**
21/3/45-12/4/45**LS**
13/2/46-27/4/46**HG**
25/5/47-24/6/47**LS**
28/10/47-4/12/47**LO**
15/7/48-2/9/48**HS**
20/5/49-25/5/49**LC**
25/1/50-14/2/50**LI**
21/2/51-7/4/51**HI**
24/3/52-26/4/52**HI**
3/1/53-17/2/53**HG**
2/4/54-28/4/54**HI**
10/5/54-29/5/54**LC(EO)**
8/8/54-7/9/54**HC(EO)**
31/3/55-11/5/55**HI**
23/3/56-18/4/56**LI**
3/6/57-28/6/57**HG**
9/12/57-10/1/58**LC(EO)**
24/4/58-6/6/58**LI**
3/2/59-27/2/59**LC(EO)**
24/4/59-22/5/59**LI**
15/6/60-26/7/60**HI**
3/9/60-1/10/60**NC(EO)**

46168 THE GIRL GUIDE, at Carlisle Upperby (its last shed) in 1963. The Britannias rooted out of other Regions were beginning to congregate at Carlisle, the intention being to eradicate the last of the LM 7P 4-6-0s, both Scots and Patriots. Many of the Pacifics were in such poor condition, however, that the 4-6-0s got a short if unexpected extra lease of life. Photograph B.P. Hoper Collection.

46169 THE BOY SCOUT

Built Derby 27/10/30, cost £6,467.
Named 12/30
Taper boiler fitted 12/5/45
Original smoke deflectors 30/1/32
BR smoke deflectors fitted period ending 28/1/50
Renumbered 6169 to 46169 week ending 15/5/48

TENDERS

No.	Fitted
4254	27/10/30
3932	1933
9334	23/4/36
9035	5/10/36
9335	29/7/37
9340	23/2/63

BOILERS

Fitted	No.	From
22/3/32	-	6141
21/3/33	-	6140
16/10/34	-	6158
14/10/35	-	6141
17/2/37	-	6118
5/12/38	7239	6136
16/11/40	11031	new
6/5/43	9883	6129
Taper 102A		
18/5/45	12091	new
11/3/48	11731	6132
6/1/50	11726	6127
1/1/53	12030	-
26/3/56	12209	-
7/7/59	12527	-

SHEDS

Crewe North 26/11/30
Longsight 7/9/32
Camden 2/7/38
Crewe North 11/1/41
Edge Hill (loan) 25/10/41
Crewe North 1/11/41
Carlisle Upperby 17/6/42
Camden 2/2/44
Longsight 12/10/46
Crewe North 18/7/59
Willesden 21/4/62
Annesley 5/1/63

MILEAGES

Year	Mileage
1930	7,474
1931	83,070
1932	51,457
1933	49,224
1934	58,202
1935	70,416
1936	87,081
1937	77,936
1938	77,223
1939	79,052
1940	71,854
1941	59,096
1942	54,653
1943	61,371
1944	59,797
1945	51,832
1946	72,554
1947	61,541
1948	65,251
1949	57,819
1950	73,077
1951	69,801
1952	57,352
1953	66,395
1954	65,627
1955	61,159
1956	71,426
1957	58,523
1958	58,153
1959	60,138
1960	42,713
1961	51,052
1962	27,669
1963	11,342

Mileage at 31/12/50 1,332,980
Mileage at 1963 2,034,330
Withdrawn week ending 25/5/63
Scrapped Crewe Works 8/63

REPAIRS

7/9/31-23/9/31**LS**
8/3/32-20/4/32**HG**
14/3/33-6/4/33**HS**
28/8/33-12/9/33**LO**
5/1/34-25/1/34**LS**
13/6/34-17/7/34**HS**
6/10/34-2/11/34**HG**
3/10/35-28/10/35**HS**
6/4/36-23/4/36**HS**
18/9/36-5/10/36**LO**
10/2/37-3/3/37**HG**
13/7/37-29/7/37**LO**
2/12/37-17/12/37**HS**
28/3/38-25/4/38**LO**
22/10/38-5/12/38**HG**
6/5/39-19/5/39**LO**
2/11/39-18/11/39**HS**
22/5/40-5/6/40**LO**
25/10/40-16/11/40**HG**
12/8/41-27/8/41**LS**
15/11/41-29/11/41**LO**
17/9/42-3/10/42**LS**
29/3/43-6/5/43**HG**
16/5/44-5/6/44**HS**
21/3/45-18/5/45**HG**
9/1/46-9/2/46**HS**
15/2/47-19/3/47**LS**
3/2/48-11/3/48**HG**
20/4/48-12/5/48**LO**
5/3/49-30/3/49**LI**
21/11/49-6/1/50**HG**
22/1/51-9/2/51**HI**
20/1/52-18/2/52**HI**
29/11/52-1/1/53**HG**
18/3/53-11/4/53**LC**
8/2/54-27/2/54**LI**
11/2/55-9/3/55**HI**
14/2/56-23/3/56**HG**
9/5/57-4/6/57**HI**
27/5/58-21/6/58**HI**
26/5/59-7/7/59**HG**
25/8/60-19/10/60**LI**

BOY SCOUT on a pub crawl. 46169 approaches Rugby with Up Evereds special W712 off the Birmingham line (I'm presuming – always dangerous – that the firm was in fact the brewer of that name). This is the site of the present flyover, and a good indication of just why it was built – to avoid conflicting movements across the West Coast main line proper. Photograph Peter Groom.